The Sinking of
the *Lisbon Maru*

The Sinking of the *Lisbon Maru*
Britain's Forgotten Wartime Tragedy

Tony Banham

Hong Kong University Press
The University of Hong Kong
Pok Fu Lam Road
Hong Kong
https://hkupress.hku.hk

© 2006 Hong Kong University Press

ISBN 978-962-209-771-1 (*Hardback*)
ISBN 978-988-8083-13-8 (*Paperback*)

All rights reserved. No portion of this publication may be reproduced or transmitted in any form or by any means, electronic or mechanical, including photocopy, recording, or any information storage or retrieval system, without prior permission in writing from the publisher.

British Library Cataloguing-in-Publication Data
A catalogue record for this book is available from the British Library.

Cover image adapted from the poster for the film, *The Sinking of the Lisbon Maru*. Courtesy of Laurel Films.

Digitally printed

Contents

Illustrations	vii
Preface	ix
Acknowledgements	xi
Abbreviations	xvii
Dramatis Personae	xix
1. Introduction	1
2. The Loss of Hong Kong	5
3. Prisoners of War: Hong Kong, 1942	19
4. The Ship: *Lisbon Maru*	35
5. The Boat: USS *Grouper*	51
6. "Hot, Straight and Normal!": 1 October	63
7. "Abandon Ship!": 2 October, a.m.	77
8. The Long Swim: 2 October, p.m.	93
9. Survival and Death: 3 and 4 October	109

10.	Shanghai: 5 and 6 October	117
11.	Back at Sea: 7 to 9 October	123
12.	Japan: 10 October	129
13.	Prisoners of War: Japan, 1942 to 1943	135
14.	Prisoners of War: Japan, 1944 to 1945	163
15.	Liberation	175
16.	Reunion	193
17.	Epilogue	205
Appendix 1	Judgement: The Trial of Kyoda Shigeru	231
Appendix 2	The History of the List of the Men on the *Lisbon Maru*	247
Appendix 3	Statistics	253
Notes		255
Bibliography		285
Index		289

Illustrations

Plate section, after p. 108

1   Hong Kong harbour just before the outbreak of war
2   Garfield Kvalheim as a young submariner
3   Jack Etiemble as a boy soldier
4   Map of Hong Kong Island, 18 December 1941
5   Map of Kowloon and the New Territories, 8 December 1941
6   The Brooks family before the war
7   The USS *Grouper* — cutaway
8   The USS *Grouper* SS-214
9   The *Lisbon Maru*
10 The *Lisbon Maru* — cutaway
11 The crew of the *Grouper* in their favourite San Francisco bar, 1
12 The crew of the *Grouper* in their favourite San Francisco bar, 2
13 Map of the sinking of the *Lisbon Maru*
14 Charles Heather, survivor of the *Lisbon Maru*, and the first FEPOW Londoner to return home after the war
15 From left to right: Chris Man, Topsy Man, Geoffrey Hamilton and Martin Weedon
16 The sinking of the *Lisbon Maru*, at 08.55 on the morning of 2 October 1942, taken from the *Toyokuni Maru*, while the *Kohu Maru No. 1* takes off the final crew members from the starboard stern of the vessel (Exhibit L1 of the War Crimes Trial of the ship's Master, Kyoda Shigeru, Hong Kong, 1946)[1]
17 Drawing of the sinking of the *Lisbon Maru*
18 Wire release on the sinking of the *Lisbon Maru* picked up by the *Grouper*

19 Some of those lost in the sinking of the *Lisbon Maru*
20 Some of those lost in the camps
21 Some of those who survived the war
22 *Lisbon Maru* survivors landing at Moji, 10 October 1942
23 Formal notice of survival of Samuel Atkins
24 Formal notice of death of Charles Frederick Brooks
25 Liberation at Hirohata camp
26 Canadian repatriation card
27 Garfield Kvalheim and Jack Etiemble in front of a Mark 14 torpedo: The 'circular'
28 The 1998 reunion, from left to right: Nobby Hunt, Jim Fallace, Reg Westwood, Garfield Kvalheim, Dan O'Hanlon

Preface

> A tempestuous noise of thunder and lightning heard.
> Enter a Ship-master and a Boatswain
>
> **Being the first two lines of**
> **William Shakespeare's** *The Tempest*,
> **Act 1, Scene 1**

I am sitting in my 'study' — little more than a cupboard, but acceptable by Hong Kong standards — wondering how I will ever find a survivor from the third hold of the 'hell ship', *Lisbon Maru*.

That hold, in the middle of the vessel, had housed the Royal Artillery contingent of the British POWs being shipped, at the end of September 1942, from Hong Kong to work in the mines and docks of Japan. They had been closest to the impact point of the American torpedo that sank the ship, and as it foundered stern first — and they were the furthest aft — they experienced the most severe casualties. They held the key to the story of the worst American-on-British 'friendly fire' incident in military history.

I check my email. Out of the blue comes one from a certain Jack Etiemble: "Have just read about your book on the Internet. I was taken prisoner at Stanley whilst serving in 12 Battery, 8th Coast Regiment; I am also a survivor from the *Lisbon Maru*. By the way I was the last Royal Artillery trumpeter in Hong Kong."

*   *   *

It is one month later: I am sitting in my study, looking through some one hundred pages of my notes on the *Lisbon Maru*, and thinking that the story will be incomplete unless I can also tell it from the point of view of the boat — the American submarine, USS *Grouper* — that sank the old freighter.

I check my email. It is Jack again, the man from the ship. He has answered more of my interminable questions and has added a postscript: "By the way I correspond with and have met a crew man from USS *Grouper*."

Acknowledgements

> With the help of your good hands.
> Gentle breath of yours my sails
> Must fill, or else my project fails,
> Which was to please. Now I want
> Spirits to enforce, art to enchant;
> And my ending is despair
>
> *The Tempest*, Act 5, Scene 1

In 1990, when I first started gathering material that eventually resulted in this book, there were perhaps one hundred survivors of the *Lisbon Maru* still with us. When I began the serious work of putting the book together, in January 2003, I only knew of nine. In March, that number had dropped to eight. In July, seven; October, six. Although I eventually found a handful of others, I had tackled the subject just in time.

The veterans and, more recently, their descendants, have been without exception extraordinarily helpful and willing to share information. In particular, I would like to thank:

Veterans of the Battle of Hong Kong and the *Lisbon Maru*:

Frank Bennett, Hong Kong Signals Company (second hold). Frank was the penultimate survivor of the *Lisbon Maru* who made contact with me, and was able to confirm many important details from other sources.[2]

Jack Etiemble, Royal Artillery (third hold). Jack and his wife Ruth were kind enough to work with me for several months to put Jack's wartime 'biography' together. As one of the few survivors from the third hold, his story was particularly valuable.

Tom 'Taffy' Evans, Middlesex Regiment (second hold). Tom — based in Manila, Philippines today — lived in Hong Kong until his retirement. My wife is also from the Philippines; we have many mutual acquaintances.

Bert Garradley, Royal Artillery (third hold). Although I never had the opportunity to talk to Bert directly, Jack Etiemble contacted him on several occasions to review questions I had sent.

Wallace Hastings, Royal Navy (first hold). Just when I thought I had tracked down every survivor, Wallace got in touch. His recollections, especially of the Osaka Stadium hospital, were unique.

Alf 'Nobby' Hunt, Royal Navy (second hold). Nobby, still around at a ripe old age despite severe wounds sustained during the fighting for Hong Kong, was a fount of information, and supplied many photos and documents. My only complaint was that as a Royal Navy man, he should have been in the first hold!

Garfield Kvalheim, US Navy (USS *Grouper*). Gar (or Val, to his Navy friends), and his wife Fran were enormously helpful during my research. We corresponded for months, until I had built up a complete biography of Gar and his experiences aboard the *Grouper*, and could use it as a counterpoint to Jack's story. Having lived all over the world, today Gar and Fran have settled by the sea in Washington State.

Ross Lynneberg, New Zealand Royal Naval Volunteer Reserve (first hold). Ross is another naval man, who was kind enough to share his detailed biography with me. This really brought the events in the first hold to life. Ross still lives in New Zealand today.

James McHarg Miller, Royal Scots (second hold). Miller, now living in Australia, provided useful and evocative testimony to the events, kindly conveyed by his daughter.

Dennis Morley, Royal Scots (second hold). Dennis, like Nobby, an email fiend, was helpful from beginning to end, and was kind enough to send me a number of emotive photographs and souvenirs he had kept from the POW camps.

William Grant Shepherd, Royal Navy (first hold). William's daughter kindly contacted me at a time when I desperately needed to speak to someone who was in the first hold. William then responded with wonderfully coherent memories that — added to those of Ross — brought the Navy experience into sharp focus. Today, Shepherd lives in Canada.

Reg Shore, Middlesex Regiment (second hold). Reg was one of my earliest correspondents. Alas, he passed away in 2002 before I was able to complete the bulk of this research.

Bill Spooner, Royal Scots (second hold). As one of the very last survivors who Chinese fishermen pulled from the sea, days after most of his colleagues, Bill published his memoirs on the Internet some time back. When I wrote to his daughter asking for permission to quote from them, I was delighted to receive an answer from Bill in person.

Reg Westwood, Royal Engineers (second hold). Reg Westwood also passed away before this book was finished, but corresponding with him was a delight. I always liked Nobby's comment about first meeting him on a scrap of wood in the middle of the South China Sea. They remained firm friends until Westwood's death in Canada in 2003.

Children and relatives of those on board the *Lisbon Maru*:

Sue Allen, great-niece of Henry 'Harry' Withington, Royal Artillery.
Reg Banham, son of Tom Banham, Royal Artillery.
Mary Barker, niece of Thomas Hamill, Royal Scots.
Ken Blackmore, nephew of Percy Chittenden, Middlesex Regiment.
Gerry Borge, son of John Borg, Royal Scots.
Ron Brooks, son of Charles Frederick Brooks, Royal Artillery.
Keith Brown, son of 'Topper' Brown, Middlesex Regiment.
Anthony Bucke, son of Cyril Bucke, Royal Corps of Signals.
Mike Butterworth, son of Jack Butterworth, Royal Scots.
Shane Cavanagh, son of Neville Bede Cavanagh, HKDYP.
Greig Chisholm, great-grandson of James Johnstone, Royal Scots.
Betty Clinghan, niece of John McFerran Cassidy, Royal Navy.

June Conolly, daughter of Alexander Sim Hilton, Royal Engineers.
Isabella Cooper, daughter of James McHarg Miller, Royal Scots.
Geoff Coxon, nephew of John Robert Guille, Royal Artillery.
Moira Cuthberston, daughter of John Duffy, Royal Navy.
Les Duffy, nephew of John Duffy, Royal Navy.
Nina Elsrud, niece of Basil Eric Hunting, Hong Kong Royal Naval Volunteer Reserve.
Jean Fenwick, daughter of Bill Spooner, Royal Scots.
Doris Froggatt, daughter of Robert Atkinson, Royal Navy.
Andrew Furzer, son of Donald Furzer, Royal Navy.
Iain Gow, son of James Gow, Royal Scots.
Simon Harmon, son of Alan Harman, Royal Artillery.
Adrienne Howell, daughter of Hargraves Milne Howell, RASC.
Kay Hughes, daughter of John 'Pegleg' Goodenough, Royal Artillery.
Ian Inglis, son of John Inglis, Royal Artillery.
Glyn Jones, son of Telegraphist Thomas Theodore Jones, Royal Navy.
Douglas Langley-Bates, son of Ronald Langley-Bates, Royal Engineers.
Gareth Llewellyn-Williams, son of Henry Llewellyn-Williams, Royal Marines.
Hilary Llewellyn-Williams, daughter of Henry Llewellyn-Williams, Royal Marines.
Leigh Neve, great-nephew of James Alfred Maynard, Middlesex Regiment.
Colm O'Brien, nephew of Dennis McGrath, Middlesex Regiment.
Melanie Parker, daughter of John Sheedy, Royal Artillery.
Robin Poulter, son of William Poulter, Middlesex Regiment.
Malcolm Powell, great-nephew of Francis Florence, RAMC.
Kenneth Salmon, son of Andy Salmon, Royal Artillery.
Malcolm Short, nephew of Sidney Charles, Royal Engineers.
Moira Sommers, daughter of William Grant Shepherd, Royal Navy.
David Stanford, grandson of Fred Stanford, Royal Scots.
Sheila Stone, daughter of William McCormick, Royal Signals.
Allan Thomson, son of Victor Thomson, Royal Scots.
Barbara Tindle, daughter of Samuel Arthur Atkins, Middlesex Regiment.
Aileen Trinder, daughter-in-law of George Trinder, Royal Scots.
Paul Vaughan, grandson of the wife of Reginald Parlette, Royal Navy.
Mark Weedon, son of Martin Weedon, Middlesex Regiment.
Sue Wilkinson, daughter of Bill Spooner, Royal Scots.
Mark Williams, great-nephew of Stephen Mellows, Royal Navy.

Others who provided kind assistance and expertise were:

Barbara Anslow[3]	
Edie Badger	
Colin Day	Hong Kong University Press
Barney Deibert	Nephew of Carl Kjellin, USS *Grouper*
Roger Dingman	Professor of History, USC
Geoffrey Emerson	
Ruth Etiemble	
Suzanne Harris	National Archives and Records Administration (NARA)
Richard Hide	
Rodney Hide	
Jean Israel	
Tim Ko	
Fran Kvalheim	
Greg Leck	
David List	
Roger Mansell	Center for Research, Allied POWs Under the Japanese
Nelson Mar	
Vic Marsh	Son of Sergeant Tom Marsh, Winnipeg Grenadiers
Pat Mulligan	Son of James Patrick Mulligan, Royal Artillery
Heidi Myers	Naval Historical Center, Washington DC
Anne Ozorio	
Richard Peuser	NARA
Ian Quinn	
John Reakes	
Elizabeth Ride	Daughter of Lt. Col. Lindsay Ride, BAAG
Helen Rigby	
Brian Roberts	
Anna Rozario	
Gregg Schroeder	
Kin 'Kent' Shum	
Glenn 'Marty' Stein	
Roderick Suddaby	Imperial War Museum
Ron Taylor	
Frank Victor	
Peter Vine	Royal Marines
John R. Waggener	University of Wyoming
Jason Wordie	
Simon Yau	

I would also like to thank the people and government of the Zhoushan Archipelago for their help and hospitality.

All these people gave useful information that filled many of the gaps in my research. Any remaining errors of omission or commission are of course entirely mine.

Every effort has been made to trace the copyright holders of works quoted in this book. If anyone has information concerning any author for whom I have been unable to trace a copyright holder, I would always be happy to hear from the copyright holder and thank them by name in future editions.

Abbreviations

ARP	Air Raid Precautions
BAAG	British Army Aid Group
BQMS	Battery Quarter Master Sergeant
BSM	Battery Sergeant Major
CERA	Chief Engine Room Artificer
CO	Commanding Officer
CQMS	Company Quarter Master Sergeant
CSM	Company Sergeant Major
CTF	Commander Task Force
CWGC	Commonwealth War Graves Commission
ERA	Engine Room Artificer
FEPOW	Far East Prisoner of War
HE	High Explosive
HKDDC	Hong Kong Dockyard Defence Corps
HKRNVR	Hong Kong Royal Naval Volunteer Reserve
HKVDC	Hong Kong Volunteer Defence Corps
IJN	Imperial Japanese Navy
KIA	Killed in Action
LSBA	Leading Sick Berth Attendant
MBE	Member of the British Empire
MC	Military Cross
MIA	Missing in Action
MID	Mentioned in Dispatches
MTB	Motor Torpedo Boat
NCO	Non-Commissioned Officer
NZRNVR	New Zealand Royal Naval Volunteer Reserve

OBE	Officer of the British Empire
OC	Officer Commanding
PO	Petty Officer
POW	Prisoner of War
RA	Royal Artillery
RAF	Royal Air Force
RAMC	Royal Army Medical Corps
RCAF	Royal Canadian Air Force
RCS	Royal Corps of Signals
RDF	Radio Direction Finder
RE	Royal Engineers
RN	Royal Navy
RNH	Royal Naval Hospital
RNR	Royal Naval Reserve
RNVR	Royal Naval Volunteer Reserve
SBA	Sick Berth Attendant
SBCPO	Sick Berth Chief Petty Officer
TDC	Torpedo Data Computer
TF	Task Force
TG	Task Group
USAAF	United States Army Air Force
USN	United States Navy
W/T	Wireless Telegraph

Dramatis Personae

O Wonder!
How many goodly creatures are there here!
How beauteous mankind is! O brave new world
That has such people in't!

The Tempest, Act 5, Scene 1

British Prisoners of War aboard the *Lisbon Maru*:

Arthur Alsey	A bandsman in the Royal Scots, aged 31 in 1942.
Samuel Arthur Atkins	A private in the Middlesex Regiment, 25.
Frank Bennett	A signaller of the Hong Kong Signals Company, 25.
Charles Frederick Brooks	A warrant officer in the Royal Artillery, 41.
Jack Etiemble	A gunner in the Royal Artillery, 19.
Arthur 'Bill' Evans	A civilian nominally attached to the HKRNVR, 40.
Tom Evans	A private in the Middlesex, 26.
Geoffrey Hamilton	An officer of the Royal Scots, 25.
Wallace Hastings	A medic of the Royal Navy, 24.
Hargraves Howell	An officer of the RASC, 38.
Alf 'Nobby' Hunt	A seaman of the Royal Navy, 23.
John Inglis	A bombardier in the Royal Artillery, 25.
Ross Lynneberg	A seaman of the Royal New Zealand Navy, 21.
James Miller	A private in the Royal Scots, 26.

Dennis Morley	A private in the Royal Scots, 23.
Dan O'Hanlon	A seaman of the Royal Navy, 22.
Alan Potter	An officer of the St John's Ambulance, 43.
William Poulter	A CQMS in the Middlesex Regiment, 33.
Andy Salmon	A gunner in the Royal Artillery, 23.
William Shepherd	An engine room artificer of the Royal Navy, 22.
Henry 'Monkey' Stewart	Commander of the POWs on the *Lisbon Maru*, 42.
William Spooner	A private in the Royal Scots, 25.
Alf Taylor	A lance corporal in the Royal Signals, about 25.
Martin Weedon	Commander of B Company, Middlesex, 26.
Reg Westwood	A sapper of the Royal Engineers, 24.
Robert Wright	A private in the Middlesex, about 28.

Japanese crew aboard the *Lisbon Maru*:

Niimori Genichiro	Official Japanese interpreter, 49.
Kyoda Shigeru	Captain, 43.
Wada Hideo	Officer commanding POWs on the *Lisbon Maru*, about 25.
Sugiyama	Senior commander of troops on board, about 30.
Gentoro Niioka	First Mate, about 40.
Araki Kaname	Second Mate, about 35.
Hiyama Seinoshin	Third Mate, 30.

American submariners aboard the USS *Grouper*:

Robert Hamilton Close	Engineer officer, Electrical, 29.
John R. Dykema	Comms, Asst. First Lt., 24.
Edward Rowell Holt	Torpedo officer, 27.
Garfield Kvalheim	A Machinist, 25.
John Denning Mason	First Lieutenant, about 35.
Rob Roy McGregor	Captain, 35.
Albert W. Weaver	S&A, Asst. Elec & Eng., 27.
William Winter, Jr.	Executive Officer, Navigator, 32.

1 Introduction

> Full fathom five thy father lies,
> Of his bones are coral made;
> Those are pearls that were his eyes;
> Nothing of him that doth fade,
> But doth suffer a sea-change
> Into something rich and strange.
> Sea-nymphs hourly ring his knell.
> (*Burden*) Ding Dong.
> Hark, now I hear them, ding dong bell.
>
> *The Tempest*, Act 1, Scene 2

July 2003: A typhoon is approaching Hong Kong. The trees lining the road outside my study are leaning at impossible angles, leaves flowing away from their branches in a maelstrom of airborne flotsam and jetsam. They relax for a moment, the screaming wind at my window dies down, and then they jerk forward again.

*   *   *

In the middle of this tempest, I am trying to summarize the story that I will spend the next two years writing:

> On the seabed east of Shanghai, some six miles from the easternmost islands of the Zhoushan Archipelago, lies the rusting hulk of a sunken freighter. Its hull is ripped open by

the jagged impact of a torpedo; its holds are lined with skeletons.

Launched in Japan in 1920, the old ship sailed the seven seas for more than twenty years as the *Lisbon Maru*. She was sunk by the American submarine USS *Grouper* in October 1942, but the sinking did not just deprive Japan of essential war materials. Unknown to the Americans, it was also carrying almost two thousand British Prisoners of War captured at the fall of Hong Kong ten months earlier.

Over 800 died in the sinking; a further 90 died of shock, wounds, and sickness before the month of October was out. Over 100 more would never see Britain again, succumbing to the rigours of the Japanese POW camps.

In more recent wars, 'Friendly Fire' incidents in which American forces accidentally attacked British have been cruel but relatively small in scale; the two-man crew of an RAF Tornado here, eleven men in a Warrior armoured fighting vehicle there. During the first or second world wars, such incidents were seldom fatal; before the days of 'first strike, first kill' weapons, one could normally defuse a blue-on-blue incident before anyone got hurt.

In this case, however, less than a year after America's entry into the Second World War, there was a far greater tragedy than had been seen in any other war. Just one torpedo hit its target and led to the death, then or later, of more than one thousand British servicemen.

Yet, the American submarine captain was never blamed. He was simply doing his job, neatly and professionally, when the wrong ship happened to pass his bows.

This is the story of that ship, the war that brought the two craft together, and the fate of all those on board all the vessels concerned.

I had been familiar with the name *Lisbon Maru* for many years. While writing the history of the wartime defence of Hong Kong against Japanese invasion,[4] I had taken it upon myself to assemble a complete list of the Colonial garrison there as it was in December 1941 (some 14,000 men and women in all) and trace their fates. Repeatedly the Commonwealth War Graves Commission's records recorded deaths as 'lost in the *Lisbon Maru*'. More than seven hundred bore this label, and later research showed that many others listed as dying on the first or second of October 1942 had in fact lost their lives on the same vessel. More than half as many people had perished on this dirty little ship than had been lost on the *Titanic* thirty years earlier; but while the latter had spawned eternal interest and the world's biggest box-office success, the former had been completely forgotten. The scale of the tragedy took some time to dawn, but finally I realized I was looking at the biggest American-on-British friendly fire incident in military history.[5]

And tragedy is the right word. Although my earlier work had been strictly focused on the events of December 1941, a constant trickle of people contacted me to ask for details of their relatives who had been lost ten months later on the *Lisbon Maru*. So many had died (having had little or no contact with their families since the beginning of the Pacific War) that there was constant confusion about the exact date and place of death of those many who — weakened by the sinking, wounds, malnutrition, disease, exhaustion, shock and cold — may have survived the sinking by a week or two. A number of these families were desperately searching for a booklet written in the 1960s by one of the survivors, Geoffrey Hamilton. Entrancingly entitled "The Sinking The Of [sic] *Lisbon Maru*", it was the only work available on the subject. Finally, a relative of a man who had been on board the ship was kind enough to post me a copy. I waited in great anticipation, only to find that it was just some thirty pages in length, and had been quoted from in so many other works that it added little to my knowledge of the story.

It was a tragedy, too, for the American submariners. Hugely courageous men, they were almost the only effective Allied force in the Pacific in 1942. The eastern seas had become a dangerous place for the Allies, and the ability to strike back at Japanese shipping — even on a small scale — was as vital for morale as Doolittle's airborne attack on Tokyo. The crew of the *Gato*-class American submarine, USS *Grouper*, which sank the *Lisbon Maru*, learnt of its human cargo and their fate almost the first moment they surfaced to recharge their batteries (having been subjected to depth-charge attacks by the Japanese non-stop for some forty-eight hours after the attack). The submariners lived with this knowledge for the rest of their lives.

For me, the starting point of the serious research was the compilation of a complete list of those who had lost their lives on the ship. For the majority of the army's fatalities this was simply a matter of typing up the *Lisbon Maru* entries from the Sai Wan Bay Memorial, in Hong Kong, to those with no known graves. The Royal Navy, as always, was a harder task. They commemorate their unburied dead not at the place of their loss, but at their home ports. Assembling all these names required months spent trawling through the Royal Navy's complete lists of fatalities for October 1942.

But what of those who had survived the sinking? Personally, I have never been satisfied by the fact that in the United Kingdom there is little official recognition of the suffering of families damaged by war, and the servicemen themselves are only commemorated if they die on active service. The experience of war is itself so destructive that those forced to endure it also require remembrance, and never has this been so true as for those unfortunates who became Prisoners of War of the Japanese.

Here I received unexpected aid. In November 2002, a friend of mine, Elizabeth Ride (the daughter of Lieutenant Colonel Lindsay Ride who led the Combined Field Ambulance during the Japanese attack on Hong Kong, and then escaped from prison camp to form the clandestine British Army Aid Group in China) presented me with a complete list of Prisoners of War in Hong Kong. This list had been marked up to record all those who had embarked in the *Lisbon Maru* and other transportations to Japan.[6]

The list itself — compiled by an unimaginably brave Chinese gentleman, who worked for the Japanese as a clerk at the POW camp and took a sheet or two home every night to type up for the British spies — was a fascinating document in its own right.[7]

Finally I had a complete list of all those who had embarked on the vessel on 25 September 1942.

*   *   *

A sudden gust of wind screams insanely at my window. The rain is so hard that I can hardly see the trees now, and each drop spawns more mist as it slams into the water already cascading down our hill. The list of men is in front of me as I write. Saying 'nearly two thousand men' is easy. Looking at their names and ages — and for more than half, their deaths — is not.

2 The Loss of Hong Kong

> There, sir, stop.
> Let us not burden our remembrances with
> A heaviness that's gone
>
> *The Tempest*, Act 5, Scene 1

Surveying the smoking ruins of the once proud Crown Colony of Hong Kong, Gunner Jack Etiemble of His Majesty's Royal Artillery threw down his bugle and his trumpet and stamped them flat with his best Ammunition Boots. The order to surrender the village of Stanley — the last part of Hong Kong Island holding out against the Japanese invaders — had just come through, and Jack had blown the retreat and last post as ordered. It was 26 December, Boxing Day, 1941; he was eighteen and knew now that he would spend his nineteenth birthday (and how many others?) as a Prisoner of War.

Five thousand miles away, a twenty-four-year-old American, Garfield Kvalheim, was slaving away in the boiler room at the submarine receiving station at Goat Island, California.[8] An adventurous young man, officially listed as a deserter from the Royal Canadian Air Force which he had crossed the border to join in an unsuccessful attempt to become a pilot, he was a fresh submariner waiting for transfer to submarine duty on the old S-28 (operating out of San Diego, but at that moment undergoing repairs at Mare Island).[9] But, like it or not, while he was waiting, the station's old oil fired boilers had to be run to furnish steam and hot water for the site. Still smarting from the attack on Pearl Harbour just days earlier, the United States Navy was not in the business of wasting resources.

Although he did not know it, Kvalheim would spend his twenty-fifth birthday trying to kill Jack Etiemble.

These two men would not meet for a further ten months, and even then, they would have no opportunity to greet each other. Instead, they would be at opposite ends of a torpedo's brutally short voyage; but against all odds, they would indeed meet face to face in the fullness of time.

As the victorious Japanese marched Jack away from Stanley in a column comprising some two thousand British, Canadian, and Indian POWs (with the dependable soldiers of the 1st Battalion the Middlesex Regiment in the van), the young Gunner looked at the debris of war all around. Like many others on that march north through the battlefield of Wong Nai Chung Gap, still littered with the bodies of those who had died in the fighting days earlier, he thought they had already lived through the closest brush with death that they would ever experience. He was wrong; the adventures he and his colleagues would relate from this short but intense period of fighting were little compared to what they would be forced to endure some ten months later. Automatically keeping step in the column, Jack cast his thoughts back just eighteen days, to the start of the Japanese attack.

*   *   *

Unbelievable columns of smoke were billowing over Pearl Harbour, and the complement of the USS *Arizona* and other vessels — the pride of the United States Navy — were drowning as their ships settled on the ocean floor, fifty feet beneath Hawaii's glorious clear blue waves. The great Pacific War, which started with Japanese torpedoes and would end with American nuclear bombs, had begun.

Almost simultaneously, the Japanese attacked the Philippines, Malaya, Wake Island, and Hong Kong.[10] Malaya, and then Singapore, held on until 15 February when the famously 'impregnable' fortress surrendered in a surprise move that left even Winston Churchill shocked. In the Philippines, on the Bataan peninsular and then finally the island of Corregedor, the American defenders held on in increasingly horrifying circumstances for an unbelievable five months, but the first Allied territory to fall to the Japanese had been Hong Kong.

The authorities there were under no illusions. They knew the attack was coming, and in 1940 ordered all women and children of the British Garrison (and of the business community) to evacuate to Australia.[11]

The family of Master Gunner Charles Frederick Brooks, who lived in Stanley where Brooks worked with the huge coastal guns of the Royal Artillery, were among the evacuees.[12] Ron Brooks, his son, described the journey thus: "In 1940 my mother, Emily Brooks, my brother Geoff and I were evacuated (I think on the *Empress of Canada*) from Hong Kong to Manila. I remember sitting in the back of an army truck with a canvas top being driven away from the ship, silhouetted against the skyline, in pouring rain. We cannot have been long in Manila. We lived for a while at a US Army camp and then were billeted in a Spanish hotel 'Las Palmas del Mallorca'. We then travelled on the MV *Awatea* to Australia. I can remember my fifth birthday (6-Aug-40) was on ship off Thursday Island — I think it had paused to ship mail from the atoll. My mother would have been forty years of age and [my brother Geoff], ten.

We arrived in Melbourne and were billeted with other evacuees in a guesthouse in the northern country suburb of Croydon. The guesthouse was pretty basic with an outside bucket privy. I started my first school in Croydon, and I guess Geoff went to the same school. I can remember taking part in the Christmas show and learning to write on a slate. I can also remember having a tooth extracted under anaesthetic on the kitchen table of the guesthouse. My mother had a friend at the guesthouse, Fossie. Miss Foster had been a schoolteacher at Stanley."

As the evacuation illustrated, British Intelligence was excellent in Hong Kong. Not only did they understand the seriousness of the situation, they also knew which day the invasion would begin. With all front-line positions fully manned on 7 December 1941, there was no doubt that the attack was coming; Intelligence predicted that it would take place within twenty-four hours.

As expected, the Japanese crossed the border from China into the New Territories early on the morning of 8 December.[13]

Frank Bennett was just one of nearly two thousand men from Hong Kong's garrison who would later find himself a prisoner on the *Lisbon Maru*. A signaller in the Hong Kong Signals Company, he remembered the start of the attack more clearly than any other incident. Born in Portsmouth in 1917 as the eighteenth child to his family, he had joined the Royal Corps of Signals as a boy. Stationed in Victoria Barracks in the heart of Hong Kong, he looked up that morning and saw bombers filling the sky: "Nobody seemed to know what was happening. It was thought to be an exercise to keep us on our toes." Then Japanese bombs started falling and the truth dawned.

Within thirty-six hours of the commencement of hostilities, on the Chinese mainland opposite Hong Kong Island, one Japanese infantry regiment was looking down from Needle Hill just to the north of the Gin Drinkers Line. The latter was a long, weakly constructed, and undermanned snake of pillboxes, barbed wire, and trenches upon which Hong Kong's hopes of defending the New Territories rested. Built in 1937 and in a state of poor repair, the original plan had been simply to abandon this line, together with all of the mainland part of the Colony, to the invaders. However, the arrival of two extra battalions of Canadian infantry just three weeks before the attack had led to a change of tactics. Now the Gin Drinkers Line, stretching from coast to coast across the New Territories, was to be defended by three infantry battalions, with the 2nd Battalion the Royal Scots in the western sector, the 2/14th Punjabis in the centre, and the 5/7th Rajputs in the east.

Noting that the strongest point of this defensive position, the so-called Shing Mun Redoubt, was undermanned, the Japanese decided upon an immediate attack. Within hours the Redoubt had fallen.[14]

The Royal Scots there had no choice but to fall back to a weaker position to the south, little more than shallow fox holes scraped into the rock hard earth, around the summit of Golden Hill. Next morning a fierce battle developed on the hill's peak. Caught up in this brutal fighting was a young Scot by the name of James Miller.

Born in Glasgow on 26 October 1915, his father (also James) served in the army in the Great War, and later worked in Munitions. Miller's mother died when he was a baby, and his father put him into a boys' home in Glasgow. From there, he joined the army.

"At dawn, the platoon was awakened with the warning to be absolutely quiet and to be ready for immediate action. Seemingly, the Japs had advanced during darkness to a position only 100 yards away from us and settled down for the night. We had the element of surprise; the order came to fix bayonets. It was to be hand-to-hand combat and no mercy to be shown. I would think that all of us would have prayed silently to God and hoped we would survive this battle. The order to charge was given. With our hearts pumping and the adrenalin flowing through, we raced towards the enemy. It was a complete surprise, as the enemy had not spotted us until we were on them, then it was man to man. All I can remember is a mist in front of my eyes, my heart pounding, as I cut, thrusted, and used the butt of my rifle against any of the enemy that came my way."

But the Japanese had been victorious elsewhere and had broken the line. Clearly, it would now be impossible to defend the mainland. General Christopher Maltby, in command of Hong Kong's forces, made the only logical decision: the garrison would evacuate all personnel back to Hong Kong Island.

Watching the defeat and the evacuation from the veranda of Number Three ward at the Bowen Road Military Hospital on Hong Kong Island — suffering, like many of the garrison, from malaria — was Robert Wright of the Middlesex Regiment: "When I reached the hospital it was in a state of confusion. The wards overflowed with sick and wounded, and there were insufficient beds to accommodate the endless stream of fresh arrivals from across the harbour. Mattresses were laid out on the floor, and I was allotted one of these. The systematic bombardment of Hong Kong by Japanese artillery and aircraft was at its height, and amid this chaos, doctors, nurses and orderlies, went about their duties diligently and efficiently. Even in the miasma of malaria, I was bound to admire them. They were truly magnificent."

By early morning, 13 December, all Hong Kong's garrison (minus a handful of men who had been killed or captured during the short mainland campaign) had withdrawn to Hong Kong Island itself. There they rejoined the other three infantry battalions, the Canadians of the Royal Rifles of Canada and the Winnipeg Grenadiers, and the machine-gunners of the 1st Battalion the Middlesex Regiment. Together with the remainder of the garrison — the Royal Artillery, the Royal Navy, the Hong Kong Volunteer Defence Corps (HKVDC) and all the supporting units necessary to keep an army functioning in an isolated territory — they waited for invasion. The Japanese, in no hurry to mount a risky amphibious attack, called twice for surrender. Twice their call was refused, and the defenders spent the next week being steadily bombed and shelled, watching their defensive positions being eaten away around them.

Ross Lynneberg, a Telegraphist of the New Zealand Royal Naval Volunteer Reserve, remembered this bombardment well. Born in Wellington, where his father worked as a soap salesman, he was an athlete specializing in boxing and swimming. With his hopes of joining the Royal Air Force stymied by his risk-averse parents, he joined the Naval Reserve instead while working as an office boy at the Assurance Company. With the coming of war he was sacked: "I was immediately awarded the 'DCM' (Don't Come Monday) by my employers", and, being unemployed, he was eventually mobilized. Lynneberg arrived in Hong Kong (via Singapore) the day before hostilities commenced.

Attached to the nerve centre of Hong Kong's garrison, Fortress Headquarters, for wireless duties, he found himself in a Japanese bomber's bombsight: "One of the targets for the dive bombers was the entrance to the underground HQ. During one of these raids as I was leaving through this entrance I saw a dive bomber coming straight down at me — saw the bomb leave as it pulled out of the dive and time stood still as I watched it coming straight at me. Then when the bomb seemed only a few hundred yards away it swept over my head to explode on the top of HQ."

With their bombardment reaching the point of diminishing returns, and under pressure from Tokyo to win a quick victory and make their forces available for battles elsewhere, the Japanese put their invasion plans in order. On the dark night of 18 December, made even more impenetrable by smoke from burning oil installations and a paint factory, three experienced Japanese infantry regiments of the 38th Division began to cross the harbour in small boats. Waiting for them, split into two Brigades, East and West, were Hong Kong's defenders.

The invaders fell upon the 5th Battalion of the 7th Rajput Regiment — tough, professional soldiers from the old British Indian army — who, after returning from the Gin Drinkers Line, had been tasked with defending the North East Shore of the Island. Smashing through these positions, the attacking Japanese then pushed west until stopped by men of the HKVDC and the Middlesex, and south until they encountered the Winnipeg Grenadiers and more HKVDC troops defending the Wong Nai Chung valley that bisected the Island.

From that moment, all was confusion. Thrown into the fray, the 2nd Battalion the Royal Scots lost many men in desperate, fragmented, counter-attacks in the centre of the Island. Royal Artillery units were either overrun, or took their place in the line as infantry. Royal Naval personnel left their ships, embarked in lorries, and drove to the front line. Royal Engineers picked up their rifles and, with RAF men at their sides, joined the counter-attacks.

The Royal Navy ordered Hong Kong's small but powerful flotilla of Motor Torpedo Boats into the harbour to try to interrupt the flow of Japanese infantry across the water from Kowloon. On board MTB12 was Alf 'Nobby' Hunt, who would be very lucky to survive the next hour.

Born in 1919 in a small village five miles from Stratford on Avon,[15] his father looked after a stable, training hunting and racehorses. It was always Hunt's ambition to travel and see the world. Luckily, the brother of one of the stable owners was Admiral of the Fleet Sir Lionel Halsey, who was also Hunt's godfather. Hunt used to carry his spare gun for him when he came up to go shooting in the local woods. At fourteen he was not old enough to join the Navy, but Halsey knew the boy was keen on going to sea and found a place for him in a merchant navy training ship at Liverpool. There, Hunt learnt seamanship and communications and, memorably, was part of the guard of honour when King George the Fifth opened the first Mersey tunnel. At age fifteen, Hunt joined HMS *Ganges* near Ipswich and trained to be a wireless operator. After sixteen months, the Navy posted him to HMS *Royal Sovereign* on a Mediterranean cruise. Then he transferred to HMS *Royal Oak*, another battleship, and spent two years patrolling the coasts of Spain during the civil war, looking after the interests of British merchant shipping from bases in St Jean de Luz, Bayonne and Palma. At the end of 1938, a more exotic posting materialized, to Hong Kong and HMS *Cicala* operating on the West River up to Canton and Waichow, and around the Pearl River delta, on anti-piracy patrols.

Now he found himself hanging on to the speeding MTB12 for dear life, standing on the outside of the bridge with a pair of earphones on and a remote-controlled Morse key (and a stripped Lewis gun), next to the skipper who was standing inside the bridge.

Rounding Green Island — marking the westernmost part of the harbour — at top speed, the MTB proceeded east into the hotly contested waters. Getting closer to the Star Ferry pier, they came under sustained attack from field guns, mortars, machine guns, and rifles. Japanese fighters swooped down to strafe them; suddenly a shell made a direct hit on the bridge.

Hunt: "The skipper and the First Lieutenant were both killed outright, as was the coxswain on the wheel. The engine room P.O. came up on deck, said 'What's happening Nobby?', shook hands with me, and was then hit by machine gun fire and fell overboard. I was hit at the same time; a bullet through my steel helmet made a deep groove across my forehead and I must have gone unconscious for the next thing I can remember was swimming around in the water."[16]

Managing to struggle through the harbour waves to Kowloon, he crawled into a storm drain. Lying half submerged, he found that he had two bullets in his left leg, one in his left upper arm and some shrapnel wounds in his back. Japanese soldiers approaching in a sampan captured him and tied him up with barbed wire, until a senior officer arrived and ordered him released.[17]

Another young sailor, William Grant Shepherd serving on HMS *Tern*,[18] had a very different experience. Born on a Scottish farm north of Dundee in 1920, his career began as an apprentice maintenance mechanic in a textile plant before he joined the navy in 1940 as an Engine Room Artificer. Drafted to Hong Kong early in 1941, he served with Hunt on HMS *Cicala* before transferring to *Tern*. Initially, on 19 December as his gunboat was being scuttled, his worries focused on his dress uniform:

"I remember having a concern for a new dress uniform I'd never worn, and my concern extended to deciding to wear it as I left the gun boat, having no idea what was in store as we were ordered to join the land forces in an attempt to defend the Colony. I recall taking up position on [Bennet's Hill in the southern part of Hong Kong] and spending the night trying to get some sleep under cover of a large army truck. When daylight broke a group began attempting to reach Aberdeen Industrial School, and it was during this attack that I was hit by a Japanese sniper's bullet. A CPO from HMS *Tern* came to my aid. In retrospect, one of my reactions to what he found necessary was rather humorous considering the predicament we were in. He found it necessary to rip the seam of my pants on the injured leg and because of this I was upset at the damage to my 'tiddly suit'."[19]

Also heading towards Bennet's Hill was William Poulter of the Middlesex Regiment. A regular soldier, he had met and married his wife Dorothy (Doff) in 1935 while stationed at Colchester in Essex, and the following year their son Robin was born. In 1938 they were sent to Hong Kong, stationed at Nanking Barracks, Sham Shui Po, living in Jubilee Buildings, "which were married quarters and were the finest that we had ever been in." His Company Headquarters were at 11 Shouson Hill, and the Company's task was to hold a line of pillboxes from Brick Hill to South Bay. As Company Quarter Master Sergeant, his role was to serve these positions with food and ammunition.

"I set out from Shouson Hill to take some food to our men on Bennet's Hill and we ran into a Jap ambush. We fought our way passed it, and I managed to stop some pieces of a hand grenade, and my driver was minus a piece of his ear. I was not seriously wounded. I got pieces of grenade in my neck and shoulders, a scratch on my head, and my legs were pitted. I remembered at the time that the grenade hit the ground

I saw an orange coloured flash and said to myself 'Bill, you've had it.' I was rather surprised to find that I was still on my feet."

He managed to continue to the Aberdeen Industrial School, and stayed there until the surrender doing roof guard and supplying his men on Bennet's Hill with food whenever possible.

As the Japanese pushed inland, fighting continued all over the Island. Soon the invaders had managed to separate West and East Brigades. Japanese forces marching south squeezed East Brigade down into Stanley, while other elements heading west pressed West Brigade towards the central business district. In furious encounters, many men had lucky escapes

Lying in his hospital bed, listening to the Japanese guns getting closer and closer, was Londoner Dennis Morley of the Royal Scots. Born in 1919, after leaving school he took an apprenticeship at Philips Radio at Mitcham, Surrey. Having the urge to travel and find out how people lived in other countries, he decided on a career in the services. He joined the Royal Scots Regiment as a band boy, and was posted to the 2nd Battalion in Lahore, India.

In 1938, the 2nd Battalion were posted to Hong Kong, which the army then considered the top posting in the world. Being in the band he had plenty of outside engagements, though felt that "anyone who had any sense knew that the war would hit sooner or later."

Once the Japanese attacked, Morley fought on the Mainland, and in the defence of Wong Nai Chung Gap on the Island. By 23 December, he was in hospital at St Albert's Convent.[20] That morning, the Japanese finally took the position: "The first thing I knew of the Japs taking over was that word I would remember for the next three years and eight months, 'kura!'[21] and Jap soldiers with fixed bayonets rushing about and menacing us. They soon left thank goodness. We later learned that a dead Jap officer was in the morgue covered with a Jap flag. This had saved our lives."[22]

At the Royal Naval Hospital in Wanchai, straight down the hill from St Albert's Convent, another man, Leading Sick Berth Attendant Wallace Hastings, also lay in bed. Born on 4 August 1918 in Dartford, Kent, he was one of seven children, with five sisters and a younger brother. His father was a journeyman barber employed locally, but later he established his own business in the town. On leaving school, Hasting's first employment was as an Apprentice Storekeeper at a local motorcar agent. His father (Wallace Hastings senior), however, knew better and decided that a career in the one of the armed forces would lead to a better future for his boy. To this end, he consulted Hasting's former headmaster who agreed to re-admit him to school for further study. The goal was to prepare him to sit the College of Preceptors Examination required for admission to the Royal Air Force apprentice school; but having no real enthusiasm for a service career, Hastings deliberately sabotaged his finals and failed.

Aged sixteen and a half years he joined the Vickers Armstrong Munitions Factory as an unskilled labourer making bomb boxes. After continued criticism and pleas from his father, at eighteen years of age he finally decided to enlist in the Royal Navy and signed on for twelve years at Chatham Barracks. "I chose the Sick Berth Branch merely to have a peaked cap and 'square rig' uniform rather than a pillbox and bell bottomed trousers!"

After basic training at HMS *Pembroke* and RNH *Gillingham*, his first draft came in 1939 to HMS *Tarantula* on China Station, thence to *Seamew*, and finally to Hong Kong's naval base station, *Tamar*.

Unlike Morley, Hastings had been able to take no part in the battle ("I regret to have to say that my contribution to the battle for Hong Kong amounted to nil") as he was in hospital having his tonsils removed. All he could do, as fierce fighting came within a hundred yards of the hospital on all sides (Morrison Hill, Mount Parrish, and Wanchai Market) was listen to the guns and the screams getting closer and closer ...

The struggle was becoming grim. More than ten percent of Hong Kong's small garrison would be dead before the surrender, with thousands more wounded with no hope of receiving modern medical care.

The half-trained and under-equipped Canadians of the Winnipeg Grenadiers and Royal Rifles of Canada fought the Japanese to a standstill at certain spots, and made madly courageous frontal attacks on them at others. The 1st Battalion the Middlesex Regiment, famed for finding humour in the worst situations, seldom fell back an inch whatever pressures the Japanese brought to bear. And 3 Company, HKVDC — comprised entirely of Eurasians of whom little was expected — held the Japanese on the strategically important hill known as Jardine's Lookout until almost every man was dead or wounded.

On the south side of the Island, the glamorous Repulse Bay Hotel, the haunt of celebrities such as Ernest Hemingway during pre-war times, came under siege. Its strategic position at the bottom of the road that split the Island in two, north to south, made it a natural target. Its guests — an amazing mixture of socialites, refugees, millionaires, and military men — reported that the Japanese were on the road outside on the morning of 20 December. Tom 'Taffy' Evans, a seven-year veteran of the Middlesex Regiment, ended up at the hotel at that time.

Born in Ipswich, Suffolk in 1916, Evans had joined the army in 1934 at Mill Hill Barracks, London, and was happy to be posted to Hong Kong ("HK Very cheap. My pay per week 16 shillings for pocket. Could live well.") He was a dispatch rider, but soon found himself in the thick of the fighting. Attaching himself to Peter Grounds, a young lieutenant who was leading an attack towards the garage of the hotel — into which they had just seen the Japanese dragging British prisoners — he was inches from him at the time the young officer was shot.

Evans: "He was killed by what I think was a sniper, which came from the garage across the road from the hotel, which the Japs had occupied the night before. We were with others, alongside the wall outside the main door, engaging in fire. Peter was hit in the head, next to me. We took [him] into the hotel but were told he couldn't last."[23]

It was all for nothing. Such courage in a force without air cover, without hope of being relieved, and outnumbered by a remorselessly experienced foe, could not prevail. At best, the Battle of Hong Kong had been a part of an overall war of attrition that the Japanese could never win. The Hong Kong Garrison had tied up and dented experienced Japanese resources that, in the long term, could never be replaced.

The Garrison's surrender, on Christmas Day 1941, was, however, honourable. Even the battle-hardened Japanese had been surprised by the fierceness of the resistance, which saw a rag-tag grouping of local Volunteers, British and Indian regulars, raw untried Canadians, and Royal Navy able seamen acting as foot soldiers, fighting gamely despite the fact that they knew the situation was impossible. The only hope for Hong Kong had been to stall the invaders until help could be sent from Singapore. However, once the news of the sinking of HMS *Repulse* and HMS *Prince of Wales* came through, that hope faded entirely; Singapore was facing a disaster of its own. A rumour began of a Chinese army heading to the relief of Hong Kong, but as the pockets of resistance on Hong Kong Island were squeezed tighter and tighter, few had any doubts as to the reality of their defeat.

The last shots in the defence of Hong Kong were fired in the early hours of 26 December 1941, a few hours after the surrender had actually been signed, in the picturesque village of Stanley on the south coast of the Island where Jack Etiemble, Charles Brooks and their comrades manned the huge coastal guns.

After the surrender, Geoffrey Hamilton,[24] a Hong Kong Volunteer who had been drafted into the Royal Scots to replace an officer killed earlier in the fighting, brought his men out of the line near Wanchai Gap. Hamilton wrote: "On arrival at Magazine Gap on the way to the Peak we found a field ambulance under the command of an excitable and not very sober officer, who, not having heard of the surrender, considered us to be deserters and waved his revolver at us. As explanations had no effect, I felt obliged to tell him that if he did not put his revolver away he would be killed. We then placed Tierney[25] in the ambulance and also my CSM Matheson who was suffering from malaria and had a head wound ... On our way to the Peak we passed the Jardine's Corner police station which was burning fiercely. Ammunition and grenades were exploding in the flames, and bullets and pieces of shrapnel were flying around, but we were so tired and depressed that we could only stumble slowly past. Fortunately no one was hit. On arrival at the assembly point in the Peak Garage we had a meal, our first hot meal for many days".

In the aftermath of the fighting, the defenders took stock. They had lost over 1,500 dead, with many more injured, from a force that had never exceeded 14,000.[26] Eighteen days of fighting had left all of them exhausted and undernourished.

They sat and waited for the Japanese to take them prisoner. They felt lucky to have survived the battle. They had no idea that they were to be led to a captivity in which disease, malnutrition, cruelty and the *Lisbon Maru* would kill almost twice as many as the bullets, bombs, shells, mortars and bayonets of the fighting.

*   *   *

Wives and children of the garrison were left to worry. For those families who had stayed in Hong Kong, there was initially little news. However, the grapevine soon began to function and stories of who had been lost, and who survived, circulated rapidly. But isolated from all information in Australia, evacuated families tried to continue with normal life, waiting desperately for news.

Ron Brooks, now separated from his Royal Artillery father by some three thousand miles: "I don't know how long it was before we moved to quite a nice flat (for those days) in the seaside suburb of St Kilda. I think that quite a number of evacuees were moved to St Kilda. I can remember playing with other evacuee children who lived in a small hotel nearby. Being the seaside playground for Melbourne, St Kilda probably had quite a lot of accommodation in flats, guesthouses and small hotels. Our flat was first floor, with a downstairs entry hall from a veranda. It had a lounge, two bedrooms, kitchen and bathroom and a large open balcony at the rear. It was one of a group of eight purpose-built flats in two blocks of four. An Austrian Jewish lady (Mrs Kirsner) who had two teenage daughters owned the blocks. They were refugees and lived in one of the flats. It was a regular errand for me to take the weekly rent around. The flat was very well situated at 332, Beaconsfield Parade. This was a long boulevard, which ran along the coast from Port Melbourne to St Kilda. By Number 332 the Parade consisted of two one-way roads separated by a wide strip of lawn, perhaps fifty yards, planted with palm trees. Later in the war a zigzag line of trenches was dug in the lawn. Opposite us was a promenade, the swimming club changing rooms and a bathing beach. The large St Kilda Park began close by.

Geoff and I went to the St Kilda primary school situated next to the terminus of the electric railway line from Flinders Street station. It was within walking distance from our flat. Geoff must have moved on fairly quickly to the Technical School (I think in Albert Park). Geoff suffered quite a bit from bad asthma attacks and this had quite an affect on him throughout his life. Geoff and I must have had a pretty good time there. We were free to wander all over St Kilda (even after the American soldiers arrived) and Geoff had a bike, my envy! I think at first my mother was also quite content apart from the separation from my father. I remember she had a few friends in St Kilda and seemed reasonably settled. That changed with the fall of Hong Kong, Christmas 1941, when the real worry of what had happened to my father began."

*   *   *

Hong Kong had fallen, and had been, for the time being at least, completely cut off from all outside communication.

3 Prisoners of War: Hong Kong, 1942

> Confined together
> In the same fashion as you gave in charge,
> Just as you left them; all prisoners, sir
>
> *The Tempest*, Act 5, Scene 1

On 29 December 1941, Jack Etiemble and slightly over two thousand men captured with East Brigade in Stanley marched over Wong Nai Chung Gap, under Japanese orders, to North Point at the centre of Hong Kong Island's north shore. They were a mixed bag of Gunners, Middlesex, Royal Rifles, Volunteers, Royal Navy, and stragglers from many other units. It was not a pleasant stroll. Many men, captured a few days earlier in the fighting at Wong Nai Chung Gap, had already been marched north along this same track. Those wounded who could not keep up with their comrades had been taken aside and executed at the side of the road, where their bodies had joined the remains of others killed earlier in the fighting.

A Winnipeg Grenadier NCO on that earlier march recalled: "Men were falling now who could not get up and the others were dragging them. Orders must have been given to cut these men loose for we heard screams and later passed the bodies of unfortunates who, after being freed, were bayoneted and left by the roadside. I thought of falling down for good, come what may, but hearing these screams I decided to keep going as long as my weary and stiffened limbs would allow. I was past feeling heat, dust, or wounds. I was smothered in a sort of coma. I, like the rest, just staggered along, at every few paces trying to avoid a stumbling companion. The big Englishman was in serious difficulties. In spite of the pleadings, mutters and curses from our group he continued to fall down. Each time he would be butted by the rifle of the guard, pulled to his feet by the others and made to stumble on. This is where I first met that phenomenon of misery and captivity. The greater misfortunes of others often tend to mitigate one's own sufferings. The big Englishman, being beaten each time he fell, received most of the attention of our guard. His falling also gave us a breathing spell. But finally he could rise no more. We were halted. Wire cutters were produced. The Englishman was cut loose and kicked to the side of the road. I heard his scream of agony as they bayoneted him and threw his body over the cliff."[27]

At the end of the march, at North Point, a refugee camp awaited Jack and his comrades. Built three years earlier to house Chinese refugees escaping the fighting against the Japanese in their own country, it had been the scene of considerable shelling during the eighteen days of conflict, and starving civilians had looted what little of value remained. All that was left for the Prisoners of War was filth. Dead horses — victims of the Japanese invasion along this stretch of seafront — framed the gate, and soldiers' bloated bodies floated in the sea, gently bumping against the harbour wall.

Robert Wright, just out of hospital after his attack of malaria: "Two days of hard work resulted in North Point looking more or less presentable. Life there, however, was anything but enjoyable. Throughout our stay there, we were hit by gales and bad weather, and as our hut was nearest to the sea, and in the open, it had to take the brunt of the storms. The rain seeped in, the high winds threatened to deprive us of our roof, and when the sea was in ill humour we became water logged. In North Point, was the shadowy shape of the evil things to come."

Soon after dawn on the next day, the bulk of the defeated defenders — some seven thousand who had been captured with West Brigade in the central and western parts of the Island — gathered in turn in Victoria.[28] In the early afternoon, they boarded ferries to cross to Kowloon. On landing, the Japanese guards split them into parties of five hundred, and led their prisoners off haphazardly. Some troops heard their Japanese captors struggling with the words 'Sham Shui Po', and guided their 'guides' in the right direction. To many of them these barracks had previously been home, and on arrival they joined many men who the victorious Japanese had captured earlier in the fighting. Later, the convalescent wounded, returning from the various military hospitals that dotted the Colony, joined them in turn.

Signaller Frank Bennett: "We had been warned before leaving our own barracks, to take only essential items with us. This advice was from our CSM Peter Wigzell,[29] who I believe had been a POW during the Great War. On top of what each man decided to carry he was issued with an item for the Company, be it office equipment, kitchen equipment or food. All items were tabulated and the recipient was bound by military law to hand it in at the other end. It was amazing how much equipment was dumped during that march but, at the end, every piece of office equipment was handed in."

According to an HKVDC Gunner with the party: "Our first impression on entering Shamshuipo was of space, order, and reasonably substantial buildings — with a grateful recognition of the survival of grass and trees. Seen close to, the picture abruptly changed. The barracks had been one of the first targets of the Japanese air attack, and a stick of bombs had been neatly laid across Jubilee[30] from corner to corner. Many of the huts had been gutted. And far more disastrous than any bombs had been the ravages of looters, who had swarmed into the camp after the British garrison withdrew from Kowloon. There is something terrifying about the thoroughness of Chinese looting. To anyone of imagination, it reveals a level of stark poverty undreamed of by most Europeans."[31]

Like North Point, everything was gone apart from bricks and concrete. Sham Shui Po had become a sterile shell of a camp. Royal Scots Lieutenant Hamilton recalled: "We were very cold sleeping on the concrete floor in January without doors or windows to keep out the wind. I was wearing shorts and long puttees[32] and at night used to wrap the puttees round my body to conserve heat. We were also very hungry."

The Japanese sent the Indian units to a separate POW camp, Ma Tau Chong,[33] but they interned the Hong Kong Police, who had been sworn in and had fought as militia, as civilians in Stanley Camp.[34]

The new authorities gathered the families of the fighting men together on 4 January and housed them in unsanitary 'short-time' hotels on the Sai Ying Poon waterfront in the north west of Hong Kong Island.[35] On 21 January, they finally transported them to their permanent internment camp — at Stanley, the very battlefield on which so many husbands and fathers had died. But Stanley would not be a bad camp, as camps go. Rations were never as generous as the internees needed, and the overcrowding was a constant trial, but there was little sadism on the Japanese side and diseases would never take control to the extent that they did in the POW camps.

A civilian nurse and young mother remembered: "When we moved to Stanley a nurse gave me a basket-cradle for Nicholas. An armed Japanese soldier watched impassively as I attempted to breast-feed my baby. The dusty journey in a truck was tedious and bumpy, with frequent stops and searches. Our arrival was chaotic and unorganized. With the help of friends, we somehow got through the first night without light and with very little food or water, on the crowded floor — an ordeal for a hungry baby who hardly stopped crying all night. The source of his food supply was already beginning to fail as a result of the turmoil, and for him this was the beginning of ten weeks of slow starvation which would have been fatal but for the timely arrival of Red Cross supplies of powdered milk — thanks to the efforts of Doctor Selwyn-Clarke."[36]

Outside Hong Kong, the families of fighting men had been waiting for news. Newspapers worldwide reported the fighting in Hong Kong, and the Christmas Day surrender. Since then, there had been silence. Suddenly, thousands of official letters arrived; addressed to the POWs' next of kin, the lack of assurance that their subjects were alive brought consternation to every family that received them. The Brooks family in Australia received their first such letter less than a month after the surrender:

The War Office — 20 January 1942

Madam,

With regard to the information already communicated to you by the British High Commissioner's Office, Melbourne, I am directed to inform you that according to the records in this Office your husband, No. 1410996 Warrant Officer (Class 1) C. F. Brooks, Royal Artillery, was serving in Hong Kong when the garrison capitulated on the 25th December 1941. Every endeavour is being made through diplomatic and other channels to obtain information concerning him but it is regretted that in the meantime, it will be necessary to post him as "Missing".

Immediately any information is obtained it will be communicated to you, and in this connection I am to request that you will be good enough to notify this Office of any change of your address. Should any news reach you from other sources it will be appreciated if you will communicate with this Department.

              I am,
              Madam,
              Your obedient Servant[37]

Ross Lynneberg, the New Zealand naval signaller, was initially interned at Sham Shui Po: "After almost a month (on 26/1/42) the naval personnel were assembled and sent back to HK Island to [North Point Camp] used earlier by Chinese refugees but since the surrender occupied by the Canucks ... [38] The Chinese who watched us changing camp were not the scornful, spitting crowds of a month earlier — in fact they were a very sorry looking mob. The route we took was about one mile around the shore line which for the whole distance, was covered with 'good nips' (dead Japanese soldiers) washed ashore — some areas many bodies deep and well protected by a thick black coating of flies and an unholy smell.[39]

On our arrival at the camp we found a self-appointed and promoted 'Naval Officer' in control[40] — fortunately this individual died later in Japan thus obviating a court-martial at the end of the war. In charge of us was the commander for the China Station who quickly had this fictitious officer's naval rank rings removed.

In this camp were over one thousand Canadians so with our naval ratings the strength increased to two-thousand-odd. The food here was for a while better than the previous camp having three small meals a day — two were rice and to build us up we also had canned foods, whale meat, Chinese preserved duck eggs and vegetables."

By the end of January 1942, the Japanese had split the POWs across three camps. On Hong Kong Island, at North Point, were in fact more than 1,500 Canadians[41] with a number of Royal Naval personnel, and the crew of a Dutch submarine captured off Malaya (who had arrived on 1 February). In Kowloon, the Indian regulars were settling down at Ma Tau Chung, while the bulk of the regular British and HKVDC forces were trying to adapt to conditions in Sham Shui Po.

Their new environment took some adjusting to, with the diet being the biggest complaint. Some men simply could not accept that rice was now the staple (and there was little enough of that). Early attempts at cooking rice in bulk did not make it any more appetizing for them, as the grains at the top generally stayed raw, those at the bottom burnt, and the few in the middle were too little to go round.

According to a senior HKVDC officer: "There were thousands of troops and the only rations we got, I discovered, were rice. They had the Royal Engineers in the cook house cooking rice and the queue was so long. I managed to approach the ration officer to say, 'Look, you give me the rice, and we'll cook it ourselves,' which he did, and being local born in Hong Kong, some of us knew how to cook rice. Those who didn't, knew how to eat the rice though."[42]

Gunner Jack Etiemble: "The Royal Artillery cookhouse had in fact been a bedroom and our cooks had to boil our rice in the bath! For a while it was just rice, some of our officers complained stating that we must have vegetables; next day a truck came loaded with chrysanthemums, the Japs said you wanted veg, you eat. I must say it did make a change."

With the poor nutrition and unhygienic conditions, disease soon became rife. Dysentery sometimes raged out of control, pneumonia was not uncommon, and vitamin deficiency diseases such as dry beri beri[43] slowly crept up on almost every man. As malnutrition and avitaminosis[44] spread amongst the prisoners, death became a daily part of life.

Robert Wright of the Middlesex Regiment: "Curiously, [the Japanese] willingly attended the funeral of some dead man, humbly said 'Very sorry', but refused to accept responsibility for the deaths taking place daily, although most could have been prevented by them, and at a comparatively slight cost."[45]

After food and disease, boredom was the other main concern.

Hamilton: "It was difficult to find any way to pass the time. Cyril Jones[46] had a pack of cards and we used to play bezique for hours. For a time I was invited to play bridge with my C.O. Colonel Simon White, and two other Colonels, but I did not much enjoy playing in such distinguished company, especially as the Colonel always blamed me if we were defeated."

In April, the Japanese decided to move the officers in Sham Shui Po to another POW Camp on Argyle Street. At the same time, the Naval contingent left North Point and returned to Sham Shui Po.

New Zealander Lynneberg had been at North Point until this time: "The huts in which we lived were in a very bad state having been riddled by machine gun fire during the war, many being partly demolished through artillery fire. In this camp was an example of a concrete pillbox being built with 'squeeze' resulting in the concrete being so poor that the wind was gradually blowing the sand away.[47] Time in this camp passed repairing huts, doing various school subjects, and counting how many flies one killed with one swish of the fly swatter, the tallies being in the scores.

Sleeping on concrete was so uncomfortable some of us made slat beds a few inches above the concrete, but the best effort was by Murdo

Stewart[48] who still had his seaman issue jack-knife and built a slat bed on legs well clear of the floor. Before winter set in many went sick with dysentery but fortunately very few died. One soon learnt not to give lights from their cigarettes as the Canucks would ask for a light and place their cigarette on your fag and half consume it before one realised they were using a hollow cigarette tube.

Due to the poor diet, this winter was so severe for us that we wore all the clothing we possessed, and stayed in bed for days and nights except for collecting meals and numbering for the Japs. After three months at this camp, many were showing signs of malnutrition, even though our commander was very helpful and made constant demands on the Japanese quoting International Law. This resulted in the officers being separated from the ratings when we returned to Sham Shui Po on 18/4/42 making it much easier for the Japs to deal with us. This move took place on a rainy day when we were stood for hours on the parade ground ankle deep in water, with many a blow to further lower our morale and were compelled to empty our small kits and bedding into the water with the Japs pretending to search through the heaps. After a very tiring day we were back to our earlier camp again being searched and counted before going to the huts and sleep. As it was several days before the weather fined up allowing the clothing to dry, tempers were very brittle.

The huts were still in as bad a condition as when we left three months earlier, the only changes being the creation of long benches for use as common beds and the erection of an electric fence. There was one at the camp we had just left which was very efficient for one morning one of the Jap dogs was found dead on it. This new fence was used by the Japs to torture Chinese who were near the fence trying to sell things or girls wanting to see their men friends. These unfortunates would be gathered together and bound with wire leaving a long loose end. After saturating the group with water this would be thrown over the electric fence, the pitiful noise wrung from the Chinese being similar to the squeals of frightened pigs."

More letters from the British authorities were now starting to get through. Financial matters may not have been the highest priority for the family of Sam 'Leny' Atkins of the Middlesex Regiment at that moment, but army formalities dictated that they still had to be taken care of.

>
> Address reply to MINISTRY OF PENSIONS   Telephone
> The Secretary   WAR SERVICE GRANTS   St Annes 2300
> And quote the   Heyhouses Lane   Telegraphic address
> Following number: Lytham St. Anne   "Millalac. St.Annes"
> E 3210 A   Lancs
>
> May, 1942.
>
> Madam,
>
> ATKINS, S.A. Pte. 6213420, Mdx. Rgt.
>
> With reference to the War Service Grant which you have been receiving, notification had been received that on War Office authority your Family Allowance will continue in payment until 9th August, 1942.
>
> It has, therefore, been possible to authorize payment of you War Service Grant up to that date.
>
> An Order Book covering the period from 11.5.42 to 9.8.42 has been sent to the Post Office at Finstock B.O. Oxon and will be handed to you in exchange for PE 45C.
>
> I am, Madam,
>   Your obedient Servant
>
>   For Secretary
>
> Mrs. M.E. Atkins
> School Road, Finstock,
> Nr. Charlbury, Oxford.[49]

Unaware that events in mid-Pacific were about to change the course of the war, early June 1942 may not have meant too much to Jack Etiemble, Charles Brooks, Sammy Atkins and their fellow POWs. Ill, hungry, and bored they had little to write home about, and as yet no chance to do so. On 3 June, Private Francis Jennings of the Hong Kong Dockyard Defence Corps died of acute enteritis and heart failure. On the fifth Signalman John Little followed him, and on the ninth Bombardier Joseph Rodgers, both from dysentery.

Jack Etiemble: "After six months, conditions in Sham Shui Po were very bad. Many POWs were suffering from dysentery. It was heartbreaking to see men you have known for a couple of years being reduced to almost skeletons, and now another curse had emerged Pellagra causing skin to peel off tongues, testicles etc.[50] I know the feeling for I was one of those who suffered. Another curse was 'Electric feet'. All of these could have been avoided with a better diet. At the time strong rumours were going around, later found to be true, that an officer and three sergeants were collaborating with the Japs,[51] also rumours that some of us will be heading for Japan before long. Deaths still occurring on a regular basis."

Robert Wright: "I was at Sham Shui Po for six months. In that time I knew nothing but hopelessness as a prisoner-of-war. This was the beginning of months and months of torture, suspense and suffering, and of starvation, disease, brutalities and killings."

As time passed, morale suffered because of the poor conditions, the lack of news from outside, and the complete invisibility of Allied forces.[52] However, just a few months after Hong Kong's surrender, while the Hong Kong Prisoners of War were still adjusting to their new circumstances, a strategically decisive battle was in progress three thousand miles away in the middle of the Pacific Ocean around a remote island called Midway.

One of the vessels involved in the battle, on her first war patrol, was a brand-new American submarine. None of the POWs in Hong Kong would have heard of her at that time, and even if they had, there was no reason that any of them should have guessed that their paths might cross so dramatically a few months later.

*   *   *

During the Battle of Midway, little changed in Hong Kong. Several more POWs died, victims, mainly, of the unremitting malnutrition and its direct effect on health and morale. Food was constantly in their thoughts. As one young prisoner from the Middlesex Regiment wrote:

> You know, Lord, how one must strive
> At Shamshuipo to keep alive.
> And how there isn't much to eat –
> Just rice and greens at Argyle Street.[53]
>
> It's not much, God, when dinner comes
> To find it's just chrysanthemums.

Nor can I stick at any price
Those soft white maggots in the rice.
Nor yet those little, hard black weevils,
The lumps of grit and other evils.

I know, Lord. I shouldn't grumble
And please don't think that I'm not humble
When I most thankfully recall
My luck to be alive at all.

But, Lord, I think that even You
Would soon get tired of ersatz stew.
So what I really want to say
Is: if we soon don't get away
From Shamshuipo and Argyle Street,
Then please, Lord, could we have some meat?

A luscious, fragrant, heaped-up plateful.
And also, Lord, we would be grateful
If you would send a living boon

And send some Red Cross parcels, soon.

Jack Etiemble: "Our diet was so bad that we had only enough energy to go from the billet to the cookhouse and back and avoided doing anything strenuous. Conditions were so bad men were dying of dysentery. It was terrible seeing men fading away ... In fact everyone was working out when he would die, if he was the last one left."

William Spooner of the Royal Scots, working in the camp hospital, had memories almost identical to those of Etiemble: "It was so pitiful a sight to see. Once strong healthy men in their prime, reduced to wrecks, shambling about the camp in rags, blood and mucous running down their legs. Despair, pain, sometimes resignation on their faces, until they inevitably joined the ranks of those who had lost all expression."

Robert Wright experienced this miserable disease for himself: "Towards the end of June, I contracted dysentery and was admitted to hospital, although there was no treatment to be had there. I was there three weeks and was so ill I felt sure I must die. Day after day, but half conscious, I lay on my iron bed, while men all around me were dying. I cannot describe the panic and torment to which I fell victim at that time. The flesh shrank from my bones, my eyes became caverns and my cheeks hollowed. There was little comfort to be had, and no medicines."

Wright was lucky. A diet of burnt rice scrapings and rice water pulled him through. But he was one of the few to escape alive from the 'agony ward'. Those who entered were tempted to believe themselves doomed; fear of disease had become almost as destructive as the diseases themselves.

Men invented different ways of surviving, mentally, the privations of POW life. One young lieutenant, Alan Stanley Potter of the St John's Ambulance, used his love of the sea to keep his spirits up. In the camp, looking out over the waves that splashed the sea wall behind Jubilee Barracks at Sham Shui Po, he wrote these words:

> My prison window opens out
> Upon a vista wide,
> An island studded harbour set
> With hills on every side,
> And right ahead, aye, calling me,
> A passage to the open sea.
>
> My prison house is fenced around
> With lines of knotted wire,
> And weapon'd guards keep vigil there
> To foil my heart's desire.
> 'Tis naught, for fancy lets me free
> Through yonder channel out to sea.
>
> When morning breaks along the hills
> And floods the bay with light,
> I rise from my dream-haunted bed
> And first direct my sight
> Where running tide goes flowing free
> Through that blest channel, out to sea.
>
> And when the sun, a flaming ball,
> Stoops Westward to his bed,
> And Tsing-I-Isle stands castle-like
> Against the flaming red,
> The sunset streamers beckon me
> To sail that passage out to sea.
>
> When night enshrouds the silent camp,
> And slumber holds me fast,
> 'Midst all the dreams of distant ones
> That conjure up the past,
> The constant vision comes to me
> Of that near channel out to sea.

Though comfort small this place affords,
My constant joy is found
In all the sweep of hills and bay
That rings the camp around.
And, for supremest luxury,
I have my passage out to sea.

In selfsame manner in our life
In narrow limits cast,
In action cramped, with vision wide,
Our mortal days are passed.
But freedom for Eternity
Waits through that channel out to sea.

Potter would have his chance to take that channel out to sea, but it would cost him his life.[54]

The War Office had also been busy writing. Now, after seven months, families began to receive their first official notifications that their loved ones were still alive:

War Office Welfare Officer – 10 July 1942

Dear Mrs. Brooks,

On the 8th of July I forwarded to your address the notification that your husband is a prisoner of war. Evidently there has been an error in delivery and I attach herewith copy of the notification.

Yours sincerely

[The original letter of the 8th is enclosed]

8 July 1942

Dear Mrs. Brooks,

I am pleased to advise you that official notification has been received from the War Office that your husband 1410996 Warrant Officer I, C. F. Brooks, R.A., recently posted as Missing, is now Prisoner of War.

Yours sincerely

The War Office – 14 July 1942

Madam,

With regard to the information already communicated to you by the British High Commissioner's Office, Melbourne, I am directed to confirm that a report has been received from official sources, stating that your husband, No.1410996 Warrant Officer Class I. C. F. Brooks, Royal Artillery, is a prisoner of war in Japanese hands. No details have yet been received regarding his camp address or prisoner of war number, but as soon as any further information is received, you will be informed immediately.

I am, Madam,
Your obedient Servant

Not long after, for some lucky families, the first brief letters from the POWs themselves arrived; though not all had enough energy to write.

Charles Frederick Brooks
Hong Kong Prisoner of War Camp S. (undated)

Dear Em,
 I am quite well and keeping fit. Conditions are terrible here (illegible).[55] The summer is on the way and it has begun to warm up. How are you and the boys keeping, quite well and happy I earnestly hope. Do not worry over me. I shall be O.K. Let them know at home that I am safe. I will write as often as possible. So Cheerio.
All my love,
Charlie

By the beginning of August 1942, a total of 186 of those imprisoned in Hong Kong[56] had died of wounds, disease, or other causes since the surrender. Then came two new shocks, one upon the other.

The first was Transportation. Treated as just another rumour for several months, the term was familiar to many Londoners as an ancient punishment for misdemeanours — transportation to the Colonies (and particularly Australia) had been a favourite sentence of some judges of the previous century. This new transportation, hastily arranged at Japanese insistence, was to take 616 POWs aboard the *Fukken Maru* to work for the war industry in Japan itself. She left Hong Kong on 3 September, those on board having been hand-picked as the trouble-makers who would not bow down to Japanese authority — the 'hard men', as they were known.

Robert Wright: "Commanding officers of units in [Sham Shui Po] were ordered to submit the names of men who were recalcitrants. Among them were included those who, two months before, had refused to sign the 'no escape' paper[57] ... As they boarded the Ferry, which took them to a much-dilapidated coastal ship we gave them the 'thumbs up' sign of encouragement. They sailed that afternoon ... No one relished the prospect of leaving Sham Shui Po for Japan, as it was to us an unknown country."

The second shock was diphtheria. A widely feared child-killer in earlier years, an effective treatment was well known by 1942. Unfortunately, though the Japanese had no shortage of the required serum, they did not make it available in POW Camps. Spooner: "On top of all the foregoing diseases, we had an outbreak of diphtheria. Outbreak is a very mild term to apply to a disease that choked, or stopped the hearts of 90% of those that caught it."

Normally transmitted by contact with respiratory droplets from infected persons, the incubation period of this highly contagious choking disease is two to five days. The bacteria primarily infect the nose and throat, and produce a toxin that causes tissue damage around the areas of the infection. It can also spread though the body, carried by blood to other organs — particularly the heart and nervous system — which can be damaged in the same way.

Not surprisingly, diphtheria spread rapidly in the crowded and unhygienic conditions of Sham Shui Po, with five men per day dying at the epidemic's peak. However, before the death toll reached that level, news began to circulate of another transportation. This, again, was no mere rumour.

Hamilton: "After spending five months in Argyle Street Camp about half the officers were moved back to Sham Shui Po[58] and told that we would be moved to a 'very beautiful country', which we guessed would be Japan. There was much debate as to whether this would be favourable from our point of view. We thought conditions might be better, but it would mean that we would not be released until the end of the war. We had not given up hope of a relieving force retaking Hong Kong."

Friendly forces were indeed approaching. A lone American submarine that had started her second war patrol at Midway on 1 September had been on station in her assigned area since the fifteenth. On the twentieth, she silently turned towards Shanghai.

4 The Ship: *Lisbon Maru*

> In few, they hurried us aboard a barque,
> Bore us some leagues to sea, where they prepared
> A rotten carcass of a butt, not rigged,
> Nor tackle, sail, nor mast the very rats
> Instinctively have quit it. There they hoist us
> To cry to th' sea that roared to us, to sigh
> To th' winds
>
> *The Tempest*, Act 1, Scene 2

For the second transportation, the Japanese demanded two thousand 'fit' men. As well as providing slave labour for the docks, mines, factories, and ports of Japan, this would free up enough space at Sham Shui Po camp for North Point camp to be finally closed.[59]

Wright of the Middlesex, who was in Captain Martin Weedon's B Company: "This was a most difficult time for our officers. They refused to select men who were obviously unfit for the journey and, in the end, the Japanese took the responsibility of choosing men for the draft". Both Wright and Weedon would be included.

Men anxiously waited for the public posting of the list of 'draftees'. Unlike the previous draft, they included many officers who had been moved to Argyle Street camp some five months previously, and a few hundred Royal Naval personnel. However, the majority of men were regular army Other Ranks[60] already at Sham Shui Po, and one of the names that appeared on the list was that of Jack Etiemble of the Royal Artillery. He was still a young man and had already had enough of the Spartan and brutal POW experience in Hong Kong.

Etiemble: "After several months I needed dental treatment. Our Dental Officer had brought some kit with him, and had a look and said he hadn't got any filling so he had better pull it out. He sat me in a chair and a couple of POWs held me, a quick pull, and it was out. Japs were still committing atrocities, for not bowing to them; made to stand holding a fire bucket full of sand above your head. Two young Chinese waved at us, the Japs saw them and called them, two of the guards took them through the camp onto a small jetty. One sentry took them to the end and pointed to things in the harbour, the other ran up and bayoneted them and tossed them into the harbour, then left laughing and joking. Later, small work parties were sent to Kai Tak[61] filling in bomb holes. I got a hiding for not handing over my watch, when the guard demanded it. Life continued in a similar vein until boarding the *Lisbon Maru*."

Born in Jersey on 27 June 1923, Etiemble left school at the age of fourteen. His father was a builder, but Jack — like Garfield Kvalheim — wanted to see the world. He joined the Royal Artillery in September 1937, trained for a year at Woolwich, and passed out as a trumpeter in September 1938. Sailing for Hong Kong in HMT *Dilwara* in December 1938, he joined 8th Coastal Regiment, becoming a Gunner on his eighteenth birthday, and helped man the big 9.2-inch guns that defended Hong Kong's famous harbour.

Etiemble had been due to leave Hong Kong in January 1942, but the Japanese attack had spoiled his plans. Now, unavoidably delayed by nine months as a prisoner of war, he would finally be leaving — but bound for Japan.

Once the draftees knew they would be on the move, many took the opportunity to send a quick letter home. Sam Atkins, whose family most recently received communication from the government about his financial affairs, was one:

S. ATKINS
HONG-KONG, PRISONER Of WAR
CAMP S.
24 SEPT. [1942]

DEAR MARIE
THIS IS MY 2nd
CARD TO YOU AND I HOPE

> THAT BY NOW YOU HAVE
> RECEIVED IT. I AM QUITE
> ALL RIGHT, AND AM LONGING
> TO SEE YOU AND THE CHILDREN.
>   WE ARE ALLOWED TO
> WRITE 3 TIMES A YEAR
> SO YOU MUST NOT EXPECT
> (illegible   ) AND
> THE LIMIT IS 200 WORDS.
>   GIVE ANNE, BARBARA A
> BIG KISS FOR ME & KEEP
> CHEERFUL DARLING.
>   WE ARE MOVING TO ANOTHER
> CAMP AND I WILL LET YOU
> KNOW MY NEW ADDRESS WHEN
> I ARRIVE,
>   YOUR LOVING HUSBAND
>   LENY ATKINS

A lucky few found their names on the list but were declared too sick to embark. They remained in Sham Shui Po.[62]

Painfully swollen with the arrival of the returning officers and the naval contingent, Sham Shui Po's POW population was straining at the wires. Inoculated, vaccinated, numbered, and photographed, the Japanese deemed Etiemble and the other chosen men ready for their voyage. Then they issued new kit (a pair of boots, canvas shoes, underwear, shirts and shorts, two blankets, a mess tin, eating utensils, an overcoat and a haversack) to every man who would board.

At four in the morning of 25 September, with the weather still warm and humid, the draftees hastily swallowed a rushed breakfast of rice and fish, and were issued with two small sugarloaves as emergency rations. Then they made their way to the Jubilee parade ground of Sham Shui Po camp for assembly. Formed up in groups of fifty under section leaders, they waited. The wait was so long that some men devoured their sugarloaves even before they left the camp. Finally, 'The Pig'[63] arrived to address the men, interpreted by Niimori Genichoro. He told them that Wada Hideo would be their commander on the vessel, and he had a guard of some twenty-five men. Commanded by Sergeant Major Hayashi, the guards included two medical orderlies — Sergeant Majors Takahasi and Ueyama — and a Sergeant Kohima who was in charge of rations. The remainder consisted of two further sergeants and eighteen privates.[64]

Jim Fallace of the Hong Kong Royal Naval Volunteer Reserve (HKRNVR):[65] "The draft paraded at 5.30 a.m. on the 25th of September 1942, from then on no man was permitted to leave the parade. At 7.30 a.m. the Japanese general, O/C all camps, arrived and said a few words, in which he told us that we would be going to a better climate than Hong Kong and that we would have to work hard and that we would have to behave ourselves."

The column of some 1,865 men[66] moved from Jubilee Parade Ground to Bamboo Pier, where each prisoner was sprayed with disinfectant, before boarding one of a shuttle of ferries taking them out to a rusting old freighter moored off Stonecutters Island to the south.

The ship they were ferried out to was not a prepossessing sight. As they neared it, they saw the name *Lisbon Maru* for the first time, painted in white on the ship's bow in both English and Japanese. The *Lisbon Maru*,[67] like her two sister ships (the *Lyons Maru* and the *Lima Maru*), was a freighter displacing some seven thousand tons. Built for Yokohama Dock Company Limited as Hull Number 70, the *Lisbon Maru*'s keel was laid on 15 October 1919, and the vessel was launched on 31 May 1920.[68] Her early career is unclear, but on 5 May 1934, she turned up at San Francisco with a cargo of Japanese immigrants, and in 1938, she was photographed in the Thames Estuary near London. From June until the end of August 1942, British spies recorded her as being in dry dock at Taikoo, Hong Kong. According to British authorities in Chungking, "She had been damaged[69] by a mine or torpedo explosion amid ships just in front of the boiler room." When she left Hong Kong, at the end of that month, she was carrying a cargo of lead bricks and other metal. A captured document shows that she was then used as a troop carrier,[70] and on 4 September 1942, she was recorded at Guadalcanal. In her twenty-second-year afloat, the old freighter was under the command of Captain Kyoda Shigeru.

Merchant Marine Captain Kyoda Shigeru was a forty-two-year-old family man, with two sons and two daughters waiting for him back home in Japan. He had twenty years' service behind him, having first served as a Third Mate for the NYK Line from 1922 (he graduated from the Marine School on 1 December 1921) to 1926. Promoted to Second Mate in 1929, he finally became First Mate in 1939 before assuming his first command, *Morioka Maru*. It did not last long. A sea mine sunk this

4,469-ton freighter off Sasebo, Nagasaki Prefecture, on 4 March 1942. Kyoda's next appointment was captain of the *Calcutta Maru*, but on 1 May the American submarine USS *Triton* sighted his vessel, together with five more Japanese freighters and two escorts. She fired two torpedoes, and both hit the leading ship — *Calcutta Maru*. *Triton* then fired two more torpedoes at the next freighter in the convoy, but both missed. Passing under the Japanese vessels, *Triton* fired two more torpedoes at the damaged ship. One missed or failed to explode, but the other hit and broke her back. She promptly sank. Having been sunk twice in less than two months, Kyoda was given command of the *Lisbon Maru* on 9 September 1942, and came aboard the vessel on 15 September.

A total of 1,676 tons of freight had already been loaded. Most (copper, scrap iron, bismuth ore, cotton, gold dust,[71] lead, aluminium, manganese ore, tungsten and leather) was bound for their first stop, Osaka. However, thirty-two tons of the cargo consisted of five-inch high-explosive shells bound for Tokyo.

The Second Mate, Araki Kaname, was also on the bridge, though sick with dengue fever. He had joined the Nippon Yusen Kaisha line in 1927. Having previously served as Third Mate on the *Chikuzan Maru*,[72] he was now one of twelve officers[73] on the *Lisbon Maru*.

From the bridge, these two experienced men watched the POWs board. They intended to transport the prisoners, and the Japanese troops who would board later, to Osaka with the majority of the cargo. From nine in the morning, to three in the afternoon, the launches shuttled the POWs to their vessel.

It is unlikely that Kyoda would have been familiar with John Masefield's "Cargoes", but these words would have been familiar to most of the approaching POWs from their schooldays:

> Quinquireme of Nineveh from distant Ophir
> Rowing home to haven in sunny Palestine,
> With a cargo of ivory,
> And apes and peacocks,
> Sandalwood, cedarwood, and sweet white wine.
>
> Stately Spanish galleon coming from the Isthmus,
> Dipping through the Tropics by the palm-green shores,
> With a cargo of diamonds
> Emeralds, amethysts,
> Topazes, and cinnamon, and gold moidores.

> Dirty British coaster with a salt-caked smoke-stack
> Butting through the Channel in the mad March days,
> With a cargo of Tyne coal,
> Road-rail, pig-lead,
> Firewood, iron-ware, and cheap tin toys.

Looking up from the launches, despite being in the northernmost latitudes of the Tropic of Cancer, they would have surely have identified the *Lisbon Maru* as a Japanese equivalent of the Dirty British coaster.

Frank Bennett of the Hong Kong Signals Company: "We were in groups aboard launches, shoving off from a small jetty at the end of the officers' block. The first thing that struck me as we approached was the gun up on the bow. This gave cause for discussion as to whether the ship could be classed as an armed merchantman, and could be sunk on sight."

Motor Torpedo Boat survivor Alf 'Nobby' Hunt, who had barely had time to recover from the serious wounds he sustained during the fighting:[74] "We boarded a lighter that took us out to the *Lisbon Maru*. The Navy were ordered into the No. 1 forward hold, the Middlesex Regiment, Royal Scots and a number of the smaller units into No. 2, the main hold, and the Royal Artillery into No. 3 hold abaft the bridge. After much pushing and shoving it was discovered that No. 1 hold was packed to capacity and about a dozen of us RN personnel were put into No. 2 hold. All the holds had two levels, and each level had been made into two tiers of roughly hewn wood to provide accommodation for the maximum numbers to be transported. Unfortunately, when we were ordered below, the only room available was on the ballast at the bottom of the ship, on the keel. The ballast consisted of foul smelling hessian sacks filled with sand. They smelt of rotting veg, urine and were dumped at all angles. Many had burst open and one could see the evidence of rat infestation everywhere. The only light was from a single dimly lit light bulb and from the hatch opening above."

Sick Berth Attendant Wallace Hastings of the Royal Navy: "On board the ship the RN contingent were directed to the forward hold as it was considered that they could withstand the possible 'pitching and tossing' that might occur at sea. I personally greeted this with trepidation as I always succumbed to *mal de mer* at the slightest ripple. I was with a group of Sick Berth ratings from [Royal Naval Hospital] Hong Kong and *Tamar* and Surgeon Lieutenant Jackson RNVR. Names of the ratings that I remember: Ken Baggs, Thomas Eccleston, Thomas McCready, Reginald

Bailey,[75] Norman Hendy, Ronald Howson, Daniel Lewis, Allen Pemberton, Gwynfor Thomas, John Allison. On descending into the hold we found a corner port side/forward bulkhead on the second tier platform and settled in."

Finally, the lighters sailing the short route between the ship and the pier had completed their task. All the selected POWs were aboard.

The Royal Navy, Hong Kong Royal Naval Volunteer Reserve (HKRNVR), Merchant Navy, Royal Naval Dockyard Police and Hongkong Dockyard Defence Corps (HKDDC) — 362 men in total — were squeezed into the first hold under command of Lieutenant J. T. Pollock. A total of seventeen other naval personnel, including Alf Hunt, had transferred themselves to the second hold.

The Royal Artillery and elements of the Hong Kong and Singapore Royal Artillery (HKSRA) were pushed into the third hold under Major 'Zazz' Pitt, but again a few of the 380 men allocated to this hold could not physically squeeze in, and were put into Number Two instead. A handful chose to swap holds of their own accord.

Bombardier John Inglis: "As a Scot, all my life I'd had various premonitions of some sort or the other and I felt quite sick with horror at the thought of being trapped in that hell-hole, and turning to my two best friends — John 'Ramp' Bowen and Rodney 'Giddy' Giddons — said that I wasn't staying down there and was getting out, fast. Saying that the Japs would kill me if I tried to get out, I replied that I'd chance that and just went. To my great relief they followed me and once on deck, we made a mad dash for another hold. There were screams and shouts from the Japanese who were shepherding the luckless prisoners into the holds. Ignoring the orders to return to our former hold, we literally fell down the ladders."

They did not yet realize how lucky they were to be out of the third hold, the stern-most of those occupied by POWs.

The second hold, the biggest, contained 1,075 men,[76] mainly from the 2nd Battalion, the Royal Scots Regiment, and 1st Battalion, the Middlesex Regiment. However, this hold was also home to the many smaller units in the draft: the Royal Engineers (RE), Royal Corps of Signals (RCS), Royal Army Medical Corps (RAMC), Royal Army Ordnance Corps (RAOC), Royal Army Dental Corps (RADC), Royal Army Service Corps (RASC), the overflowing sailors and gunners from the first and third holds, and even a few unfortunate civilians and policemen who had never been transferred to the civilian internment camp at Stanley.[77]

Bennett's Hong Kong Signals Company was one of these smaller units: "It was here that I saw my nephew Les Smith. He was a member of [40th Fortress Company Royal Engineers]. There was no time for me to converse with him as we were being ushered forward to a wooden staircase which took us down into the hold. This seemed vast and gloomy. Against all four walls (I think the naval term is bulkheads) had been constructed a two-tier platform which was covered in a thin rush matting. Each man was allotted about eighteen inches. In our hold were about 600 men. I well remember being next to Busty Phipps (he came from Portsmouth)."

This hold was under the command of Lieutenant Colonel 'Monkey' Moncreif Stewart, commanding officer of the 1st Battalion, the Middlesex Regiment, who was also in overall command of the POWs.

However, as Lieutenant Howell of the RASC pointed out: "One cannot say that Colonel Stewart was in command of the 1,800 men, except by his soldierly example and by the respect in which he was held for his dogged retreat, against eight to one odds and lasting over a week, through the two mile shambles of Wanchai, during the defence of Hong Kong in 1941. The person in command was a brutal, callous Japanese interpreter named Niimori who had lorded it over us in the POW camp for the last nine months."[78]

Captain Martin Weedon of the Middlesex described the accommodation in this hold: "[Number two hold] was divided into two tiers, the upper occupied by the Middlesex Regiment, Royal Engineers, and Royal Corps of Signals, and the lower by the Royal Scots and Royal Artillery ... There was communication from the lower to the upper tier by means of two wooden ladders, and from the upper tier to the deck by three ladders."[79]

Robert Wright of Weedon's Company noted that, in the top tier of number two hold at least, the living space had been divided by rough wooden slats into 'cubicles' measuring twelve feet by twelve, each holding about twenty men. In Wright's cubicle were Arthur Iles, 'Typhoon' Gale, George Iszard, William Steele, Frank Meakin, William Hughes, and Richard Tivey. The adjoining cubicle housed the beri beri victims, including William Bowles, Percy Hatchett, Walter Hayward, and Thomas Gorman.[80] On the lower tier, men just slept where they could in the bottom of the hold.

Conditions in all three holds were very similar. There was rampant overcrowding, and there were no toilet or washing facilities below decks.

Ross Lynneberg reported from number one hold: "It was impossible for everyone to lie down at the same time so many of us took turns and many were unable to sleep for more than a few minutes due to their beri beri." Arthur Alsey, a bandsman of the Royal Scots, found a similar scene in number two hold: "By 3 pm 500 are crammed in bottom hold, 600 on top. No washing arrangements. 12 WCs on top deck, 4 urinal pipes. No leaning over the side."[81]

Jack Etiemble experienced no better in number three hold: "All I could see was a mass of bodies all jammed together, luckily I managed to find enough space to lie down. I had just got myself sorted out when down came a BSM who told me to move as he wanted that space. I refused and he then ordered me to move and once again I refused. Two sergeants asked me what was wrong, I told them, they then told the BSM that we were all POWs and he must find another space."

Not knowing when they would sail, they settled down as best they could. But many men who had seemed 'fit' when they boarded, started to develop worrying symptoms in the cramped and unhygienic conditions on board.

Jim Fallace of the HKRNVR: "It is estimated that at least 75% of the draft had some sickness or other, among which prevailed dysentery, diphtheria, beri beri (wet and dry), pellagra, many had diarrhoea and very bad skin diseases. Beri beri and Pellagra were most prominent owing to the inadequate food and absence of vitamins. In the former the men were suffering most excruciating pain in the feet which caused many sleepless nights. It must be born in mind that right until the last day when the ship left men were being removed back to the camp as Diphtheria suspects."

Fallace's colleague Arthur Evans: "We were on board two days before we sailed and on the mornings of the 26th and 27th diphtheria suspects were being sent off the ship back to the camp. Directly we arrived on board the dysentery cases and other sick men needed segregation, and the only thing to do was to put them on the steel decks, in any space that could be found between the various hatches, etc., and there they laid on their blankets with a tarpaulin cover over them when it rained."

The first night on board the stationary vessel passed relatively well. Those on board woke to still seas and calm weather on the morning of 26 September.

Bandsman Arthur Alsey: "Fairly good sleep. Up at 6.30. Beautifully cool. 1/2 loaf bread and sugared tea for chow at 9 am. Stayed on deck from 9.30 to 2 pm. A lovely smell and sight of frying steaks in Jap galley … Everybody below by 8 pm. Sharrock[82] gets the lads singing with borrowed squeeze box. The heat below is stifling. My feet ache far into the night."[83]

Alf Hunt: "On the afternoon of the 26th, a large number of Japanese troops came onboard and occupied the upper part of the hold. They all appeared to be in good spirits, laughing and joking amongst themselves, probably with the thought of going home."[84]

The Japanese soldiers were 778 men of a Japanese battalion, under their commander Lieutenant Sugiyama, heading back to Japan, and then for further battles against the Allies.[85]

These men were the last passengers that the *Lisbon Maru's* captain had been waiting for. With everyone aboard, at eight in the morning of 27 September, the ship departed Hong Kong. The thoughts of those on board varied. For some, it seemed an opportunity, for surely conditions in Japan could not be worse that those in Sham Shui Po? Others, though, were leaving their wives and children, whether interned in Stanley or 'free' in the city itself.

Wright: "As we steamed out of Hong Kong, we were allowed on deck for an hour. It was a hot, sunny afternoon, and I found myself beside a Mr Gorston,[86] who had served with the Hong Kong police. Neither of us spoke at first, and as we sailed past Stanley Point, where we had made our last stand, I saw tears streaming down the man's cheek."

William Poulter, Middlesex Regiment, was also on deck, now recovered from his grenade wounds: "As we were leaving we were all allowed up on deck. It was with very mixed feelings that I looked at the harbour. I first pulled into Hong Kong in 1927 as part of the Shanghai Defence Force. Ten years later, I returned with my wife and son. At least they [were safely out of it now in Australia]."

Jim Fallace: "She left Hong Kong without convoy, keeping in sight of the coast practically all the way. The only vessel passed en route was a freighter proceeding in the same direction carrying railway carriages."

As the familiar skyline of Hong Kong faded out of sight behind them, the POWs settled into their new environment as best they could. Although the seas were calm, conditions were far from pleasant. The decks were overcrowded, cold, and foul. Little comfort came from the observation that there were four lifeboats and six rafts aboard, and that there was a pile of kapok lifebelts in the holds. Few men thought of shipwreck, and the lifebelts when used at all, were used as pillows.

In the morning, they received rice and tea, and in the evening rice, tea, and bully beef (corned beef), the latter thanks to Monkey Stewart who had used camp funds to buy essential supplies from the Japanese before embarkation.[87]

A few men day-dreamed of an *Altmark*-like rescue by the US Navy. Widely publicized in Allied nations desperate for some good news, a British destroyer's successful rescue of some three hundred British sailors — captured from merchantmen victims of the German battleship, *Admiral Graf Spee* and held on the German auxiliary ship *Altmark* — had given hope to many. But the Royal Navy was strong in the North Sea, the RAF in the United Kingdom had aircraft capable of locating the *Altmark* in Jösing Fjord, Norway, and once the men had been rescued, it was a short trip to return them to Leith, Scotland. The situation in the South and East China Seas was sadly different.

With that vain hope fast fading, the men settled down to a routine at sea. Reveille was at six, followed by roll call at seven. Thirty minutes later, breakfast (rice and onion soup) was served. Free time followed. In the dim light of the holds, men played games of ludo and draughts. More than a few kept diaries, or shared in reading the few books on board until they fell to pieces. A social set visited other cubicles, conducted quiz games, gambled, and sang in the evenings. In the first hold, Able Seaman Bill Deering entertained with his mouth organ and Able Seaman 'Bogey' Butler with his stories. In the third, Bombardier Denton held sway. In the second hold, Sergeant 'Dodger' Green of the Royal Corps of Signals, like many old hands, had an inexhaustible portfolio of smutty tales, soldiers for the delight of.[88] Private Micky Myles[89] had smuggled his piano accordion on board, and regaled his audience with exquisite renditions of 'Roll me over in the clover' and 'Men of Harlech', accompanied by the voice of Sapper Jones.

At six in the evening the second roll call was held, followed half an hour later by supper (again, rice and onion soup). However, for the first two days the diet continued to be supplemented by Monkey Stewart's stockpile of corned beef and cigarettes.

Only one tap was set up on deck, so no real washing was possible, though men were allowed to fill their water bottles twice a day. The toilets were narrow wooden latrines set up at the deck's sides, projecting over the sea. Initially those wanting to use these had to ask the Japanese for permission, but very quickly, the Japanese appointed a British NCO to be responsible for the unpopular job of queue control.

Frank Bennett: "On my first visit to the benjo[90] (you went whether you needed to go or not) I was appalled at the precarious structure. It was a frame-work slung on the side of the ship with a length of 4 x 2 to sit on. One merely perched up on the 4 x 2 with your backside facing the sea, and let it go. I noticed a lot of chicken coops on deck, and quite a lot of Japanese troops further aft."

Alf Hunt: "Getting up to the upper deck, to go to the toilet when allowed, was a major problem. Avoiding treading on other bodies and negotiating the two narrow companionways or ladders was quite a hazard. Those of us that felt well enough tried to level the sacks of sand out and cover them with our single blanket, but the damp came through almost immediately. The conditions were pretty dismal, in fact grim. There were between eight and nine hundred POWs crammed into the main hold, it was very hot, the air was foul, and it was extremely difficult to breathe. There was just enough space for one to sit down comfortably, and to lie down was almost impossible without putting one legs over someone's body."

Although Monkey Stewart remained outwardly calm, he was clearly feeling the strain of being responsible for nearly two thousand men in conditions that allowed him minimum control over their fates. With a reputation for always doing what he could for the men's well-being, he carefully rationed out the cigarette stocks that he had brought onboard. A man whose authority came simply from his presence, he shocked his subordinates with a rare show of temper when one man tried to join the dole queue (of just two cigarettes per man) twice, and swore for the first time in his men's experience.[91] The strain was starting to tell, but how great it was would not become clear until later.

Diphtheria, which the medics guessed some men were carrying from the moment they were taken on board, had now broken out. By the 28th there were twelve suspected cases on the ship. Despite symptomatic sufferers having been removed back to Sham Shui Po before the *Lisbon Maru* sailed, up to two hundred others would come down with the disease. The medical personnel: Officer, Page, Lynch, Jackson, Allen Pemberton, Harry Pelham and others did their best to find space on deck for the worst sufferers.

While those on board feared disease, lack of food, and an uncertain future in Japan more than anything else, certain individuals back in Hong Kong realized that the biggest threat to the POWs' safety could come from American submarines.

Amongst these was James Patrick Mulligan of 12th Battery, Royal Artillery. One of several soldiers to hide out in Hong Kong's teeming streets in preference to becoming a POW, he simply walked away from North Point POW camp before the Japanese imposed any real security. Now he was at large in the Colony.

His son takes up the story: "I believe that my father was on Nathan Road next to a British Officers' Club when he was given the extra information that POWs were being loaded on to the *Lisbon Maru* at the last minute. A young Chinese girl gave him the information and he related the conversation to me in great detail. It was clear that he did not know the woman and was not sure if she was telling him the truth or trying to find out if he was in fact an informant. After she left he apparently ran to where he could observe the ship and confirm that it was indeed being loaded with prisoners and it had 'steam up' and was ready to go. He then went to his contact who seemed very uninterested in this updated information. He implied to me that his contact was a 'Yank' and he definitely said that the 'Yanks ignored his information and the ship was torpedoed'. I also know that he was debriefed by the Americans in Shanghai after the war and also had a very desultory debriefing from the British in Hong Kong after he returned from Shanghai.

He never mentioned the BAAG [British Army Aid Group] and I tend to think that he was disenchanted with the British Army and would therefore be loath to work with them, particularly the officer class. His stories were always about getting money and trading information with the 'Yanks' and one of his most consistent stories was about being given a great deal of money by the 'Yanks' at the end of the war and being asked to stay. He declined to stay and gave away the money, preferring to go back to England to meet the girl he been writing to before the war, and who eventually became my mother. One of his brothers told me recently that after being in the UK for a couple of years he regretted not taking the opportunity that had been offered to him in China at the end of the war."[92]

Similarly, Selwyn Selwyn-Clarke, the Director of Medical Services in Hong Kong, who was still allowed free travel in the Colony at that time, stated:

"In September, 1942, I came to know that nearly two thousand prisoners were to be shipped from Shamshuipo to labour-camps in Japan, where the chances of escape would be almost non-existent. I had seen Japanese ships entering Hong Kong harbour for the repair of damage which must have been done by American ships or aircraft, and I decided that it lay within my duty to contrive that details of the prison-transport, the *Lisbon Maru*, and the date of its sailing should reach the U.S. command through our own, so as to ensure that the vessel should not be attacked. Once before, when passing a message through Macao in order to get the International Red Cross to press for representation in Hong Kong, I had made use of secret communications. I now made a second, and my last attempt, to use the same route and it was tragically unsuccessful. Either because my information did not reach the right place in time, or by some other error the *Lisbon Maru* [was lost]."[93]

However, the British Army Aid Group, a clandestine organization set up by Lieutenant Colonel Lindsay Ride of the HKVDC after escaping from Sham Shui Po POW camp, was watching. Ride had been a Professor at the University of Hong Kong, and at the same time commanded the Field Ambulance unit of the Volunteers. An experienced man (he had been sent to France in the First World War at the age of nineteen), he lost no time in breaking out of Sham Shui Po POW camp with a handful of companions. His aim was to set up an organization in southern China to provide military intelligence, keep in contact with the POWs still in the camps, and to aid other escapers. From small beginnings BAAG grew to be a formidable force, though in autumn 1942 it was still a young organization. Nevertheless, it had many eyes and ears in Hong Kong, and they were quick to report the transportations.

The first message referring to a ship sailing with POWs at the end of September was dispatched to Ride on the twelfth of that month. It read:

> This is Duggie number 51 dated 10/9. 600 POWs from Shamshuipo shipped towards the oriental sun on the nights of the 3rd or 4th. A further cargo of 1000 POWs is arranged for the end of the month. The source of this information is the addressee of your note number 16 and the subject of my letter no 15.[94]

Just over a fortnight later, the day before the *Lisbon Maru* sailed, another of their agents sent a message to Ride in Guilin:

> "MACHIN Chungking. For [Lt. Col. Lindsay] Ride. Agent 64 dated 25/9 confirms agent 51's of 10/9. Report six hundred POWs going to Formosa [now Taiwan. This was the first transportation]. Twelve hundred going to Moji, Japan, today."[95]

Thus BAAG — in China and in contact with the rest of the world — knew that a ship with POWs onboard was sailing, but no one outside Hong Kong had access to the vital fact that the vessel was the *Lisbon Maru*. So the ship sailed on, unaware of the dangers waiting, and without any Allied submarines knowing that she carried British POWs.

For three more days, from 28 September to 30 September, the Prisoners of War onboard grew hungrier and sicker, not knowing that their voyage was about to be brought to a sudden end. The captain of the ship also came down with dengue fever, and retired to his cabin, coming up to the bridge only when necessary. Even then, he had to sit in a cane chair.

Wallace Hastings in the first hold complained: "Most of the next few days were spent below deck in total inactivity, just talking, speculating on our future prospects in Japan and sleeping; going top-side only when allowed to answer toilet needs."

Wright reported worse: "The sufferers from beri beri did not sleep at night. In agony, they moaned and cried, as they walked ceaselessly up and down to allay their pain. They cried to God and for their mothers, as they held on to the flimsy wooden rail which separated the cubicles from the chasm of the hold below. Like ghosts they moved about, exciting anger, complaint and pity as they kept us awake. With dawn their torment ended, and, exhausted, they would fall asleep."

However, even on 29 September, as Alsey — one of the beri beri sufferers — described, men were still entertaining themselves:

"Read a book of short stories. Swapped it for 'And Quiet Flows the Don'.[96] Blondie, Alf, Sharrock, and Hector play for concert sponsored by Mickey Myles who gives 10, 6, 4, and 2 packets of fags for entertainers. Some awful noises. Blondie wins first prize with 'Just a Song at Twilight'. Chatted to Hector until 10 pm. My feet keep me up all night. No lights on." Next day he continues: "Rain starts to fall and the hatchboards are covered over. The diphtheria patients are kept on deck, covered with tarpaulin. Very breezy and cold. Rice, bully, spoonful of veg and tea. Very dark — stuffy in the hold. Hector starts to tell me of his affairs which led to his marriage — his wife's six month stay in a mental hospital in Basingstoke and of the homecoming. What a trial and test for a marriage."

Some, however, had premonitions of troubles to come.

Lieutenant Howell: "It's a funny thing how a chance remark 'shapes our ends'. On the night of September 30th, lying on a Japanese straw-mat in the conglomerated No. 2 hold into which a canvas ventilator funnelled some air, we were somewhat ominously discussing shipwrecks. I had remarked that twice had I experienced such a misadventure in my thirty odd years — once with a girl friend (now my wife) during a holiday cruise when the liner struck an uncharted rock not far from Nagasaki (which years afterwards I was to see atom-bombed, only a few miles from my last POW Camp) — and a second time while travelling with a rugby football team to Shanghai, when some inconsiderate ship in the darkness off Woosung, knocked the stern off our vessel. 'Third time lucky', the Colonel's voice dryly commented, adding that it was up to me if our zig-zagging freighter ran into trouble."

*   *   *

Trouble was indeed waiting to be run into — a low, grey shape, hardly visible in the waves despite the broken moonlight — was quietly submerging a few hours steaming ahead.

5 The Boat: USS *Grouper*

> Where we, in all our trim, freshly beheld
> Our royal, good, and gallant ship; our master
> Cap'ring to eye her — on a trice so please you
>
> *The Tempest*, Act 5, Scene 1

Submarines were the great hope of the Allies in the Pacific in 1942, when there were few other cards to play.

The Allied naval losses in the Pacific battles of late 1941 and 1942 had been horrendous. The Royal Navy had lost the *Repulse* and *Prince of Wales* (as well as many other smaller craft, including Hong Kong based HMS *Thanet*)[97] off Malaya. Even worse, they had also lost the naval port installations of Hong Kong and Singapore. At Pearl Harbour the Americans had lost two battleships, the *Arizona* and *Oklahoma*, outright, with the *West Virginia*, *Nevada*, *California*, *Maryland*, *Tennessee*, and *Pennsylvania* being damaged to a lesser or greater degree. They also lost light cruisers, destroyers, the converted battleship *Utah*, various smaller vessels, and almost two hundred aircraft, but — of huge strategic importance — they at least retained the harbour facilities.

In the longer term it was vitally significant that the three US Pacific Fleet aircraft carriers, *Lexington*, *Enterprise* and *Saratoga*, which were not at Pearl Harbour at that time, had escaped. However, with these losses, and the need for a major naval effort in the Atlantic and Mediterranean seas to counter German forces in the European Theatre,[98] little but submarines were available for offensive action in the Pacific in 1942.

The standard type of American fleet submarine during the Second

World War was the *Gato* class, and its continuation as the *Balao* class. In 1940, the first six *Gato*-class boats were built (numbered SS 212 to SS 217), and these were followed by a series of sixty-seven further boats (SS 218 to SS 284).[99]

Built in the initial batch of six, the USS *Grouper*, SS-214, was a large boat. Over three hundred feet from bow to stern, and twenty-seven feet across, she could manage nine knots submerged and twenty-two on the surface. A crew of sixty officers and men could take her twenty-four torpedoes and three-inch gun eleven thousand miles at maximum endurance.

Grouper had been launched by the Electric Boat Company at Groton, Connecticut, on 27 October 1941 — two months before the surrender in Hong Kong. She was commissioned at New London on 12 February 1942 by her commander, Lieutenant Commander Claren Duke, together with fellow officers Lieutenant Close, Ensign J. R. Dykema, Lieutenant Edward R. Holt, Jr., Lieutenant J. D. Mason, and Lieutenant Commander W. Winter.

After shakedown in Long Island Sound, *Grouper* sailed for Pearl Harbour on 30 March 1942 to join the Pacific Submarine Force that was to play such havoc with Japanese shipping. Here Lieutenant A. W. Weaver joined her complement on 28 April 1942.

Attached to Task Force 7's Midway Patrol Group, together with submarines *Cachalot*, *Cuttlefish*, *Dolphin*, *Flying Fish*, *Gato*, *Grayling*, *Grenadier*, *Gudgeon*, *Nautilus*, *Tambor*, and *Trout*, the submariners aboard *Grouper* had no more idea than Jack Etiemble and his colleagues that blind chance would soon lead them to meet.

On the morning of 4 June 1942, *Grouper* received a message from TF7's Commander,[100] giving the position of Japanese carriers comprising part of a major assault force sailing towards Hawaii. Recently arrived at Midway, *Grouper* dived in the deep blue waters off the island, commencing her First War Patrol.[101]

Remaining submerged at a speed of six knots, *Grouper* set course to intercept the carriers. She manned 'battle stations torpedo' at 07.26, and five minutes later sighted a large number of planes — apparently taking off from carriers — on the horizon. Battle had already been joined, and dogfights were visible all over the sky. Still at periscope depth, *Grouper's* lookouts became aware that a Japanese fighter was approaching, strafing with machine guns and cannon. Cannon shells were exploding as they hit the sea just off the conning tower, so her commander, Duke, ordered a crash-dive. Beginning at 09.17, those on board heard ten or more explosions; *Grouper*, for the first but certainly not the last time in the long and varied career to come, was being depth-charged.

Continuing to search for the carriers, *Grouper* constantly swept the area. For the next two hours, she was depth-charged almost continuously, and at 11.40, coming back to periscope depth, she sighted smoke plumes from two burning ships at a distance of about ten miles. Believing the vessels to be the carriers again, she changed course to intercept them, diving once more to avoid further depth-charge attacks.

Before reaching the carriers, soon after 13.00, *Grouper's* crew heard several heavy explosions and changed course again to avoid the area, believing that they might have overestimated the distance to the first burning ship, and that there was a possibility that they were already under the blazing carrier that might suddenly sink on top of her. Coming back to periscope depth, *Grouper* received another message from CTF-7 ordering her to take station for a patrol a hundred miles from Midway.

*   *   *

At Midway itself, Garfield Kvalheim was no longer manning the boilers of a shore station; instead, he was suddenly about to find himself in the thick of the action. Born on 1 October 1917 in Tacoma, Washington, Gar was the son of immigrants from Norway. His mother worked as a seamstress in an elite ladies' dress shop in Tacoma, and his father was a fisherman working mostly in the cold seas around Alaska. Brought up during the depression, as a youngster he worked for a doughnut company for a dollar a week. An adventurous young man even then, one day he left a note saying 'gone fishing', and that was the end of a fine career in deep fried comestibles.

Every summer, elements of the United States Navy would anchor in Tacoma harbour, opening up their ships to visitors. Young Kvalheim was one of them, and was seized by the glamour of these vessels and a desire to see the world. He enlisted in December 1935 and served on an oil tanker until December 1939. Bored by the routine, he then decided to leave the Navy and set the world on fire. However, although the economy was improving, America was still in the grip of the depression and jobs were hard to find.

Kvalheim: "I was contacted by a civilian from Canada who was looking for volunteers to join the RCAF (England was at war at that time). I jumped at the chance since I always wanted to be a pilot. I was sent to Toronto, Canada for flight training but was washed out because of scar tissue on my left eardrum. I was sent to Windsor, Ontario to Airframe Mechanics School. I went to my Wing Commander and explained that I had volunteered for flight training and I requested a discharge. The reply was 'We are at war and a discharge is impossible'. To shorten the story, I left Canada and returned to the States and reenlisted in the U.S. Navy."[102]

By September 1941, he was serving on the converted battleship *Utah* in Pearl Harbour. Not finding such an old — and large — vessel to his liking, he volunteered for submarine duty.[103] Transferred to the receiving station at Goat Island, California at the end of November 1941 for physical examinations (and, like all American submariners, an in-depth interview with a psychiatrist) Kvalheim soon found himself transferred yet again, this time for submarine duty.

By February 1942, he had reported on board the old submarine S-28. Kvalheim: "I remember the Captain, J. D. Crowley (we referred to him as Captain Bligh). My rating on the 28 boat was 2nd (second class) Machinist Mate in the engine room. My diving station was on the stern plane ... To be a good submariner one must possess the quality of being able to get along with other people, be of sound mind and top physical condition. After Pearl Harbour, everyone was 'gung ho' to go out there and sink those Japs. Especially after the battle of Midway, there was never a thought of the Allies losing the war."

Then the United States Navy, in their wisdom, transferred him yet again. This time, at least, he was somewhere more suited to his adventurous nature. He was aboard the submarine tender USS *Fulton* based in Hawaii.

On 4 June — as *Grouper* departed for battle — he spent a normal day aboard the *Fulton*, moored at Pier S-1 Submarine Base, Pearl Harbour, where their vessel had been since mid-March. As evening fell, he sat down to watch the movie *Sergeant York* with the rest of the off-duty section. Halfway through the film, at about fifteen minutes past eight, a deafening klaxon sounded. They were to get underway immediately.

With the USS *Breese* and USS *Allen* as escorts, the *Fulton* steamed out of Pearl in less than two hours. Those on board did not yet know it, but the Japanese had severely damaged the carrier *Yorktown* with bombs and torpedoes and, in danger of sinking, her captain had ordered the crew to abandon ship. Even as the rescue force steamed towards them, most of the crew were in the water, with the cruisers *Portland* and *Russell* pulling the majority from the waves. *Fulton's* job would be to take them off the cruisers and back to Pearl.

Meeting up with the big grey ships at midday on 6 June, they steamed alongside *Portland* at eight knots, trans-shipping *Yorktown's* survivors in coal bags on high wires rigged up between the ships. All off-duty members of *Fulton's* crew helped with the hauling, as did the uninjured *Yorktown* survivors when they came on board.

Just as they managed to rig the lines to *Russell* to repeat the operation, the escort USS *Allen* reported a submarine contact. Alert officers immediately gave orders to cut all lines with fire axes, and the ships separated.

That evening *Fulton* lowered her boats and brought the last survivors on board. *Fulton*, not a big ship to start with, was now overflowing with an incredible 1,891 of *Yorktown's* survivors.

While the cruisers headed back to battle, *Fulton* steamed a reverse course to Pearl Harbour. All efforts were made to help the survivors on board; medical staff and the galley work twenty-four hours a day until they reached Pearl mid-afternoon on 8 June. Kvalheim: "I remember giving up my bunk to a survivor, as others in the squadron did. [The rescue] was handled mostly by *Fulton's* ships company personnel. We, in the squadron, rendered assistance where needed."

On 9 June, one day after Kvalheim and the *Fulton* docked at Pearl, the submarine *Grouper* arrived back at Midway to refuel and replenish her stores. From there, she then operated between Tokara Gunto, Tokara Jima,[104] and Yokoate Shima, and finally in the latter days of her patrol she cruised the shipping lanes from the Formosa Strait to Japan.

All had been quiet for a month but, at 17.41 on 6 July, *Grouper* made contact with an 8,000-ton freighter at a range of 14,000 yards and fired three straight bow shots at the vessel. They observed no explosions so at 18.07 she fired a further three torpedoes, and all hit their target. With no further contacts, *Grouper's* patrol had come to an end. She returned to Pearl Harbour via Midway on 30 July.

Here *Grouper* and her crew enjoyed four weeks of relative peace before returning to the fray. They also picked up a new commanding officer in the shape of Lieutenant Commander Rob Roy McGregor.

McGregor came from an old naval family. Born in Seattle in 1907, he had been appointed to the United States Naval Academy in 1925. There, as a Midshipman, he played lacrosse and football, and was a member of the Wrestling Squad. Graduating in 1929, he served first on the battleships *Wyoming* and *Arkansas*, followed by the destroyer *Childs*. He entered the submarine school at New London, Connecticut, in 1932 and served on three submarines before taking his first command, USS *S-36*, in 1938. Serving with the Asiatic Fleet, he returned to the United States in November 1940 to recommission and command the USS *S-1*, staying with her until taking command of the *Grouper*.

He did not have long to get to know his officers before taking them on the boat's Second War Patrol.

Lieutenant Commander William Winter, Jr., the *Grouper's* Executive Officer, Navigator, was born in June 1910. Joining the navy on his eighteenth birthday, he had graduated from the US Naval Academy in 1932, three years after McGregor.

From Charleroi, Pennsylvania, Lieutenant John Denning Mason, the First Lieutenant, graduated from the Naval Academy in 1938. He served on the battleship *New Mexico* before being posted to the Submarine School. From there, he joined the complement of *S-44*, then *Grouper*.

Lieutenant Robert Hamilton 'Boney' Close, the Engineer officer, Electrical, was born in Mount Vernon, New York, and was McGregor's junior by six years. Graduating from the Naval Academy in 1934, he served on the light cruiser *Concord* until the end of 1937. From *Concord*, he passed to the Submarine School, and served on the *S-30* and *R-11* before joining the *Grouper*.

Lieutenant Edward Rowell Holt, Jr., the Gunnery Officer, was born in Hickory, North Carolina, in July 1915. He graduated from the US Naval Academy in 1939. He then served in *Arizona* and *Cushing* before attending the Submarine School, from where he was posted straight to the *Grouper*.

Lieutenant Junior Grade D-V(G)[105] Albert W. Weaver, the S&A, Asst. Elec & Eng. was born in June 1915 and entered the US Navy in November 1940.

Finally, Ensign[106] D-V (G) John R. Dykema, the Communications, Assistant First Lieutenant was born in June 1918 and joined the US Navy in October 1941.

Replacing the *Grouper's* original captain, Claren E. Duke, McGregor found the boat's morale at a low ebb. 'Boney' Close, in a post-war letter, described Duke as follows: "My first skipper in *Grouper* was Claren Duke who had a reputation as a truly outstanding and successful peacetime submarine commander. I feel that he would have been an outstandingly successful wartime skipper but the transition from peace to war was too sudden and violent for him." However, the official summation of the *Grouper's* First Patrol Report noted: "many golden opportunities to inflict heavy damage on the enemy were missed, in that the Commanding Officer chose in many instances to use evasive tactics rather than aggressive tactics", and Kvalheim recalled: "I do remember that Duke was very strict and not popular at all. There may have been an incident when Duke was reluctant to close a target during that run. After having reviewed the patrol report I have with Captain Duke in command, there seems to be more than one reason for a morale problem. The main reason was one that plagued most of the subs early on in the war. It was faulty exploders in the MK 14 torpedoes. Reports from ComSubPac would indicate that it was a case of poor marksmanship. This was not true."[107]

McGregor penned his first words in the boat's log at the end of July:[108]

> \# Arrived Pearl Harbor July 30, 1942 from First War Patrol. Commenced refit on July 31, 1942, by submarine base, navy yard, and tender repair forces. Controlling job was installation and boring of new bearings for # 1 periscope by navy yard. Readiness for sea on 23 August, 1942. Not depermed or wiped;[109] training period 24–26 August, 1942.
>
> 28 August Underway from Submarine Base, Pearly Harbor, for assigned
> 0900 VW   area, via MIDWAY, escorted by U.S.S. LITCHFIELD.[110] Calibrated RDF. Escort dropped three (3) familiarization depth charges, distances 275, 300, 350 yards. Escort released at nightfall.

Aboard the *Fulton* as she returned from Pearl to Midway Island, Garfield Kvalheim was assigned to the *Grouper* when she paused there to refuel. Joining as the boat's new Machinist's Mate First Class in the after engine room, Kvalheim did not have too long to wait before his first real wartime submarine patrol, and *Grouper's* second. *Grouper* both arrived at and cast off from Midway, for her second war patrol, on 1 September.

1 September 0800 W	Arrived MIDWAY. Surface and air escorts. Topped off fuel and water. USS Fulton replaced gasket on flange in negative tank blow line located in #2 main ballast tank. Departed MIDWAY with surface and air escort at 1600 W. Escort released at nightfall.

For almost three weeks there was little to report. Now part of TF7's Offensive Patrol Group (together with submarines *Cuttlefish, Flying Fish, Haddock, Narwhal, Pompano,* and *Silversides*), the new captain and his crew settled down as they steamed to their patrol area.

15 September 0220	Arrived in area twelve (12) days after departure from MIDWAY. Trip uneventful. Fired .50 cal. machine gun and 10 rounds ammunition with the 3" at homemade target on 4 September. Outside of the structural test shots this is first time gun had been fired. Results good. Sighted eight (8) fishermen's lights during trip, none of which interfered with our progress. On 9 September 305 miles from CHICHIJIMA in the Bonan group had radar contact at eight (8) miles. Dove and ran submerged during daylight from then on. Sky overcast. Do not believe we were sighted. Crew was extensively trained each day during entire passage.
17 September 2000	Conducting first portion of patrol about 10 miles east of DANJO GUNTO,[111] where contacts had been reported on previous patrols and a possible route for the NOTORI to SASEBO. Sighted tanker of about 3000 tons, distance 9000 yards, angle on bow 40 Port. Made night surface attack immediately as it appeared target would be obscured in heavy rains shortly. Fired one torpedo at 1500 yards (full field in binoculars). Missed. Target passed into heavy rains at about estimated time of torpedo crossing track. Paralleled target course and proceeded at 9 knots, the estimated target speed. At this time heard an explosion in direction target. Sounded like the report of a 4" gun. Submarine was now in heavy rain, visibility zero. Continued for one hour. With no signs of weather clearing abandoned pursuit.

18 September 1004	Moved to new position during night, west of DANJO GUNTO. Sighted cargo passenger vessel of about 3000 tons, distance 10,000 yards, angle on bow 80 port. Closed on normal approach at high speeds. Echo ranged with no results. Fired three (3) torpedoes at 2000 yards. Offset 0, 1.5L, 1.5R. No hits. Target turned away three minutes later. Had abnormally high stack and was riding high. Could not identify. Decided to head for the China coast along a probable trade route. Had intended to visit off the YANGTZE and the present time seemed propitious, our presence being known around present locality.

Grouper took up a position near North Saddle Island off the mouth of the Yangtze River, about 100 miles east of Shanghai. It was, and is, an area of sea dotted with islands, and traditionally full of shipping — both fishing boats and cargo vessels going into and out of Shanghai.

Then, on 20 September while patrolling submerged, *Grouper* sighted a Japanese cargo vessel of about five thousand tons, and waited patiently for the moon to set before attacking. She started her approach at 03.15 and fired a single torpedo, hitting the ship directly amidships and breaking the merchantman's back. Within five minutes, only the bow and stern were visible. In less than half an hour, the vessel had disappeared beneath the waves.[112]

Four days later on 24 September, the submarine turned towards Shanghai. She returned to her previous patrol off North Saddle Island on 27 September and sighted another ship at a range of seven miles. This target was zigzagging and the approach was difficult. *Grouper* never came closer than five thousand yards and, with a full moon shining brightly through a cloudless sky, was unable to make an attack.

Frustrated by the elements this time, the submarine resumed her patrol with renewed determination. On the night of 30 September, McGregor decided to patrol at the south-westernmost corner of the area to which he had been assigned. They would wait southwest of the ZhongJie Shan archipelago, to see if they could intercept any shipping approaching Shanghai from the south — the direction of Hong Kong.

*   *   *

At his station in the dimly lit and claustrophobic Control Room was Garfield Kvalheim. The Control Room was the heart and brains of a submarine. The Bow Planesman and the Stern Planesman worked as a team here to control the depth of the submarine when submerged, operating two large brass wheels on the port side in the middle of the Control Room (and two little handles between the wheels), watching the depth gauges and angle gauges for clues as to the submarine's position and attitude.

Maintaining the submarine in a level condition, and controlling its overall weight, was accomplished by pumping and venting water among various tanks and the sea itself. The Trim Manifold in the Control Room provided the means for monitoring and managing the transfer of appropriate quantities of water. The water was transferred by the Trim Pump, located in the lower section of the compartment just underneath the Trim Manifold. The man on the Trim Manifold used the gauges to assess how much water was in each of these tanks (in thousands of pounds), and the Trim Manifold itself controlled the way the tanks were connected together to make appropriate adjustments in weight. All this was Kvalheim's job.

Kvalheim: "It felt really good to be operating in Japanese home waters. We had a job to do and evidently we did it well."

He continued: "I was a Machinist Mate 1st Class in the after engine room. During battle stations submerged, my role was in the Control Room on the trim manifold. During a routine war patrol, much time was spent reading and maybe playing Acey-Ducey.[113] Everything was peaceful and quiet until a target was sighted then everything came to life. If we were lucky enough to close the target for a favourable shot we had a chance for a hit. If the target zigged away or we were spotted, that was another story. If the target had an escort, we would be in for a working over with depth charges. This happened quite often. Our patrols lasted 50 or 60 days as a rule."

It was now thirty days since the start of this patrol; at least half-way through, and long enough for the possibility of men being more tired and less observant than they might normally have been. *Grouper* was patrolling on the surface, in the moonlight, when suddenly a large Japanese freighter was observed heading 010 — from the direction of Hong Kong — at nine knots.[114]

"On the night of 30th September 1942 we were patrolling off the China coast and [at 04.00 on October 1st] picked up a target heading north. We paced the ship for some time and plotted its course and speed. Due to the bright moonlight we were unable to close the range without being detected. We made what was called an end around. Full speed ahead and then just before dawn we submerged and waited."

Battle Stations Submerged. At battle stations submerged, every crewmember had an assigned station. In the quiet of the dimly lit conning tower were Captain McGregor, the Executive Officer (Lieutenant Commander W. Winter), an officer on the Torpedo Data Computer, the quartermaster who raised and lowered the periscope for the captain, and the helmsman who steered the boat. In the control room were the diving officer (Lieutenant Holt), a chief on the hydraulic manifold, a man on the high pressure air manifold, and another — Garfield Kvalheim — on the trim manifold. The sonar gear was manned, and a full complement of torpedo men was in each torpedo room. All other compartments were manned and ready for any emergency. *Grouper* had left port carrying twenty-four torpedoes, with all tubes loaded, six tubes forward and four tubes aft. She still had all but one.

*   *   *

Turned to face 180 degrees from the track she had just made, she waited silently underwater for the approaching Japanese merchantman.

6 "Hot, Straight and Normal!": 1 October

> We were dead of sleep,
> And — how we know not — all clapped under hatches,
> Where but even now with strange and several noises
> Of roaring, shrieking, howling, jingling chains,
> And more diversity of sounds, all horrible,
> We were awaked
>
> *The Tempest*, Act 5, Scene 1

There was nothing silent on the *Lisbon Maru* that night. Men groaned and writhed at the discomforts of their diseases and hunger, the overcrowded conditions, and the primitive accommodation; adding to the cacophony, a lucky few snored.

The lookouts on the bridge did not see the *Grouper* keeping pace with the ship, nor did they notice her pick up speed and slice through the water ahead. At a top speed of nineteen knots — twice as fast as the *Lisbon Maru* — she was able to gain a considerable lead and was well over the horizon when she turned around, pointing back towards the direction from which McGregor expected the old freighter to steam. He planned a torpedo attack at daybreak. To him, to the best of his knowledge, this was simply a Japanese troopship with her decks covered in Japanese soldiers.

At six-thirty, two and a half hours after the POW's vessel was first spotted by the submarine, Lieutenant Geoffrey Fairbairn of the 2nd Battalion the Royal Scots — Duty Officer for the day — visited the lower deck to ensure that the men were up and ready for the 07.00 roll call. He did not know that the captain of the *Grouper*, at periscope depth, was already watching. McGregor, looking on the reciprocal of the course he had steamed, saw that the *Lisbon Maru* had unexpectedly altered course to his left, to 060. She was now considerably further away than he had expected and no longer in such an advantageous position for attack; he would not be able to launch torpedoes at the shorter range he would have preferred. The submarine dived again and started a new approach. Still unaware of the activities in the water below, Fairbairn continued his rounds.

Located in the *Grouper's* conning tower were the two periscopes, the Torpedo Data Computer (TDC), the electric consoles, and the control panel for firing the torpedoes. There was silence, apart from quiet instructions from Edward Holt. As Diving Officer, he was responsible for maintaining proper depth at all times. He gave instructions to the bow and stern planesmen, and to Kvalheim on the trim manifold. He knew that in a choppy sea it would be very easy to broach — to break through the waves and be visible to the enemy — in which case the submarine could be in for a very long submergence under depth charge attack.

But today the seas were relatively still. The men in the *Lisbon Maru's* holds were shaking aching limbs, rubbing tired eyes, and readying themselves for a new day; a number were coughing, keeping fears about their sore throats — all too often the first signs of diphtheria — to themselves. But in the submarine, all were wide awake. At exactly 07.00, though still (at a range of just over two miles) a good deal further from his target than he would have wished, the captain finally gave the command: "Make tubes one, two and three ready for firing."

Down in the forward torpedo room, the torpedo men opened the outer doors of the three tubes, allowing them to flood. They set the depth at which the torpedoes would run (ten feet) at the tube. Fingering his locket — holding a little piece of Scottish heather, a good luck charm that he always wore during battle stations — McGregor waited patiently for the ready light to come on in the conning tower. Checking the periscope once more, and hearing a favourable solution from the TDC, the captain gave the order:

"Standby one — fire one."

At four minutes past seven in the morning of 1 October, under cover of mist, an old Mark 14 torpedo left the first tube at an estimated range of 3,200 yards from the *Lisbon Maru*. The sonar man hunched down, holding the earphones tightly to his head by habit, though in fact the whole control room was deathly silent.

"Number one running hot, straight and normal!" he reported, indicating that the torpedo was running true, and not boomeranging back towards the submarine itself as a 'circular'.[115] Forward, in the torpedo room, the torpedo men closed the outer door of the tube and the water inside drained into a tank to compensate for the weight of the tin fish that was now cutting its way, supposedly ten feet under the waves, to the *Lisbon Maru*. Holt kept the boat at a steady depth.

Ten seconds after the firing of the first tube, McGregor ordered the second, and then the third, to be fired.[116]

"Standby two — fire two."

"Number two running hot, straight and normal!"

"Standby three — fire three."

"Number three running hot, straight and normal!"

Knowing the range to the target and the speed of the torpedoes, *Grouper*'s crew watched the clock, silently counting off the 157 seconds that the water borne missiles would need to reach their target, waiting for the sound of an explosion.

As three tin fish hissed towards the old freighter through two miles of turbulent seas, the POWs on board still believed they were getting ready to start just another day.

Alf Hunt in the *Lisbon Maru*'s second hold: "On the morning of October 1st, about 7 am, most people were awake and awaiting the first meal of the day. Suddenly a loud noise — like air escaping from a tyre — was heard and one could not tell whether it was inboard or outboard of the ship. We later realised that it was a torpedo that had missed."

Another naval man, Wallace Hastings, in the first hold heard: "to port side[117] a sound which to me sounded more like a gurgling such as that when a sink finally empties."

The three torpedoes had missed their mark, but not by far. One in fact, had simply bounced off the hull.

Kvalheim recalled: "One thing to remember is that we were plagued with faulty detonators in our torpedoes early in the war. There were many hits with no explosions. We fired a total of six fish at the *Lisbon Maru*. I firmly believe that our first spread of three ran too deep. [There] was no explosion."[118]

Five men were on the *Lisbon Maru*'s bridge that morning. First Officer Niioka Gentaru was with the helmsman, Hiraoka Eikichi, and three sharp-eyed lookouts, Gahira Goro, Sugisaki Hirome, and Mizoguchi Miki.

Kyoda: "At 7.10 a.m. on October 1st the ship was attacked by torpedoes. I was awakened to shouts of 'Torpedo Attack' and I ran out of my room to the deck. That torpedo hit the centre of the starboard side but did not explode. The torpedo hit the ship, turned round, and went in the direction from where it came. A few minutes later the same torpedo turned round and sped on top of the water towards the ship. The speed of the torpedo was very slow, therefore with a hard turn the ship was able to dodge it. A few minutes later the second torpedo came at an angle of 45 degrees on the starboard bow. There were actually two torpedoes in this second attack, but the ship was able to dodge them."

In the silence of the submarine, the crew knew that too much time had gone by. There had been no explosions. Rob Roy McGregor ordered a fourth torpedo fired, but this time at a shallower depth; already, experienced men suspected a problem with the weaponry.

Two minutes and ten seconds later, travelling at a speed of 46 knots, the 1,488 kilograms monster, 6.24 metres long, slammed into the ship's stern, and 292 kilograms of Torpex[119] was a millisecond away from blowing an unpluggable hole, two and a half metres across, in the *Lisbon Maru's* hull.

Kyoda: "Then about 7.15 the fourth torpedo came at the ship from an angle of 35 degrees at the starboard bow and the distance away from the ship was 1,200 metres. When we discovered this fourth torpedo we did a hard starboard turn but we were not able to dodge it and it hit the propeller part at the starboard stern. It exploded and damaged the ship, and as a result the ship was unnavigable."

Japanese Private First Class Ito Elzu (*sic*), in hold number 7, died instantly in the explosion, pinned by a beam that came off the hatchway above him.

On board the *Lisbon Maru*, as the explosion reverberated, the POW's breakfast was being prepared. Private Bill Spooner: "Another chap [Charlie Heather] and myself were walking along the deck carrying a wooden bucket of rice and what we named 'slum', a horrible looking, evil smelling, concoction of some vegetables, thin and watery, when there sounded a dull thud from one side of the ship. Then the Japs went berserk, slapping and pushing us into the hold again."

Taffy Evans was also on deck as the torpedo struck, answering a call of nature: "Immediately those few men who were on deck using the lavatories and so forth, were ordered back into the holds, while all the sick men, whether naval or military were quickly bundled down into our hold which now contained about 400 men. The only space for the sick men to lie was on the hatch covers covering the lower hold, the hatch cover now being completely crowded with sick and baggage."

Watching the clock again, the men in the submarine's conning tower this time heard the loud explosion they had been waiting for. *Grouper* came back to periscope depth to make a quick observation — a matter of seconds to keep from being detected — and saw that the *Lisbon Maru* had changed course again, and now appeared to have stopped. They also noted that the *Lisbon Maru*'s forward gun was firing at her.[120]

Ross Lynneberg, in the first hold: "Down in the hold I could hear a swish, swish sound approaching the boat. This went past, then there was another swish, swish a rumble and a shudder as though we had run aground. All those who were on deck were driven back to the holds — the Japs then opened fire right above our hold."

Alf Hunt in the second: "A minute or so later there was a loud rumble, more so than an explosion, and a few seconds later the noise from the engines died away. Someone shouted the old naval saying, generally used in a jocular way; 'Don't panic till the lights go out'; and then, very gradually, the single light bulb slowly dimmed and went out."

Water, already pouring into the engine room, had swamped the generator.

James Miller, also in the second hold: "There was an almighty thud and the ship seemed to shudder to a halt, then start to settle down in the water. Panic seemed to spread among the crew. There was the ringing of bells, whistles and shouting and the ship's guns were blazing away."

While the men on deck heard a dull thud, and those in the forward holds heard the rumble of a distant explosion, those in the third hold were left in no doubt as to what had happened. Etiemble was in that sternmost hold, nearest of the POWs to the torpedo's point of impact: "I was lying on my straw mat in a hold way down near the bilges when I heard a torpedo whir across the ship's bows. Then I heard a terrific explosion in the coalbunker on the opposite side of the bulkhead to where I was trying to sleep. Water started to pour into the bilges below us. A Japanese sailor came down with an armful of cotton waste to plug up the hole but needless to say, it was useless."

The hole left by the torpedo was as far across as a man was tall. Water was pouring in, and as the pressure built up, any attempt to staunch the leaks was doomed to failure. Kyoda: "Then some rags were being pushed into the leak to stop the water, but it was impossible to completely stop the leak."

Etiemble: "The ship was motionless. Japanese guards were posted at the gangway, with orders that the deck was now out of bounds. Access to the taps for fresh water, and the latrines was therefore impossible."

At 8.45, *Grouper*, at a range of one thousand yards, fired a fifth torpedo with a one fathom[121] depth setting.

Kyoda: "About 8.50 the fifth torpedo came at the starboard side of the ship from a western direction. This torpedo just skimmed under the bottom of the ship and did not explode."

Taking a long time to gain the best position, exactly fifty-three minutes after firing the fifth tin fish, *Grouper* fired a sixth and last torpedo at a depth setting of zero feet — it was set to run at the surface. Just before firing the torpedo, the captain spotted a light bomber (which he claimed to be a Mitsubishi Darai 108)[122] over the *Lisbon Maru*. He immediately shouted an order. The man on the Main Ballast Control panel (unofficially known as the 'Christmas Tree' because of its red and green indicator lights) pulled the levers causing the vents at the top of the ballast tanks to open, resulting in water flooding the vented tanks and thus causing the submarine to lose buoyancy. *Grouper* crash dived. The submarine reached a depth of a hundred feet, and a loud explosion was heard forty seconds later.

Kyoda: "About 9.37 the sixth torpedo came at the portside of the ship and the distance was about 1,200 metres. The gunner on board the ship was able to put this torpedo out of action with an expert shot."[123]

Kvalheim: "We turned and got in another shot from #7 stern tube. One explosion was heard but not observed, as we had to go deep. We took quite a working over from two patrol craft. By this time things were becoming unpleasant."

It was becoming unpleasant for those on board the ship too, hearing the guns and depth charges exploding around them. Taffy Evans, having been bundled from the sunlit deck into the dark hold, had nothing to rely on but his ears: "Firing started from a gun erected on the focsle — the gun was probably an 18 pounder which we had noticed on previous days, while there was also another gun on the stern of about the same size. Some fifteen or so rounds were fired and then after a period of between half an hour to an hour, aeroplanes were heard and also the sound of bursting bombs, probably from the planes or maybe depth charges from destroyers which might have come on the scene."

In *Grouper's* Control Room was a bathythermograph. A military secret until many years after the Second World War, this instrument simultaneously recorded both the depth and temperature of water just outside the submarine's hull. It traced a combined depth/temperature graph on a calibrated card coated with carbon. As the boat descended, a stylus rubbed off the carbon from top to bottom of the card. A second control rod moved the stylus laterally as the temperatures rose and fell. A constant angle or gentle curve would mean a slow and steady decrease in temperature with depth. However, a sharp change of angle in the line being drawn as the submarine dived would indicate a thermocline — a region of sudden and significant temperature change. Sound waves are deflected by thermoclines, giving submarines the opportunity of hiding beneath them out of sight of sonar.

Watching the bathythermograph and directing the man on the large brass wheel front and centre in the Control Room (used for steering when under depth charge attack and running silent), Rob Roy remained calm. Kvalheim and the men manning the bow planes and stern planes followed his orders as the temperatures started to soar — and air quality plummeted rapidly — with the noisy ventilation system shut off for silent running. Sweating, they watched the mercury rise slowly to 130 degrees Fahrenheit.[124]

At 09.40, almost immediately after firing the last torpedo, the men on the *Grouper* heard three depth charges explode. Garfield Kvalheim's friends, Charlie Bowers the Gunner's Mate from Michigan Bluff, California; Rudy Hess, in the aft engine room; Pat Higgens, who had burnt off half his moustache in an accident on board at Midway; "Obie" O'Brian, the ship's cook, had no choice but to sit it out. They braced themselves together with their fellow crewmembers, "Wop" D'Allesantro, John Erim, Bob Glenn, Tommy Hodgson, Eric Lawler, Charlie Link, Tommy Ploe, "Frenchy" Remillard, "Pinky" Rimmer, and the others. Each took the bombardment in his own way.

Kvalheim: "Whenever we rigged for depth charging, [D'Allesantro] would head for his bunk and, being Catholic, he would lie there with his prayer beads and start mumbling and repeatedly crossing himself. We all figured if he was that close to God we were all safe."

A Japanese destroyer (the old *Momi*-class Japanese destroyer *Kuri*)[125] and several auxiliary ships had appeared on the scene and were searching for the *Grouper*.

After a suitable pause, the submarine came up to periscope depth. Seeing no sign of the *Lisbon Maru*, the captain assumed she had sunk. In fact, the vessel would not sink until almost exactly twenty-five hours later.

Meanwhile in the holds, the POWs knew that the ship had stopped and was listing. They could hear the Japanese troops running around on the deck. They heard the Japanese crew firing the front gun (the rear one having been disabled in the torpedo attack), shooting ninety-eight shells in total. They also heard a plane (no doubt the same one spotted by the submarine), and from the Japanese cheering, guessed that it was one of theirs.

James Miller of the Royal Scots: "We firmly believed the Japs would not let us drown. They could not be so heartless, that they would let 1,800 helpless men die. The ship was sinking slowly by the stern and we waited and waited for the Japs to mount a rescue mission."

This hope turned to despair as the minutes in darkness turned to hours. There was to be no rescue mission.

Sergeant William Poulter: "My own thoughts at this time were: I've been shot at with bullets and shells, bombed, had a hand grenade thrown at me and now I've been torpedoed. Maybe I'm fated to be drowned, so what, there's not much I can do about it."

Ross Lynneberg: "Our next request was to go to the latrines but this wasn't granted so the few buckets we had amongst us were used and were soon over-flowing. We asked to empty them but were not allowed so by the evening the air was thick and nasty tasting due to the smell associated with dysentery. We also learnt there was no food available …"

Large numbers of the men had dysentery, thus the holds quickly became fouled. They knew now that this was no temporary stop, and used any receptacle they could find — tin cans, hats, jars. But it was all futile.

Alsey: "No food all day, no one allowed on deck for latrine, 2 boards are pulled up from bottom of hold, and 1,100 line up for piss, men use their mess tins for shit pans".

At about 12.35, a motorboat from the *Kuri* came alongside, with the destroyer's captain aboard. He went to the bridge to enquire about damage to the ship, and Kyoda reported that the torpedo attack had injured four of his crew. The motorboat returned to the destroyer to fetch a doctor to examine the four men.

Taking note of pleas from Lieutenant Potter (the Japanese-speaking poet of the St John's Ambulance Brigade), the guards passed two empty petrol tins into the second hold. These were quickly filled and overflowed. Potter managed to persuade the Japanese to send down water, but only two buckets of extremely unclean liquid were lowered into the darkness of the hold. Desperately ill men had nothing to slake their thirst — though the seawater in the rear-most holds was now rising ten inches per hour — and the ranks of the sick were steadily growing.

Despatch rider Taffy Evans: "It should be remembered here, that the diphtheria cases were now in the hold, likewise all those with dysentery and all the other sick men."

This, in the long term, magnified the disaster. Men, stressed and weakened by wounds received in the fighting less than a year before, by ten months of malnutrition, and by the shock of the attack on their vessel, were now thirsty, starving, shocked and exposed to a concentrated mass of bacteria and viruses. These would later kill many of those who managed to survive the sinking itself.

Lieutenant Howell: "Slowly it dawned on us that the imprisonment was not a precaution against escape but fortuitously had become a calculated mass-murder of unwanted prisoners by drowning."

And drowning was becoming ever more likely. Although the POWs did not know it, by just after five that afternoon there was already eleven feet of water in the rear-most cargo hold.

Etiemble in the rear-most hold that the POW's occupied, closest to the torpedo's damage: "Then we were handed a four-man hand pump[126] and three candles and told that it was our job to keep the ship afloat."

Apart from the feeble flickering of the three spluttering candles, number three hold was now bereft of any light. The only sound, bar the squeaking of the pump and the panting of the men manning it, was the gurgle of new water seeping into the hold. Battery Quarter Master Sergeant 'Busty' Dicks egged on the pumpers, but the air was becoming thicker, foul and hot. Every few minutes a man on the pump fell in a dead faint, and was replaced by another.

Etiemble: "Although there was no panic in No. 3 hold, someone had to take control of the pumping, and in my opinion this is just what 'Q' Dicks did. As well as organising and making sure the pump was fully manned at all times, he tried to keep up morale by cracking jokes and stating: 'keep it up lads we're gaining' as he placed a bit of wood in the water, knowing full well the reality was just the opposite."[127]

Dusk was falling by now, as 1 October came to an end — not that the term 'dusk' meant anything to those who had been shut up in the lightless holds for twelve hours already. Shortly after seven that evening, the *Grouper's* captain, having stayed in the vicinity all day, decided to surface and leave the area. It being Val Kvalheim's twenty-fifth birthday, Edward Holt, the torpedo officer, made him a birthday card of a sketch of the *Lisbon Maru* crossed out. The American submariners, of course, still had no inkling of the true situation on board their victim.

Kvalheim: "At nightfall we surfaced to put in a battery charge but were driven down by the patrol boats. We tried once more with the same results. It was apparent that we could not stay submerged much longer so we finally surfaced, put all four engines on the line and were able to gain some distance between us and the patrol boats. We were later able to get in a battery charge before dawn."

At half past seven, shortly after *Grouper* had steamed away, those on board the *Lisbon Maru* again heard the Japanese running around on deck, and apparently moving heavy objects. More significantly, they also heard another ship coming alongside. Hope sprung once more. Rescue!

Howell: "After twelve hours the scene was rapidly approaching that so vividly described by Macaulay — the Black Hole of Calcutta — and then suddenly a bump and a trampling overhead; we were to be let out! Another hour passed, the sounds died away; hundreds of Japanese soldiers had been rescued from a sinking ship."

The ship the Japanese soldiers boarded was the destroyer *Kuri*, which — together with the gun-boat *Toyokuni Maru*[128] under Captain Yano Mitoshi, the Shanghai Coast Defence Commander, and the *Hyakufuku Maru*[129] — took off all the 778 regular Japanese troops on board, leaving only the 77 crew and 25 guards under Lieutenant Wada. Unfortunately, as the *Toyokuni Maru* came alongside, it crushed the two port-side lifeboats. A doctor on board crossed to the *Lisbon Maru* to supervise the treatment of those Japanese wounded in the torpedo attack. They were placed in the other two (starboard-side) lifeboats, which sailed — taking a further twelve members of the crew with them — to the escorting vessels and did not return. All four lifeboats were now unavailable to the POWs. Captain Yano decided to tow the *Lisbon Maru* west to shallower water.[130]

Together with *Kuri* and *Toyokuni* (which acted as the command ship), other Japanese vessels came to the *Lisbon Maru's* assistance. These included the gunboats *Unkai Maru No. 10*, *Tone Maru*,[131] *Fuku Maru No. 10*, and *Ikushu Maru*. The naval tug-boat *Koho Maru No. 1* was also present, as were the salvage boat *Kasajima Maru*, and the *Shosei Maru*. Including the destroyer, there were now ten escorting vessels in total.

At eight o'clock that evening, during a meeting between Kyoda and Wada, Wada suggested that Kyoda should completely close the hatches so that the POWs could not escape. Kyoda disagreed, citing conditions in the holds and the loss of life that would occur if the ship sank. This caused some argument with the military guards.

Kyoda: "I objected to the closing of the hatches. First of all, the ventilation of air would become very bad, secondly there might be further enemy attacks. If these hatches were closed and the ship was further attacked lives might be lost unnecessarily."

However, Kyoda admitted that: "In the first hold there were some 300 naval personnel and therefore if these personnel revolted it would be quite serious."[132]

After arguing the matter for an hour, they tired of the debate. Wada, now joined by Sugiyama, simply ordered Kyoda to have the hatches fastened. The captain complied and passed the order on to his first officer.

Kyoda: "Lieutenant Wada would not listen to me and it could not be helped, so I ordered the hatches closed."

While seaman fitted towlines and the Japanese started to haul the stricken vessel west, the hatches were finally closed, battened down, and covered with tarpaulin. At least, until this point, the POWs had access to shouted communication with those on deck and could just make out a small square of darkening sky high above them; but they were now entirely cut off. The air in the holds was completely stagnant. The only sound was the laboured breathing of sick and frightened men in an atmosphere that was becoming increasingly polluted.

In the second hold, Howell, the shipwreck expert, took stock: "Now as we perforce had learnt during the previous months of the callous cruelty of the Japanese soldier, we were not prepared for the next move. Machine guns were mounted to preclude escape; the ventilator shaft was cut down; the wooden hatchboards fixed in place; tarpaulin cover stretched over them, battened down, and lashed with Manila rope. Thereafter complete darkness reigned."

James Miller, also in the second hold: "Somebody shouted out that the ship was sinking. This started an immediate panic for the ladder leading out of the hold. Before anybody could get to the top, the Japs had started putting the hatchboards over the hold and the canvas covers were being battened down."

The first hold had identical treatment. Fallace: "Our wind chute was cut down and the bottom half fell on the sick lying in the hold, the remainder of the hatch boards were put on and the tarpaulin covering the hatch was chocked down thus preventing any further ingress of fresh air and putting us in complete darkness. From this time on the air became absolutely foul and together with cries and moans from the sick all night the situation became unbearable."

And Lynneberg: "With the sunset they had battened us down completely by covering the hatch with a tarpaulin and drove in wedges to keep it in place."

Civilian Arthur Evans: "The men in the hold then got a little excited when they realised what had happened and [Pollock] then got up and addressed everybody and told them to lie quietly. Smoking and talking were forbidden to conserve any fresh air that might be in the hold."

Through Morse code tapped on the bulkhead, the men in the third hold reported that water was rising and the Royal Artillery were still manning pumps, but to little avail.

Midnight passed, though most men were uncertain of the time. A few had watches with luminous dials, the only lights of any kind in the holds. In the very early hours, number one hold suffered the first fatalities. The first to die was CERA Herbert Thomas Bevis of HMS *Tamar*; the second, Shipwright First Class Cyril Alfred Lifton of HMS *Tern*. Both had been suffering from beri beri and had been dragged down from the deck after the torpedo had struck.

Jim Fallace was in that hold: "About 1 a.m. the first man died. Signals were then tapped in Morse through the bulkhead to No. 2 hold asking them to inform Colonel Stewart of the situation in No. 1 hold. Shortly after the second man died, thus adding to the discomforts."

Ross Lynneberg, also a radio operator and equally familiar with Morse, in number one hold: "It was unsettling to hear this message being tapped out in the deadly quiet of the hold."

Alf Hunt, on the other side of the bulkhead in number two hold, was listening to the tapping with Lieutenant Colonel Stewart: "We had no idea of time, but it must have been in the early hours of the morning after a night that seemed like an eternity that a tapping sound was heard. I realized — being a radio operator — that it was Morse being tapped by one of the navy boys in the forward hold onto a common connecting pipe. 'Have two dead and several dying', was the message I read. Someone in our hold started to reply and then there was a frenzied scream of 'stop that tapping' from some demented soul."

As the messages came, Lieutenant Bucke of the Royal Signals decoded them for Stewart. Signaller Frank Bennett was in the same hold, straining to hear as the tapping ceased: "Slowly the noise diminished and eventually silence. It was quite eerie. Sitting in the darkness in silence. It must have been at some time during the night that we realised the ship was starting to list. Thoughts then came to the fore as to whether we would get out, or go to a watery grave."

The situation was simple: the ship had been torpedoed, the majority of the Japanese on board had been rescued, the half-starved POWs were lying in absolute darkness below the water-line bathed in their own urine and excrement, oxygen was in short supply, and the only possible exits had been deliberately closed tight shut. Now men were starting to die, and when the ship foundered, it seemed that there would be no option; all would be doomed to drown in terror and utter darkness.

Bill Spooner: "Even in these circumstances there is always a humorist. Imagine the ship sinking, swaying from side to side, a voice shouting, 'I'm bleedin' 'ungry'. Humorist — 'Right, lay dahn and 'ave a bleedin' roll'."

In the darkness, the men tried to talk of ordinary things: football clubs, weddings, families, homes. Non-swimmer CQMS Henderson of the Royal Scots assured others in the same predicament that 'this is the time to learn'. But by now most men were too uncomfortable, scared, and ill to laugh.[133]

Wallace Hastings: "[The stench of dysentery added] to the already oppressive heat that had built up following the battening down and sheeting of the hatches some time earlier. Conversation dwindled and a state of ennui prevailed. I believe that now hopes of rescue began to fade."

"Gale was in a bad way with diarrhoea," reported Wright, and Gale was far from being the only one. Wright let him have his last few drops of water, but in the darkness, Gale mistakenly picked up a bottle of urine and took a mouthful before spluttering it over his companions.

Ross Lynneberg: "The air had now become very thick and even the fittest of us were sweating and panting, while several of the sick who had been sent to our hold were raving mad and were screaming out for air and water alternately. I myself had about a mouth full of water left in my water bottle which every now and again I'd empty into my mouth, sluice it around, and return it back to the bottle for next time."

*   *   *

And so the night passed.

7 "Abandon Ship!": 2 October, a.m.

> 'Mercy on us!'
> 'We split, we split!'
> 'Farewell my wife and children!'
> 'Farewell, brother!'
> 'We split, we split, we split!'
>
> *The Tempest*, Act 1, Scene 1

No light, no air. Stripped-off men lay blindly in their own sewerage and waited. This night no one slept. They all panted for breath; there was no water to replace their sweat. Despair had stifled most, but not all, of the remaining humour.

Bill Spooner: "It was pitch dark, there was a wooden gallery above the floor of the ship on which the bulk of the men were lying, the men on the gallery could not retain their urine or their faeces any longer so we below received them with shouts of 'you dirty bastards'."

But Arthur Alsey remembered it differently: "Middlesex piss down from deck ledge causing repeated appeals from below. In agonized indignation and frustration, a voice from below yelled 'aren't there any NCOs up there?' No reply. 'Aren't there any sergeants up there?' No reply. 'Aren't there any bloody officers up there?' A small voice replied, 'they are next in the queue'. It says a lot for our sense of humour that there was an immediate bellow of laughter from every quarter of the hold."

Exhausted and half drowned, the gunners in the flooded third hold finally stopped pumping. In the second hold, men could hear objects — clearly floating in a flooded part of the ship — crashing into the bulkheads at the back of their hold, and others further aft. The whole ship began to creak as it took on water. The flooded rear compartments settled lower in the water, raising the bow and putting the strain of the bow's weight on the hull. The metal started to groan in protest; the *Lisbon Maru* was in danger of breaking her back, and if she did before reaching shallow water, she would go down like a stone.

Lieutenant Potter and Lieutenant Colonel Stewart tried to contact the guards, but with no success; Potter had been calling out 'moshi moshi' and 'anno, neh' ('excuse me' and 'I say') for hours. There was no more hope of rescue or relief; the time had come. Stewart ordered Lieutenant Hargraves 'Ginger' Howell, RASC — he who had been shipwrecked twice before — to break out of the second hold.

Howell: "Colonel Stewart in his calm matter of fact manner then reminded me of his comment the previous night, and suggested it was about time that I did something about this particular shipwreck! Near us (though we could not see it in the utter blackness) was a vertical iron ladder rising up the side of the hold which normally would provide an exit for cargo workers. Could escape from the hold be found this was through the battened down hatchboards? 'Tommy Atkins'[134] is proverbially resourceful but I was amazed when, subsequent to a request for a tough instrument of some kind, there arrived in my hand through utter darkness by a sort of hunt-the-slipper process, a long sharp butcher's knife from some far away cook-house.[135] The muttered cursing that literally followed the handing on to me of this knife through the inky blackness, as those lying prone in its course were disturbed by proddings and tramplings, was almost funny, had it not indicated the stupor that was fast overcoming many in that airless hold. Never shall I forget the physical agony of gasping for oxygen while under the exertion of climbing to the top of that iron ladder. Then anxiously striving to find a slit through the boards; or later, spasmodically and blindly slashing at them in desperation while panting for breath. Through sheer exhaustion after what seemed hours the attempt was abandoned and I settled back to listen to the gradual crescendo of moans, blasphemies, prayers that arose from the darkness around and below me."

But Stewart was an old campaigner; he did not give up hope.

Soon after eight in the morning, Captain Kyoda — realizing that he was losing his third command in eight months — signalled to the *Toyokuni Maru*: "The *Lisbon Maru* is about to sink. I wish to have everybody abandon ship."

He received no reply. Around eight-thirty, the *Lisbon Maru* shuddered again. Clearly the end was near; the tortured old freighter and all those on board were headed for the sandy floor of the Zhoushan Archipelago.

Fifteen minutes later Kyoda was informed that a ship, the *Koho Maru No. 1*, would be sent alongside to take off all remaining Japanese guards and crew, but not the POWs.[136] The crew left, but a small group of guards — perhaps half a dozen in all, together with Kyoda and some of the ship's officers — remained on board when their colleagues jumped ship. The first and second mate, and the chief engineer, tried to persuade Kyoda to leave, but when he refused, they jumped into the sea and swam to the escorts. Second Mate Araki: "The chief engineer was with the master of the ship when he was master of the *Calcutta Maru* and the *Calcutta Maru* was sunk, and the master of the ship had a very strong sense of responsibility and the chief engineer said the master of the ship might commit suicide."

Indeed, Kyoda tied himself to the ship, fully intending to go down with it. The ship lurched, dunking him in the water, then lurched again, pulling him free of it. "I stayed as I was for a short time aimlessly. Then I untied the rope that was holding me."

Alf Hunt: "The water could be heard swilling about in the next compartment, probably the engine room, and then there were ominous noises as the bulkhead started to give. The list to port had increased, the ship, I estimated, was over about 30 degrees and the companionway ladders were almost level."

At nine o'clock, convinced that they were now in immediate danger, Stewart roused the men into action again. For the second time he gave the order to break out of number two hold. Howell took up his knife once more, and with a few colleagues — this time climbing a wooden staircase leading directly to the hatch — successfully cut his way out.

Howell: "After what seemed years someone announced by means of a watch which inexplicably had not been purloined or exchanged for food that it was 9 a.m. on the 2nd October — more than twenty-four hours in this hell hole had dragged by. Almost simultaneously, the ship gave a tremendous lurch and listed heavily to port. A bulkhead had given way somewhere. That she was sinking fast was painfully obvious! With dwindling hopes I groped in the darkness to find a way along the edge of the gaping hold that lay below and finally reached the bottom of the make-shift stairway that had once lead to the open air. Crawling up to the top where the hatchboards closed over me, I was eventually — with the aid of the butcher's knife — able to find a chink in the boards, and it was possible to scratch the canvas and finally slit it. Using my shoulders and with two others pushing behind, a board was eventually edged-over enough to form an aperture which could be squeezed through."

With his head above deck, he shouted down to Stewart in the hold, reporting seeing some islands, and a few gunners from number three hold tying to escape through portholes. Andrew Salmon — in the third hold — confirmed this, but noted: "[some of us] climb up the side of the hold by clinging onto rivets and get to the mid-decks. Others tried to get out through the port-holes, but got stuck, and for them all they could do was wait for the ship to go down."

For once, the Prisoners of War had been lucky. During the previous night, at about 22.35, they had heard the 8-inch manila rope — which the *Toyokuni Maru* was using to tow the ship — snap. Unknown to the POWs, the Japanese had found and re-fitted a similar rope at about 01.35. The towing continued. At 6.10 the second rope broke. Working quickly, the Japanese seamen replaced it some fifty minutes later with a 3.5-inch wire hawser from the *Toyokuni Maru*. This rope held until the *Lisbon Maru* came to a halt. By that time, the *Toyokuni Maru* had dragged the vessel to within swimming distance of the islands Howell had spotted. Without this tow, very few of those on board would have been able to survive. Closer to the mouth of the great Yangtze river, silt from the Chinese heartland, slowly deposited over tens of thousands of years, had built up until it was just metres below the ship's hull.

Howell: "Colonel Stewart then told me to break out on deck and ascertain the state of the ship. With providential prescience I requested that Lieutenant Potter who spoke some Japanese, should accompany me, for though we did not know it, there were six 'suicide' guards left on the ship to prevent any escape, however improbable. Wriggling out through the aperture just made, the two of us, followed by a few others who could not resist the balm of clean fresh air and sunlight, firstly cut the ropes, enlarged the exit and then proceeded to make a second air inlet and escape route just where the iron ladder emerged from the hold almost directly under the ship's bridge. The sea was by now washing over the port bulwarks and the old freighter's lurching caused a scrambled chaos in the hold below. Turning to midships, I was able to open the heavy iron doors screwed from the outside and let out some of the surviving 'gunners' from the upper section of No. 3 hold. Stark horror on the faces of a few actually wedged in the small port-holes and forced to watch the water on the well-deck lapping nearer and nearer, was a sight that at times still haunts me."

While Howell was unscrewing the bulkhead door to release the gunners, he and Potter came under fire. Lieutenant Wada, looking down at them from the passage of the saloon deck,[137] had ordered the few Japanese guards left on board to shoot the escapees.

Howell continued: "The crack of a rifle, the thud of a bullet hitting the hatch beside me quickly made it clear that we were not alone on the ship. I rapidly slid under the steel sheeting that covered the steam pipes running forward on the well deck. Lieutenant Potter was wounded, two others collapsed and several shots went into the hold[138] through the newly made opening. The faces of four guards, looking down their rifle sights appeared over the ship's bridge. A few more desultory shots at varied targets including myself were made and then I asked the wounded Potter, if he could still do so, to inform the guards that if they ceased firing we would go back into the hold. They did so, and with considerable trepidation I came out from my prone retreat alongside the steam pipes, stood up and carried Potter back to the original exit we hade made. Not a further shot was fired at us; a sitting target less than fifteen yards from the muzzles of those rifles; but meanwhile some of the gunners had not returned to their hold but had crept unnoticed to the stairway leading to the bridge."

The Royal Artillery in number three hold were in the worst situation, as the ship was settling stern first. Desperate to escape, they had not been able to afford the relatively leisurely escape tactics of the men in the other holds. There was no 'calm evacuation' here. As soon as their comrades had opened the doors, those who could sprang onto the deck.

Jack Etiemble was waiting inside the third hold for anybody who could undo the hatches or bulkhead doors and let them out: "Whilst undoing ours the Japs shot him. We managed to loosen a few more and started climbing out, the Japs were still shooting from the patrol boats, I managed to get out and was lying on the deck waiting for a break in the shooting, before sliding into the water. Just after the escape ladder gave way no one else could get out. I heard an Irish gunner shout, 'we cannot get out, let's give them a song.' They sang 'It's a long way to Tipperary'. I slid down into the water, knowing the Gunners had done their duty in spite of the adverse conditions. No water, no food, no air. They had kept the ship afloat for twenty-four hours, and no one need have died … Gunner Childs and I had climbed out just behind each other. We lay on the deck alongside the body of the Lieutenant who had been shot whilst undoing the battens of our hold. During a lull in the shooting we both slid into the water."[139]

As Howell helped the mortally wounded Potter[140] back into the second hold, Stewart asked his opinion on the future of the ship. Howell voiced his fears that it would sink at any moment.

Stewart had no choice; he ordered 'Abandon Ship.'

Lance Corporal Taylor was in that hold: "Wild panic ensued. Within seconds the ladders to the second deck were a mass of writhing, struggling bodies. Those first up discovered there was no room for them there, but others on the ladders below climbed over their backs before falling back into the bottom hold, crashing on to the men beneath them."

Initially there was a free for all, a noisy fight as panicked men struggled over use of the ladders. The only light was from the newly opened hatches two decks above, and in the rush to reach them, escaping men trampled anyone too slow or too weak to get out of their way.

Robert Wright was lying next to diphtheria-victim Hayward: "I heard Hayward calling desperately for his mother as he was crunched against the plywood of the billet."

Frank Bennett: "I have seen panic portrayed on the screen, but had never been a part of it myself. That wooden set of stairs up from the hold was absolutely packed with men. Men with one aim — to get out. What a bloody scramble, clutching and clawing at each other to gain an advantage. Some were falling back with a deafening thud as far up as the gallery deck."

Howell: "It was Colonel Stewart on the 'tween decks reiterating, in Regimental tradition, the command 'Steady!' that saved those of us in the front from being shoved by the surge of ranks behind us into the crowded hold forty feet below."

"Steady the Middlesex!" Shouted Lieutenant Colonel Moncreif Stewart, "remember who you are!"

Monkey and his NCOs quickly restored order, and queues formed at the bottom of each ladder as the ship lurched yet again; men and their possessions slid across the steeply angled floor.

Howell, having hardly had time to recover from his last spell on deck, received the usual reward of the successful. Stewart again picked him to lead the final orderly evacuation. Behind Howell, the men from number two hold raced on deck, though a few unfortunates still fell back into the holds, slipping on the urine and excrement that oiled the steep steel plates; the ship was now down at the stern (which was resting on a sandbank), and by quite an angle.

Although the vessel had originally carried four lifeboats, two sampans, six rafts, and 2,700 life jackets, only one sampan and a scattering of life jackets could be found. The four lifeboats had been lost as described, and the fate of the rafts was unknown. One sampan had simply disappeared; the other was still in place, but only one man in two retrieved a life jacket.

Howell was first on deck and made straight for the water: "I hurtled across the deck and dived in. Once more a bullet whizzed past my head. I spurted on and another bullet splashed beside me. To protect such a vital target as the head, I swam under water until breath gave out, then dipped down again and I remember wondering as I went which end they would eventually hit. By then I was not the only target as scores were in the water, but many failed to get very far. Some on deck with complete disregard of the bullets were tearing down the wooden latrines to make a raft of sorts or find a support of some kind before entering the water."

The six remaining guards were armed, and were firing down from the bridge at the POWs who were blinking in the strong sunlight as they escaped from the hatches. But even armed men were no match for the flood of desperate survivors now swarming from the second hold.

Howell credits the Royal Artillery with the demise of the guards: "The firing suddenly lessened because, as it turned out later, the released gunners had reached the bridge and in a maniacal dash had overcome the guards and mangled them."

In a more colourful account, Sergeant "Porky" Betts (the Middlesex battalion heavyweight boxing champion), Corporal Dan Cavill, Lance-Corp "Pancho" Panting, Private "Darkie" Hope, Private "Chopper" Hatchett, Private Harry Whitehouse, and Bandsman Johnny Hymes are said to have thrown the guards overboard with no further loss to themselves.[141]

According to at least one observer, Hope, Panting, Hatchett, Whitehouse then made for the captain's cabin. Here they found two bottles of Suntory whisky. On empty stomachs, the effects were huge and almost instantaneous. Ringing the ship's bell continuously, Panting (wearing the captain's cap and a Union Jack that he had found somewhere) kept up a running commentary: "Any more for the Skylark? All ashore that's going ashore!"

Fuck 'em all, fuck 'em all,
The Long and the Short and the Tall,
You'll get no promotion this side of the ocean
so come on my lads fuck 'em all!

There may be some truth in this, as Ross Lynneberg reported: "Before leaving the *Lisbon Maru* I remember a lad floating away on a partly submerged wooden deck toilet shouting and waving a bottle of looted liquor from which he kept taking swigs."

Dennis Morley agreed: "Yes, I seem to remember some singing going on. I was more engrossed with giving and fitting, [to] what seemed to me at that time an old man, my life jacket. Ah! The confidence of youth; I often wonder if he survived."

William Poulter added: "There were some islands about five miles away and there were five or six big tugs standing by, so it looked as though everything would be OK. Nearly everyone had a life belt or something to hang on to and I had a certificate from the 'Royal Life Saving Society' so I was not too worried about going into the drink. Two or three men were up on the bridge and ringing the ship's bell and a few more were standing under it having a smoke before going into the water. Everything was nice and orderly. I stepped into the water, which was not very warm, and swam away from the ship."

But most men were still trying to escape from the holds. To get out, the men at the bottom of number two hold had to negotiate two sets of ladders: the first to the second deck, and the second to the open air and freedom.

Robert Wright tried to reach the first gangway, but was pushed away again and again by the crush. He looked up and saw 'Busty' Eaton[142] lowering his belt to him. Busty pulled him up to the next level. Now Wright had to scale the second gangway. There was a seething mass of struggling men at the bottom. The strong got through, and saw from the deck that the sea was already full of men swimming in circles, or holding onto wreckage.

Robert Wright: "Men were running about, not seeking immediate means of saving their lives, but with the aim of looting the ship. Not far away were half-a-dozen auxiliary vessels of the Japanese navy, there, I assumed, to pick up survivors."

Alf Hunt, who also escaped from the second hold: "I made my way to the starboard side and looked aft. The stern of the ship was under water, some were dashing around, and others were ambling around as though it was a holiday cruise. 'Always abandon ship on the opposite side to which it is sinking' is the navy maxim. This, when it is possible, is to avoid suction from the sinking vessel. In my estimation, it was about twenty-five feet down to the water and there were many swimmers, swimming around amongst the flotsam. Timber from the hatch covers was still being thrown overboard and I considered it was too dangerous to dive or jump because of the objects and swimmers in the water, so I decided to slide down a rope hanging down the ship's side. The barnacles on the ship's side and bottom scratched and cut my legs but the water was marvellous. Lovely and cool."

James Miller, who appears to have left the second hold after Hunt: "When I got out of the hold, I could see bodies floating face down, all around. The hold was filling rapidly now and the ship was beginning to go down quicker. I was pushed overboard by the mad rush to get off as she sank lower and lower. My first reaction as I hit the water, was self-preservation. I saw a hatchboard floating near me and immediately struck out for it. I was a good swimmer, but I was in a very weak condition and this hatchboard was going to be my lifesaver."

Frank Bennett: "Skeats Langley,[143] our MT Sergeant, grabbed me. 'Let's make a raft,' he suggested. We collected a hatchcover (a hell of a lump of timber), tied a piece of rope to each ring bolt to hang on to and carried our prize up the slope of the deck to the top rail."

Some men in number two hold were by now too weak to escape. Bombardier Inglis: "I owe my life to four gallant Royal Scots who asked me why I was just sitting there. Hearing that I couldn't move because of my badly swollen legs and feet,[144] they picked me up and laboriously carried me up the ladders to the deck. One even apologised that there were no life jackets left!"

Captain Cuthbertson of the Royal Scots was the last to leave number two hold, first descending to the hull to check that all living men had left.

Howell: "What can be said of the courage shown by the Adjutant of the Royal Scots who, having once escaped from that fast flooding hold voluntarily, went back to that he could solace some of his men who lay injured below, for the rickety stairway from the lower hold had collapsed under the weight of those who scrambled to get out. Some had plummeted forty feet. Some had been dead for hours. To whom he could, this Captain Cuthbertson gave a drink — a last cigarette rifled from the ship's store — a splint of wood for a broken leg or just a kindly word. He was later swept out of the hold by a surge of water as the ship finally went under."

It is not clear who opened the forward hatch, letting the POWs out of the first hold, but Howell believed it was probably the gunners whom he had earlier released from the third hold.[145]

The experience of the Navy men in this hold was similar to their comrades in the second.

Lynneberg, Royal New Zealand Navy: "I made my way on deck to find it over-crowded, with the sea breaking over the hatch next to our vacated one, the stern was well under with the bow well up. I stood for a few minutes then asked why they weren't taking to the water, and was told by many that they couldn't swim."

Fallace, Hong Kong Royal Naval Volunteer Reserve: "I picked myself up and dived over the side. All this time shots were heard which seemed to come from an auxiliary off the stern. Whilst swimming clear of the ship, shots were heard to hit the water in my vicinity."

Grant Shepherd, Royal Navy, with his 'quarters' midships against the rear bulkhead: "Possibly 15 minutes before escaping the hold I felt for the only time during 3 years and 8.5 months as a POW that my life was over. Unfamiliar though I was with the act of praying, I prayed fervently at that time. I don't know if that enabled me to escape the hold, but I did so following the efforts of those unknown to me who worked hard for some time and were able to remove the hatch covers from my position near the centre of the rear bulkhead. I followed other escapees up a stairway forward of my position and on the port side."

Wallace Hastings, Royal Navy, who, uniquely, had somehow managed to sleep the previous night: "I suppose that during the night we slept on and off and I can remember waking up and experiencing difficulty in rising to the sitting position because of the increased list to port. Looking across the hold to starboard the ladder to the upper deck was fully occupied by prisoners and at this time the ship gave a sudden movement and — whether the hatch covers were removed within or without the hold I do not know — but access to the upper deck was achieved. In the scramble that followed one or two of the heavy battens were dislodged and fell into the hold injuring one or more of the prisoners below. There followed a burst of gunfire from above which ceased after a short while."

The final evacuation of number one hold was as calm and disciplined as that of the second, with Lieutenant Pollock returning to it to retrieve the funds of which he was in charge. Sick Berth Attendants had even wrapped in blankets the two men who had died during the night.

Arthur Evans: "By the time the first of the naval contingent had scrambled out on to the deck, it was seen that the military from Nos. 2 and 3 holds were already out of their holds, and hundreds of men were already in the sea swimming in the direction of five or six Japanese auxiliary craft which were cruising slowly between the ship and the land which could be seen faintly in the distance. When the naval men got out of the hold some jumped over immediately into the sea, and some of these were shot at by the Japanese, while others crowded together with some of the military men on the bows of the ship."

Seeing a man with a water bottle, Evans went into the hold to collect one too, and then took it to the Japanese crew's quarters to fill it. There he found their rice, still warm from the quick breakfast, which had been interrupted by evacuation.

The RAMC, led by Staff Sergeant Ross,[146] collected some forty sick and injured — from all holds — on deck for first aid.

The naval men, spared the horrors of the flooding of the third hold and the drowning men stuck in portholes, stayed calm. Being familiar with all things ship-like, they were in less of a hurry to jump into the sea than men of the other units.

Grant Shepherd: "The first thing I saw on the upper deck was blue sky and calm water. Minutes later many of us were hugging each other, almost hysterical after 24 hours in what most of us must have thought was our final voyage. After approximately fifteen minutes we became more composed — so much so that a few individuals went back into the hold, mistakenly believing that the ship was going to stay in its listing position. This mistaken belief led to a few more going down with the sunken ship. About half an hour after reaching the upper deck, the ship started its plunge to the bottom and it was at this point that I jumped from the starboard side, not knowing what was to follow as I was a very weak and inexperienced swimmer."

Leading Sick Berth Attendant Wallace Hastings was one of those in no hurry to leave the ship: "Dr Jackson told our group to hold back until it was safe to move. This proved to be sound advice, as I believe that those unfortunates that left the ship immediately came under fire from boats lying off. We stayed below for some time until no sounds could be heard from above and then climbed out. The scene above was much as depicted in the drawing [see the 'Drawing of the sinking of the

Lisbon Maru']. The ship's stern was below water almost to the funnel and the sea off the port side awash with debris and many bobbing heads of the swimmers. The day was bright and sunny, the sea quite calm and as there appeared to be no further active submergence we decided to search for food or water having not eaten for almost 48 hours. We struck gold! This was in the shape of a small keg of sugar which was rapidly emptied by the handful thus providing energy for the coming endurance swim."

Alf Taylor of the Signals also found the sugar: "The deck was pitched at a very steep angle. We were desperately in need of water, but could find only a sack of white sugar which had been slashed open. We ate a little and found that in our dehydrated state we could not swallow it. The sunshine was brilliant, and the sun sparked across the calm sea like a carpet of dazzling diamonds. The air was like wine after the foetid stench in the hold."

Civilian Arthur Evans: "I saw one lifeboat being lowered by the army. It was on the port side, just near the bridge, I should think a little behind the bridge, and I watched the army lower it successfully and row off."[147]

Evans did not know it, but that sampan was carrying a very important passenger.

At ten-thirty, just ninety minutes after Stewart gave the order to abandon ship, the *Lisbon Maru* finally started to slip beneath the waves. Major Leighton William Walker, second in command of the Royal Scots, was seen giving his lifebelt to a non-swimmer, and that, in fact, was the last time he was ever seen. Waves breaking over the deck washed the sick and wounded there into the sea with everyone else. Hope, Panting, Hatchett, and Whitehouse, the Middlesex die-hards who had so much fun drinking captured Japanese whisky and serenading the departing POWs, disappeared forever as the seas close over the boat.[148]

Wallace Hastings witnessed the ship's end from close quarters: "We were sitting at rest probably discussing the best way of conserving our strength for the coming ordeal, when one eagle-eyed companion stated that the ship's stern was beginning to slip away and that she was about to go under. At this, we immediately dived off and struck out as fast as we could to escape the inevitable suction to follow. The noise of escaping air and the snapping of hawsers under strain rang in our ears as we swam for our lives. Unfortunately, some of the poorer swimmers were taken down, but most recovered. One thing I can remember most vividly which has not been mentioned by anyone else. On feeling it safe to pause, I turned to view the final demise of the *Lisbon Maru* and to my amazement her mast was still above water and sitting on the cross branch was one of the survivors. I believe that SBCPO Allison was injured by a breaking hawser and we learned some time later that he had died as a result."[149]

Frank Bennett was also still in the water nearby when the ship finally succumbed: "There was a terrific noise as the air blew out and the water rushed in, then I was in a seething mass of bubbles. Remembering tales of being sucked down by a sinking ship I struck out under water. I bumped into one or two things, and when I surfaced the ship had settled with two mastheads still visible above the water."

By this time almost all the men, save those who had died in the night or been shot by the Japanese, those who had fallen from the ladders back into the holds, and the unfortunate Royal Artillery men who hadn't made it out of hold three, were clinging precariously to the masts or in the sea.

Howell watched the final escapes from the vessel from his viewpoint amongst the waves: "The water was not excessively cold, the sea was calm and a bright sun shone. I stopped swimming and looked back at the ship. By now she was down at the head and even those who could not swim at all were being forced to leave her. The last I saw of her was with masts etched against the skyline. Soon hundreds, apart from a few optimists who had scrambled up the rigging, were struggling in the water and thanks to the current of an autumnal tidal-bore providentially running strongly into Hangchow Bay, they were all being borne swimming, floating, or drowned, towards the island I had first seen."

Now it was an endurance test. The islands that Howell had spotted were not too far away, but the hydrodynamics of the area were (and are) ferociously complex. The mighty Yangtze — at nearly four thousand miles in length, the third largest river in the world — poured into the shallow waters of the archipelago, through a gigantic sieve of islands, large and small, placed at impossible angles, into the East China Sea. Currents crossed and mingled constructively and destructively, first heading in one direction, then another in an eastern maelstrom.

Ross Lynneberg: "During the night the ship had been towed to within about eight miles of a group of islands, and as I could see the waves breaking high on the cliffs I decided to swim to the ships (four small Jap tugs and patrol vessels) which were lying about one to two miles away. To reach the boats I had to battle across a fast running current which was a benefit to those heading for the islands but a hindrance to us making for the boats. Amongst my possessions was my navy Mae West life jacket, but as I had picked up a Jap life jacket when I first came on board I felt sure it would work, whereas my Mae West made of rubber might have perished. Jack Rix had no life jacket so I passed over my naval one."[150]

At 10.47, the vessel finally disappeared beneath the sea's surface; looking back, the men in the water could only see the crosstrees at the tops of the masts.

Jim Fallace: "After swimming for about 100 yards I looked back and observed four auxiliary transports in the vicinity of the ship. None of these vessels attempted to rescue the men in the water or those still aboard the torpedoed vessel. I continued to swim on and after a short while I heard small explosions and on looking round I saw that the transport had sunk leaving only the tops of the masts showing above water. After this, the auxiliary vessels began to circle the men swimming and picking up one or two here and there and ignoring the remainder. I myself attempted to board three of these vessels but on one occasion was thrown back by the wash."

Arthur Evans: "When the ship finally sank and I looked round, somebody in the sea yelled out 'Are we downhearted?' and everybody yelled out, 'No.' There were hundreds of heads all over the sea."

Alf Hunt was swimming in sea water again for the first time since being blown off his Motor Torpedo Boat in Hong Kong's harbour: "My first thought on entering the water was to put some distance between myself and the ship and I headed for one of the several ships that were in the vicinity. Many heads were bobbing around in the water and there appeared to be rifle fire from some of the ships, directed at the swimmers."

Taylor: "Hundreds of men had taken to the water and a swift current was running westward towards some islands about four miles away, which looked rocky and dangerous. Four Japanese auxiliary transport boats were slowly circling the *Lisbon Maru*. As the swimmers approached them, I heard rifle shots and small arms fire. The Japanese were picking off our men, one by one, using them for target practice".

For the first hour or so, in fact, Japanese soldiers on these ships fired at the men in the water,[151] and kicked back the few men who managed to reach them and tried to climb on board. Then they started charging groups of men, knocking some off their rafts or from precarious holds on flotsam, and threatening others with their propellers.

James Miller: "I noticed several small ships approaching. I was horrified to see these ships, ploughing through groups of swimmers and then machine-gun fire could be heard. The survivors were being massacred and there was nothing could be done to stop it."

Jack Etiemble: "All swimming around together, we saw Jap patrol boats shooting men in the water, made to pick up one Gunner [Gunner Childs] then kicked his head in and threw him back into the water. I was swimming about 50 yards behind him, a Jap patrol boat picked him up, kicked his head in and threw him back. I did a smart about turn, managed to avoid some rifle shots, and continued swimming around."

Another Gunner, Haywood, noted: "I swam with my colleagues to the merchant ship which was a Japanese armed trawler. Whilst in the water we were fired on. We got to within a few yards of the trawler and a rope was thrown overboard to us which was caught by a Marine Pierman,[152] whose address I do not know. As he was being pulled aboard, a Japanese soldier leaned over the side and shot him in the thigh. He fell into the water. I decided to swim to the islands."

Signalman R. Parkinson: "We swam back. Able Seaman Chilcroft and I found a small piece of wood." As a foretaste of the experience of many men in later hours as the weaker slip from their holds, Chilcroft would drown before another POW finally hauled Parkinson onto a Japanese patrol boat.

Howell: "The will to hold on is, one would have thought, virtually indestructible, and yet within the next half hour I was to see an Oxford Swimming Blue throw up his arms and just sink out of sight because twenty-six hours of darkness and fetid air was too much for one liable to claustrophobia."

*   *   *

The sun was now at its zenith; it was noon.

8 The Long Swim: 2 October, p.m.

> Now would I give a thousand furlongs of sea for an acre of barren ground — long heath, brown furze, anything. The wills above be done, but I would fain die a dry death.
>
> *The Tempest*, Act 1, Scene 1

At this moment, some 1,750[153] British Prisoners of War were in the water. Non-swimmers unable to find anything to cling to disappeared first, but for those who could swim or who had adhered themselves to the plentiful flotsam, the situation — initially — seemed survivable. The sea temperature off Shanghai at the end of the summer is not unpleasant, the weather was calm, and initially most men were in sight of others.

But it was now over an hour since the ship had sunk, and most men had been in the water for more than two; not a single one had yet been rescued.

John Inglis: "To my relief I saw a Japanese Naval Officer throw a rope towards me. I swam towards it and with all my remaining strength began to haul myself up the side and reached the top and hung on grimly to rest before making the final attempt to gain the hoped-for safety of the rescue vessel. The Japanese Naval Officer disappeared but his place was taken by a soldier. 'Give me a hand' I begged and then to my surprise and horror, not to mention fear, he began to try to batter my hands. I swung from hand to hand, dodging the blows while I cursed him roundly. He stopped doing this, much to my relief, and I looked up as I saw a glint of a bayonet. This he fastened quite deliberately to his rifle and leaning over, he made every effort to bayonet me. I'd had enough and with a cry of 'bastard!' I pushed out and away and dropped once more into the sea."

Bill Spooner: "There were a few Jap naval ships in the area and they threw life lines over the side. Some of the drowning men climbed up them. As they climbed, the Japs gradually lowered the lines to the sea again. If any of the POWs managed to reach the deck rails, a shot would ring out, and a body would fall into the water. After this, we kept clear of the Jap ships."

Alf Hunt: "The ships were of various sizes; one was steaming among the swimmers intent on running them down. None seemed to be making any attempt to pick up survivors, so I headed for land which could be seen in the distance."

Time moved slowly, but eventually most of the Prisoners of War realized that as they had already been in the water for several hours, there was little likelihood that they were going to be picked up in a hurry. They continued to try to swim, or paddle themselves to the green and rocky islets they could see above the wave tops. They did not know it yet, but these were the easternmost islands of the Zhoushan Archipelago on the East China Sea outside Hangzhou Bay, to the northeast of Zhejiang Province.

*   *   *

The Zhoushan Archipelago is an oceanic maze of rugged islands, waves, and currents. China's leading fishing ground and the largest of China's offshore island groups, it consists of over six hundred islands ranging from small uninhabited outcrops to larger populated land masses. Their names evoke the sound of the spray of waves hitting rocky shores: Daishan, Liuheng, Jintang, Taohua, Zhujiajian. Zhoushan Island, the largest of all, has an area of 524 square kilometres.

At the junction of warm and cold currents, the sea surrounding the islands is shallow and fertile, the outpourings of the Yangtze and Qiangtang rivers providing abundant sustenance for a wide variety of fish. Even today, the waters are famous for large and small yellow croakers, cuttlefish, and hairtails. With its scenic peaks and temples, Putuo Island is one of the four famous sacred hills of Chinese Buddhism, but at the south easternmost extent of the Archipelago are five distant, seldom-named islands. These five, Huangxing Dao, Miaozihu Dao, Qingbang Dao, Xifu Shan, and Dongfu Shan — remote enough to form, between them, their own mini archipelago called Dongji — were about to witness the most tumultuous event in their long history.[154]

*   *   *

In a seaborne diaspora, the survivors made random groupings as the currents threw them together then pulled them apart. Lance-Corporal Thomas Rolfe found himself on a piece of wood together with Sergeant 'Porky' Betts and BQMS 'Busty' Dicks from the third hold. Able Seaman Bill Tuffs and Marine Jake Croft sat back to back on an upturned hatch cover. Having one singlet between them, they wore it turn by turn. Sergeant 'Pedlar' Palmer, Corporal Jim Picton, and Corporal Harry Pelham spent four hours floating on a mattress before they were picked up. Sergeant James Thomas Edwards drifted past on a raft; Gunner Arthur Hemmingfield was last seen sharing a plank with another.[155]

John Inglis: "Reaching and passing other swimmers I came across one, a member of my own battery, Gunner Spiller. He had a huge grin all over his face as he did his doggy-paddle and held in each hand a bundle of chopsticks. 'What the hell have you got there, Spiller?' I asked. 'Souvenirs Sarj', he grinned happily. 'Souvenirs?' I gasped incredulously. 'Aye Sarj. *Lisbon Maru* souvenirs Sarj!' Now how the hell do you get a fellow down who thinks of souvenirs on occasions like this?"[156]

Robert Wright: "It was then that I heard someone calling my name. It proved to be Lieutenant Witham who, completely naked, was hanging on to a flimsy piece of wood."

Wright swam off to find a lifebelt for Witham, who had been wounded in the legs in the Hong Kong fighting, passing Sergeant Green and other men hanging onto a floating latrine from the deck. When he returned, there was no sign of Witham, but Private Hare floated past on a small raft; some men were lucky, some not.[157]

Bill Spooner: "The currents were so strong that the makeshift rafts our chaps were on kept going out to sea then back towards the far distant coast line again. I had managed to get onto a small, square cork raft, after swimming for about an hour (I think). At first, I was the only occupant. Later, I was joined by two exhausted chaps on their last gasp. I helped them onto the raft as best as I could, and the raft carried us out to sea; in again, out again, in again. It was a bright sunny day (weatherwise). The chaps on the makeshift rafts were passing us in opposite directions."

At this point, the experiences of those who would survive took three different paths.[158] The stronger swimmers would reach these islands under their own power, while those still at sea would either be picked up by Chinese fishermen from the islands, or — possibly because the Japanese now realized there *would be* survivors — by the Japanese patrol boats.

Hunt fell into the first category: "The sea was warm with a long rolling swell and swimming conditions were good. I managed to get hold of a vegetable crate and made good headway towards the shore, greatly assisted by a strong current going inshore. The land turned out to be a group of islands and unfortunately, some of the swimmers failed to make land and were swept out to sea by the strong tide flowing between the islands. The islands were very steep and rocky with one small sandy beach, only a few yards wide, which I managed to struggle ashore on. I estimate I had swum about four miles in four hours."

Together with Private Donny O'Donnell, Wright also swam towards the Dongji Islands.[159] Perhaps two hundred men in total arrived on these rocky outcrops under their own power. The challenge in trying to reach the islands was the crosscurrents that could sweep even the strongest swimmers away and out to sea.[160] Even those with the endurance to fight the currents then faced the challenge of landing and clambering up the steep and rocky cliffs.

Bombardier Inglis: "As I got closer I saw a number of the men trying to swim into a very small bay, but seeing how the swell was turning into the waves and dashing them against the rock face with some force, I called out to tell them of the danger. Many turned away but one or two still persisted in going in. Recognising one in particular as Major 'Jimmy' Officer of the RAMC I called and called again to him telling him not to go in but he just shook his head wearily and continued splashing inwards. I was in no state to follow and help, but could only watch in horror as he was picked up on the crest of a wave and smashed against a cruel grey rock with devastating force. He disappeared under the wild white waves for a moment or two, then a second wave picked him up and once more he was dashed against the wall of rock."[161]

Howell, as the first man off the ship, was in the first group of swimmers to reach the larger island. In the Shanghai dialect,[162] he explained to the local Chinese fishermen that the drowning men were British rather than Japanese. Until this moment, the Chinese islanders had been watching the drowning 'Japanese' with little show of emotion, but on hearing Howell's news they immediately launched a rescue attempt. Within moments, their sampans were in the water, heading for the POWs.

One of the fishermen, Shen Agui, recalled: "All the men in my family rushed out of the house and we saw a big ship in the sea with its back part in the water. We decided to see what happened."

Another, Guo Ade, added: "First we saw some wooden blocks and cotton floating on the water. But to our surprise, we found many people in the sea, yelling something."

Shen: "Blue eyes, yellow hair and white skin. We had no idea they were British, but we could see they were foreigners ... Qingbang launched about thirty boats, and rescued some 200 men."[163]

Fallace was one of those who benefited: "On one particular occasion whilst assisting a comrade in difficulty, we reached within five yards of one [Japanese auxiliary vessel] but no notice was taken of our plight. I sang out to one man who had managed to board a cutter towed by this vessel to throw his lifebelt over and which I gave to my comrade, Cadet Laloe,[164] HKRNVR, I then swam to shore assisting Laloe and eventually was picked [up] by sampans within a few yards of the island on which we landed where I stayed for the night."[165]

Taffy Evans remembered: "Later I was picked up (almost had it by then) by a fishy-smelling boat, then placed on a shore. I and others were helped to a shed full of nets."

CSM Soden had a similar experience and ended up in the same shed: "At around dusk we were picked up by two Chinese in a lone rowing boat. One of them took my shirt and CSM's badge off my wrist, leaving me only with my 'fundoshi', the small piece of cloth covering my privates. ... We were led to a warm shed full of fishing nets where women fed us hot vegetable soup and rice with bits of fish. The following morning a Chinese woman gave me an old overcoat for which I was most grateful."

Alf Taylor was swimming with Private Ferris of the Middlesex (who had a broken back and was paralysed from the waist down — presumably he was one of those who fell from the ladders): "By 6 p.m. that evening, we began to draw near to land, which proved to be several islands sticking out of the sea. It was obvious that unless we wanted to be swept through the channel between the islands, we would need to start working towards the edge of the rip. This meant trying to make a landfall on the weather shore, a dangerous undertaking, but one that had to be made as there was no guarantee that if we got caught in the tide race between the islands, we would never be able to get out of it and make a landing on the lee shore." As they swam on, they too were rescued by a Chinese boat, and dumped on the shore of the island. Crawling by himself to a village higher up, Taylor explained that Ferris was lying paralysed on the beach. Using a door as a stretcher, several villagers fetched him in.[166]

One Chinese fishing boat picked up Andrew Salmon and Ernest Plowman; another rescued Robert Wright and Bandsman Geary. On their island, they found eighty-five or more POWs including Sergeant Robins, Sergeant Hobson, and Privates Benningfield, Wood, Nelson, Jones, and Green. They also found a fluent Chinese speaker[167] attempting to organize a mass escape. Signalman Topcliffe was there too, having saved Christopher Man on the way.

Apart from Captain Man, other officers present included Major Innis RE, Lieutenant R.M.M. King, and Lieutenant Howell. Those on inhabited islands were clothed and fed by the local villagers.

Robert Wright was one of many who were amazed by the kindness that a relatively poor Chinese fishing community could show these half-drowned men: "A Chinaman who saw my sun-burned body smeared a strange concoction over my back, chest and shoulders, and handed me a quilted coat to protect me from the cold night. They strapped up the broken ribs of the Royal Scot,[168] and fed him tepid soup like a baby. They even shared the last of their tasteless tobacco with those who thought a smoke the world's finest luxury. These Chinese certainly showed, in action, the full meaning of good will and sympathy."

Shen Agui: "We housed them in a temple and in ordinary houses. They used body language to show they were hungry — rubbing their tummies. But they didn't know how to use chopsticks — they used them like forks."

The Japanese patrol boats, sure now that they had picked up all the Japanese survivors, started changing their strategy and picking up prisoners. Whether the cause of this change was that they believed the *Grouper* was no longer in the area and a danger to them, or simply that they realized that some POWs were going to survive to tell their story anyway, made little difference to the men in the water.

Jack Etiemble: "For some reason or other sometime in the afternoon the Japs started picking up survivors. I had been swimming or floating for six or seven hours when I was picked up, I was given a raw potato to eat, it tasted heavenly, my first food for nearly forty-eight hours."

James Miller: "I had been about ten hours in the water ... How helpless can people feel, in the face of such adversity, it would take a miracle to save us now. This miracle duly took place in the shape of a large Chinese fishing fleet coming into view. The Jap ships started to pick up survivors. I was one of the lucky ones who was picked up."

Wallace Hastings remembered the whole swim, from leaving the *Lisbon Maru* until being picked up by the Japanese boats: "The weather was bright and warm when we started and the sea calm. In the distance a very long way off were boats of some sort and further away almost indistinct the bluish haze of land. Having discarded most of our clothing and footwear to prevent drag I had on just a pair of Y front underpants and using the lazy man's side stroke began to swim not knowing whether we too would be shot, picked up or reach the distant shore. Time passed and making very slow progress, the boats and land appeared to be as far away as when we started. One felt extremely dispirited especially when fellow swimmers unable to carry on submerged not to be seen again. The increasing fatigue was only overcome by a strong will to live. Some hours later, I cannot guess how long, as we neared the Japanese boats they began to pick us up. By this time, almost devoid of physical strength, we had to be hoisted aboard."

New Zealander Ross Lynneberg had a similar experience: "On reaching the first [Japanese] boat I found a group of lads on one side, over which were hanging ropes purposely tied so they could not be reached from the water. Then after a while the propellers started to turn and the stern of this ship was turned towards us, the result was that those who were near exhaustion were sucked under while the rest of us managed to swim away in time. I then looked around for a more likely boat but after chasing a couple more, only to have to swim away to avoid being caught in the screws, I decided to make one more try and if not successful to make for the islands. This last effort was successful and I hauled myself onboard. Many of the boys weren't strong enough to haul themselves up or fit a bowline over their shoulders so one or two of the fitter ones would go down and tie a rope around their chests while we on deck pulled them up."[169]

Many POWs, after a few moments recovering from their ordeal on the decks of the Japanese ships, joined in with the rescue efforts and started dragging their comrades aboard.

William Grant Shepherd was hauled to safety in this manner: "When in the water I was mostly alone and occasionally hanging on to floating wreckage in an attempt to alleviate fatigue. I was pulled aboard one of the boats by a POW who was previously rescued. His is one name I remember;[170] he was Pipe Major Duncan Rankine of the Royal Scots regiment."

Dennis Morley: "After the shooting stopped I was picked up by a Jap naval vessel. I was given a cup of green tea and a cigarette. I then helped to pull other men on to the vessel."

Hamilton: "One of [the Japanese on the vessel] threw me a rope and pulled me alongside. I gave a heave to climb the rope, but to my astonishment nothing happened. I was quite unable to climb the rope which normally would have been an easy exercise. A British officer on board named Walkden lowered another rope which I tied round my chest with a bowline, and he and two other troops hauled me up. We then organized teams of three to pull up others, but many drifted by with their faces in the water."

It was not so simple for Poulter: "I swam to the nearest tug and they threw ropes over the side for the men to hang onto. There must have been about twenty men hanging on to ropes on my side of the tug. The tug started to move and gradually increased its speed until it was going flat out. It towed us for about five miles and then stopped. There were only three of us left on my side of the tug and one man was dead. He had got the rope around his neck and it had strangled him. The two of us that were left were not exactly feeling full of the joys of spring either. I was still hanging on to my rope when some order or signal was given, and the Jap sailors motioned for me to come up on deck. I managed to climb up the rope but just as I was putting my leg over the rail I was stopped by a sailor and not allowed to go any further. I managed to help some other men up to the rail but when one of my own officers needed my help, my strength was not up to it. I managed to pull him just out of the water, but not one inch further. The tug started moving again and he shouted at me to let him go. I felt rather badly about it, but he turned up later and was all right."

However, as Frank Bennett reported on approaching a boat, the Japanese naval personnel could be helpful: "I swam amidships where there was a rope-ladder with wooden rungs, hanging down. I grabbed the lowest rung and hooked my arm over. I looked up, and it was like looking up the Eiffel Tower. 'God!' I thought, 'I'll never get up there'. Suddenly a Nip face appeared over the side, urging me to come up. I shook my head. It was taking all my strength to hang on. Then another face appeared. A short conversation was held, and the two Nips heaved up the ladder with me hanging on the bottom rung. I was pulled unceremoniously over the side and onto the deck. One of the Nips tore a great lump of calico, thrust it at me and indicated that I should give myself a good rub down. It was then that I realised that I was absolutely starkers."

Staff-Sergeant Ross and Surgeon-Lieutenant Jackson had tried to keep the wounded and sick together when they were finally washed off the sinking vessel, though they had lost a few. Now, finally, this group was also picked up and taken aboard a Japanese patrol boat. Jackson was particularly concerned about Able Seaman Thomas Eccleston who had a wounded leg that had turned gangrenous. He operated on the boat as it cut through the surf, with only a blunt razor blade as an instrument; Eccleston lived.

The Japanese picked up many others, including Reg Westwood, Dan O'Hanlon, Captain Weedon, Lieutenant Graham, and Lieutenant Bucke.

But one officer, the much-loved commander of the 1st Middlesex, 'Monkey' Stewart, had a characteristically classy rescue.

Lynneberg explains: "Before the *Lisbon Maru* finally sank some of the boys checked out the bridge, no doubt with loot in mind, and discovered a flat bottom punt in which the colonel [Stewart] and another officer or so were rowed over to the [Japanese ship] I was on. Unlike us, they were fully clothed and, as they came alongside, they stood up showing the lads how good it was to be rescued in such a novel manner. Unfortunately one of them blundered, their punt capsized and they had to swim the last few yards, much to our amusement."

Frank Bennett remembered the incident slightly differently: "Unbeknown to them the boat had been spiked and filled with water. It was a comical sight to see four men rowing with an officer sat in the stern, all up to the waist in water but still sat in the boat."

By this time, the Japanese had picked up most of the men still alive in the sea in the vicinity of the sinking. But with men separated so widely on different islands and ships, no one was in any position to attempt a roll call; at that time it was far from obvious that the currents had already swept so many away.

* * *

On the islands, free again for the moment, the men who had swum there or been taken to their shores by the fishermen's boats, took stock of their new situation.

Alf Hunt, exhausted after his long swim: "Being extremely dehydrated my first priority was to find water and scouting around found a trickle of clear water coming from the cliff face and forming a pool on the beach. The water tasted like nectar and all of the hundred or so people who had come ashore had their fill. It was only after climbing the roughly hewn steps to the top of the cliff that we found that the water was coming from a small bamboo shed being used [as a toilet]."

The survivors on this smaller island buried the body of a Japanese soldier washed up on the beach, and met a local fisherman and his son who appeared to be the sole inhabitants. These two men came out of their hut and led the British POWs to their food store and fed them rice and sweet potatoes.

Bombardier Inglis: "Returning to the hut, the soldiers with varying expressions of satisfaction on their faces pressed around the two Chinese, all using the word 'dingho' (very good). The old man's face lit up and he beamed at the obvious show of thanks. Using signs while he spoke, the son managed to convey the fact that on the other island with the lighthouse there was plenty of food and clothes."

Promising to return for the others in the morning, the two fishermen departed with five of the fittest POWs to the next — larger — island.[171] It rained, and the temperature started to fall.

By sunset on 2 October, the rescue was all but over. Almost all of those who would survive this stage had either been picked up by the Chinese fishermen, or by Japanese patrol boats, or had swum under their own steam to the islands.

Although a handful of men would still be lucky enough to be recovered from the sea alive, some 828[172] would never be accounted for. Approximately eighty-one[173] had gone down with the ship, a few of the others were shot in the water or mown down by Japanese shipping, but the majority — alive or already dead — were still simply drifting out to sea. One by one they would sink to the bottom, or be washed lifeless onto uninhabited shores.

*   *   *

And who were they, this majority? Let these lost men and their families speak for themselves:

William Arthur Barlow was the son of Mrs B. Bromley and stepson of Mr Bert Bromley of Jacksdale Street (Stone Row), Jacksdale,

Nottinghamshire, UK. William was a scholar at Jacksdale Council Schools, later taking up employment at Codnor Park Forge, Ironville, Derbyshire. He joined up at the age of eighteen and progressed through the ranks to become Battery Sergeant Major, 12 Coastal regiment, Royal Artillery at Hong Kong. He was an excellent sportsman and was a trained Army Boxing Instructor. He was a sprinter of no mean ability and an expert swimmer. But he did not survive.

William James L. Boyes of HMS *Tamar* had joined the navy as a Boy Artificer in July 1919; he had become an Engine Room Artificer (ERA) Apprentice in 1920, and worked his way up from ERAV in 1922 to ERA 4 in 1923 and ERA 3 in 1926. Up to 1929, he had served at sea on HMS *Indus, Carysfort, Eagle, Curlew, Ceindre, Emperor of India,* and *Benbow*. By the time that the *Lisbon Maru* was sunk by the USS *Grouper* he was a Chief Engine Room Artificer with twenty-three years of seagoing experience behind him. But no amount of experience could help him this day.

Charles Frederick Brooks enlisted at Great Yarmouth into the Royal Regiment of Artillery on 11 February 1915 as a boy soldier. He was posted to Hong Kong in 1937 after service in Ireland, Gibraltar, and Malta. He married in Cork in 1927. He was at that time stationed at Fort Carlisle with the Royal Artillery guarding the fleet port of Cork Harbour (Southern Ireland became a Free State in 1921 and Cork was a "Treaty Port"). His first son Geoffrey was born in 1930, and the second, Ronald, was born in Malta on 6 August 1935. The family moved to Hong Kong in 1937 and Brooks' wife and two children were evacuated to Melbourne, Australia, on the *Empress of Canada*. While he was floating away, the last letter he wrote as a POW in Hong Kong was still making its way to his family.

As Royal Engineer Sergeant **Sidney Charles**, born in Gillingham, Kent, on 13 April 1900, drifted away from his companions, he must eventually have realized that he would never see his wife, Alice, whom he had married in 1931, and son, David again.

From Lossiemouth, Scotland, forty-three-year-old Chief Skipper **Andrew 'Andra' Flett** of Hong Kong's boom[174] vessel HMS *Bargate* also disappeared that day. His sister, Isabella, did not know of this new loss yet, but she was no stranger to the tragedy of war. Eighteen months earlier she had lost her husband, John Gault, to the sea when his fishing vessel *Kinclaven* sailed out of Aberdeen and was destroyed by a mine or raiding German aircraft on 27 March 1941.

Thomas Hamill, of the Royal Scots, wounded on 21 December 1941 during the fighting for Hong Kong Island, was born in 1914 in Tayport, Fife, Scotland. A friend last saw him drifting away alone, surrounded by sharks. Twenty-eight years old, he left two brothers (John and George) and seven sisters (Elizabeth, Ellen, Mary Jane, Margaret, Janet, Catherine, and Martha).

Ronald Langley-Bates was born on 26 July 1901 in Leicester. His father was a grocer and they lived at 77 Raymond Road. He joined the Royal Engineers on 1 November 1922. In 1929, while stationed at the barracks at Brompton, he married Kathleen Ivy Cox-Rogers at St Lawrence Church, Warborough, Oxford. He was posted to Hong Kong as a WO1 (Clerk of Works) with the 40th Fortress Company and spent a good deal of time supervising the building of the pillboxes that dotted the island and would be so important to its defence. With the exception of a brief holiday back in England, the family remained in Hong Kong until just before the war. He had three children (Douglas, born in 1930, Derek, 1932, and Denise, 1933) who, with the advent of war, were evacuated with his wife to Australia.

Percy Albert George Robinson was the second generation of his family to be captured by the enemy. His Canadian father (also named Percy) had served as a Private for six years prior to the First World War with the West Surrey Volunteers. Percy Robinson senior had enlisted on 22 September 1914, and sailed for Great Britain on 3 October 1914. He went with his battalion (2nd Canadian Infantry, Eastern Ontario Regiment) to France on 8 February 1915. Little over two months later, on 24 April, he was wounded through both lungs and became one of only around two thousand Canadians to be taken prisoner by the Germans. Twenty-six years later — in the new war — his son, a Sapper in 40 Fortress Company, Royal Engineers aged just twenty-two, had also been captured — but by the Japanese. He would not share his father's luck.

Frederick Samuel Stanford, born a true cockney in 1901 within the sounds of Bow Bells, was the son of a prosperous shopkeeper in Dagenham. Being a free spirit, he left home towards the end of the First World War to travel around the UK, ending up in Glasgow. With a strong desire not to follow into the family business at such an early age, he enlisted for the King's Shilling and found himself recruited by the Royal Scots. This was a rarity for the time as the regiment usually only took on Scotsmen. Here was a Sassenach, 5'7", complete with 'Estuary' accent, joining a predominantly Scottish regiment. Although not tall, he was a quiet, but firm man whose authority came from his confidence and bearing.

Being well-educated, and despite leaving home at the time that he did, he became an instructor at Glencorse, teaching illiterate soldiers how to read and write. He married Alice McGowan from Largs, against family wishes (both sides!) after seeing her working in a Glasgow cinema as an interval singer and usherette. Despite his confident bearing and forwardness, he could not bring himself to ask Alice out directly, often choosing a third party to pass messages. Finally Alice, by way of a message, told him that if he wanted to court her, then he should ask her himself! She says in her own memoirs that in all the years of marriage and deep love for him, her overriding memory of him was his smartness. He would always be well presented, whether in civilian or military clothes.

He rose steadily through the ranks over the years to Company Sergeant Major and was posted to India with C Coy 2nd Battalion Royal Scots in the mid-1930s. Alice was renowned in India, and the Regiment, for being the first ever wife to give birth to triplets. Unfortunately, they all died within two weeks of birth due to a lack of medical knowledge and facilities in the mountain barracks where they were based. The life they led as a family during the inter-war years was one of typical imperial Britain; easy postings, ceremonial activities, a good life with servants, and a batman.

Stanford was posted to Hong Kong just before the war broke out. He evacuated a newly pregnant Alice and his two sons (Frederick, the older, and John), to Australia whilst he stayed on in Hong Kong to serve out his time and receive his discharge papers. He was due to leave the Army after twenty-two years of service, but his plans were shattered when the Japanese invaded Hong Kong. Looking forward to leaving the army, to pick up his family and retire to run either a pub or shop, he was never to see his family or his dream again.

Royal Scots Sergeant **George Trinder**, born on 23 February 1904 in Yorkshire, had enlisted at Hull into the Royal Scots in January 1924. He reached the dizzy heights of Acting Lance Corporal four months later, but soon reverted to Private. Posted to 2nd battalion in July, with military conduct rated as exemplary, he then swiftly climbed through the ranks (Lance Corporal, Corporal, Lance Sergeant, Sergeant, Warrant Officer III,[175] Warrant Officer II — Company Sergeant Major) until becoming Regimental Quarter Master Sergeant in September 1941. His pregnant wife, Lena Emily, and his two sons, Bernard (then seven years old) and George (four years old) had been evacuated from Hong Kong in July 1940 to Manila via the ship *Empress of Japan* (later renamed *Empress of Scotland*). He would never even see his third child, Charles, who would be born there later in the month. Trans-shipped via the *Awatea*, the family finally landed in Brisbane, Australia.

Just ten men from all the hundreds of those who the currents swept into memories that day, unbeknownst to their families or the Allies.

But, late that day, an American monitoring service picked up a strange and garbled Japanese radio message. Sent to the Japanese China Seas Fleet, it read:

> From: HO MU SI (Garbled) 2 Oct/2208 1942
> To: (CHINA SEAS FLEET) JN-25-D-10
> Info: I WE RE (Garbled)
>   (65th GUARD FORCE, Wake)
>   (2nd CHINA FLEET)
>   (HONG KONG AREA SPECIAL BASE FORCE)

NU YA TA
(Translator's note. Message fragmentary.)
Unit SHANGHAI (53253x) AREA FORCE Action Summary #____
(1) With regard to the enemy submarine which made a torpedo attack on Army trans(port?) ship (56652x) (LISBON MARU?) 1 October, in the eastern (68266x) area a search and attack was made immediately, extending through 1 and 2 October, with ships and float attack planes, but results are unknown.
(A) Anti-submarine operations ____ (42834x) (48741x) 917 G 132 G134 G #1 ____ MARU.
(B) ____ float attack planes, total number 16.
   (2) As for the (ship) (56652x), ____ is in direct command. 131 ____ by means of the HAYASHIO,[176] in spite of bad weather, immediately ____ and ____ towing. 2 October 1045, on a bearing of 136–17 miles distant from ____ (____ (compass bearing) 30) about 10 meters.
   (3) Condition of rescued survivors of the foregoing is as follows:
(A) ____ (#) (among them 1 dead, 1 ____), whereabouts unknown 1.
(B) ____ all.
(C) Among the 1800 prisoners, besides ____ interned, investigation is being made.[177]

The first indication that there were prisoners on board the stricken vessel had reached the outside world, but in the seas off Shanghai, the tragedy was still far from over.

Hong Kong harbour just before the outbreak of war (Captain T. A. James, EA)

Garfield Kvalheim as
a young submariner
(Garfield Kvalheim)

Jack Etiemble as a boy soldier (Jack Etiemble)

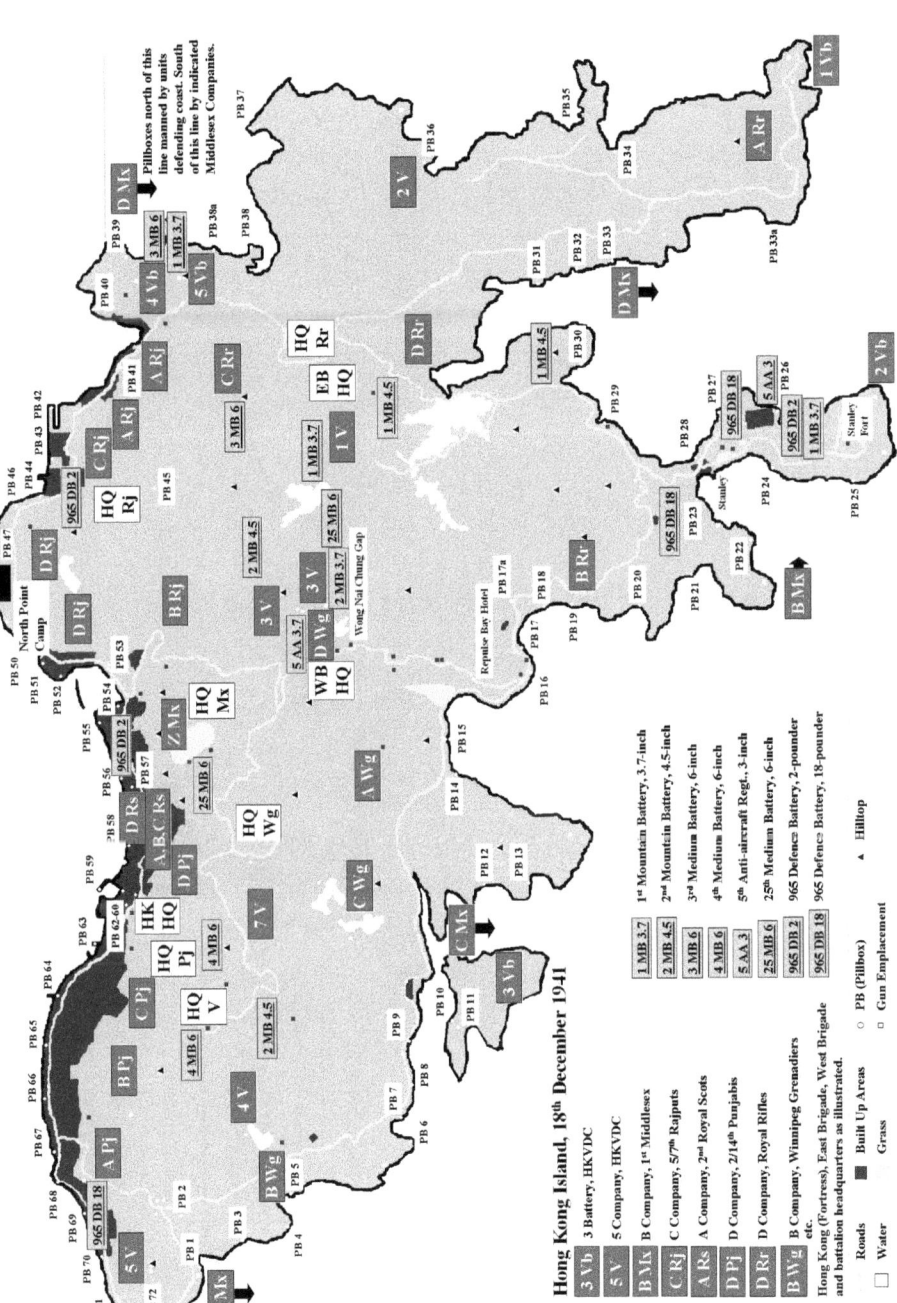

Map of Hong Kong Island, 18 December 1941 (Tony Banham)

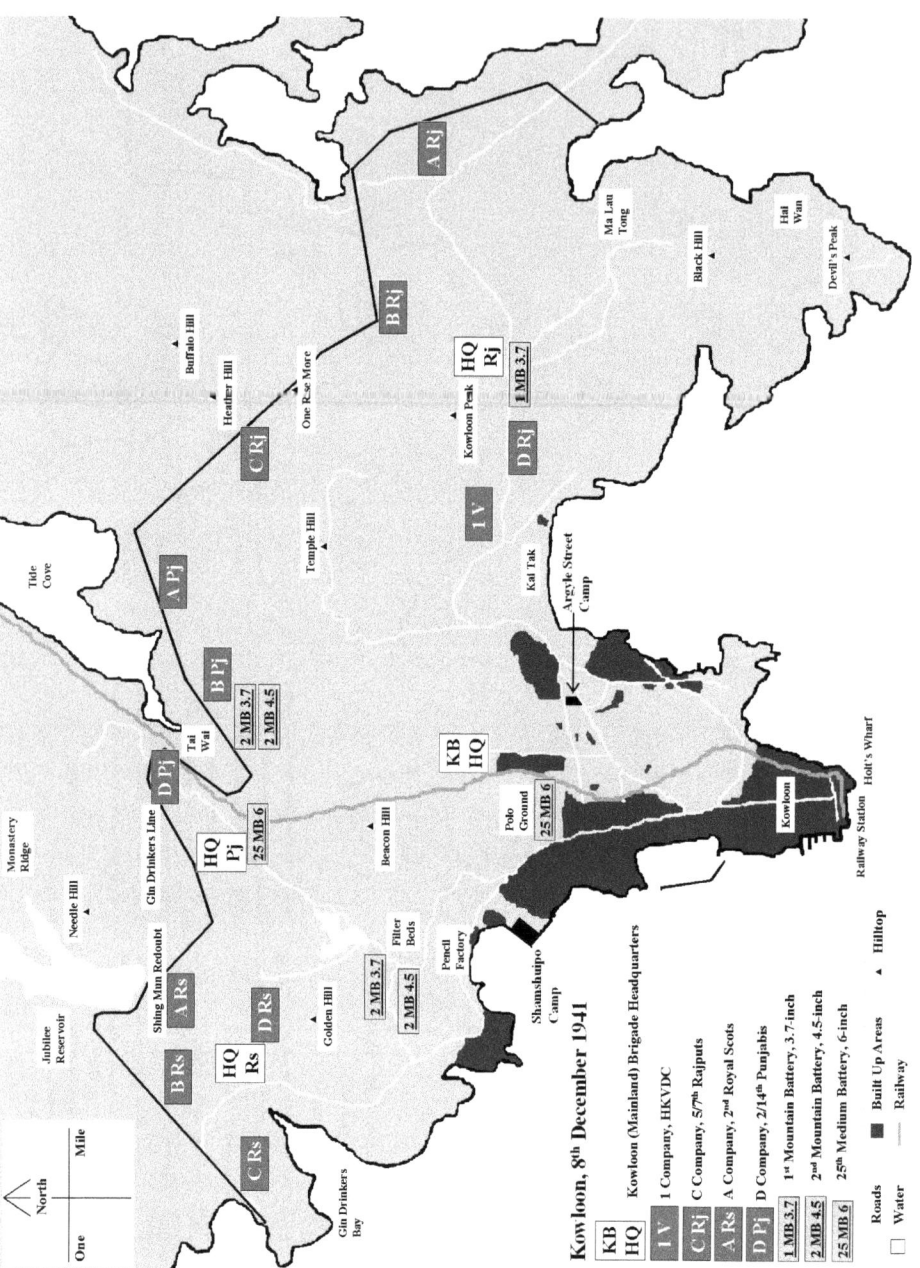

Map of Kowloon and the New Territories, 8 December 1941 (Tony Banham)

The Brooks family before the war (Ron Brooks)

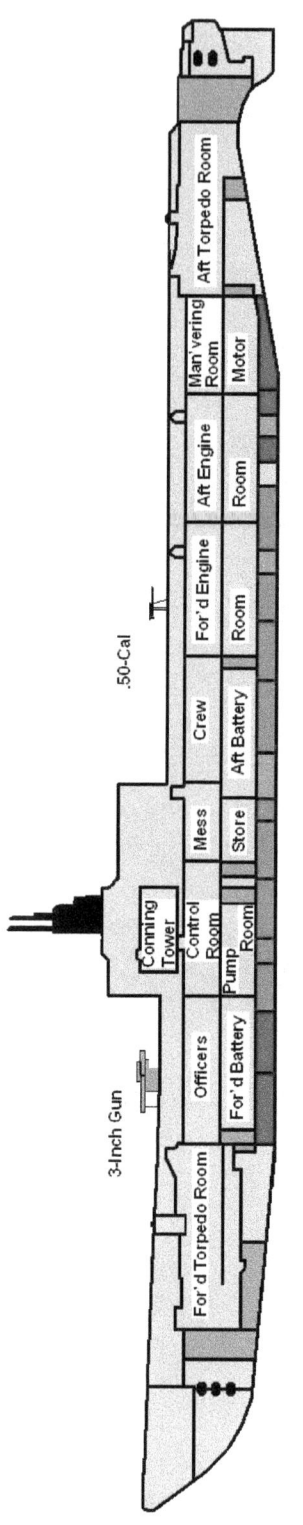

The USS *Grouper* — cutaway

The USS *Grouper* SS-214 (SUBNET, J. Christley and R. Sminkey)

The Lisbon Maru

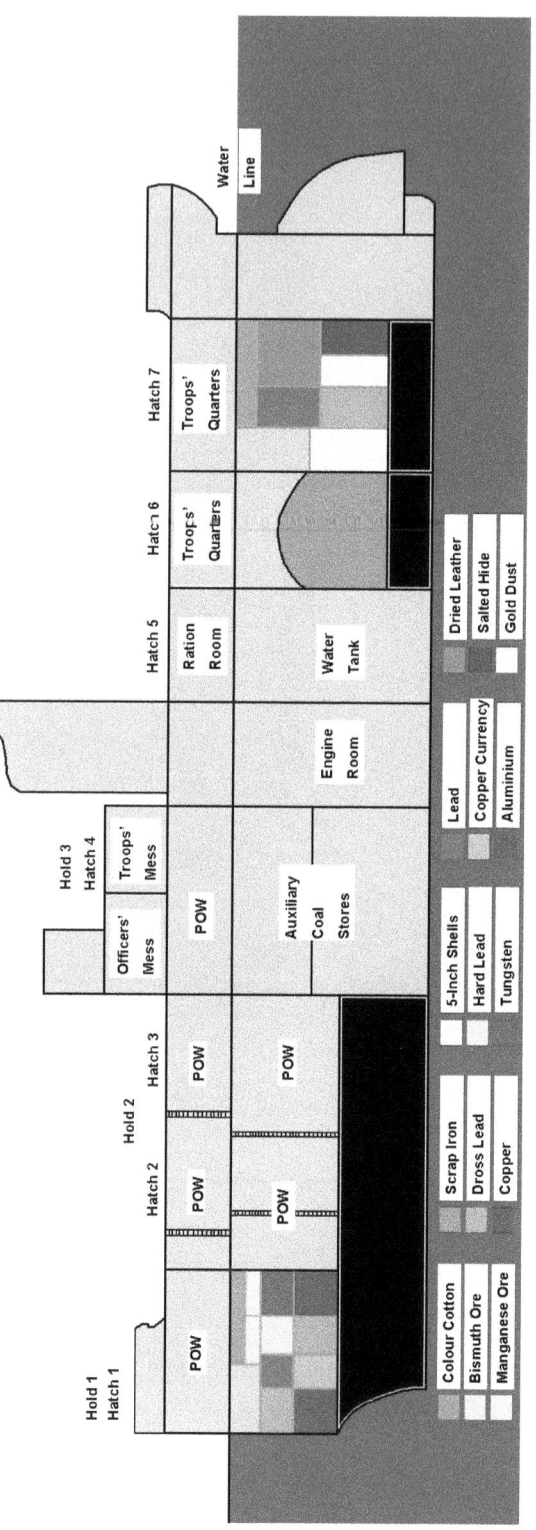

The *Lisbon Maru* — cutaway (based on the original in PRO 235/1114)

The crew of the *Grouper* in their favourite San Francisco bar, 1 (Garfield Kvalheim)

The crew of the *Grouper* in their favourite San Francisco bar, 2 (Garfield Kvalheim)

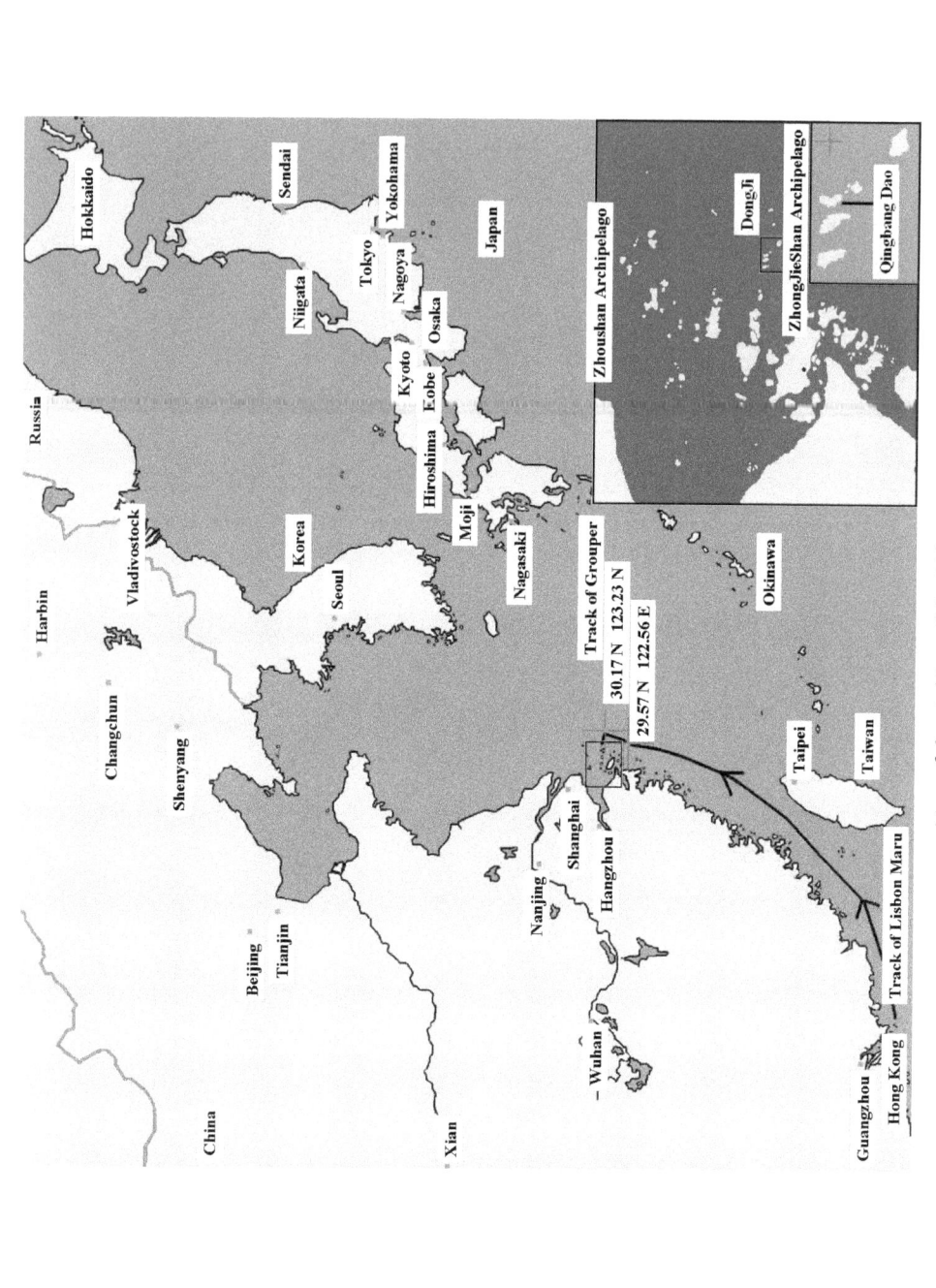

Map of the sinking of the *Lisbon Maru*

Charles Heather, survivor of the *Lisbon Maru*, and the first FEPOW Londoner to return home after the war (IWM photograph HU93201, courtesy of the Imperial War Museum, London)

From left to right: Chris Man, Topsy Man, Geoffrey Hamilton and Martin Weedon (Hilary Hamilton)

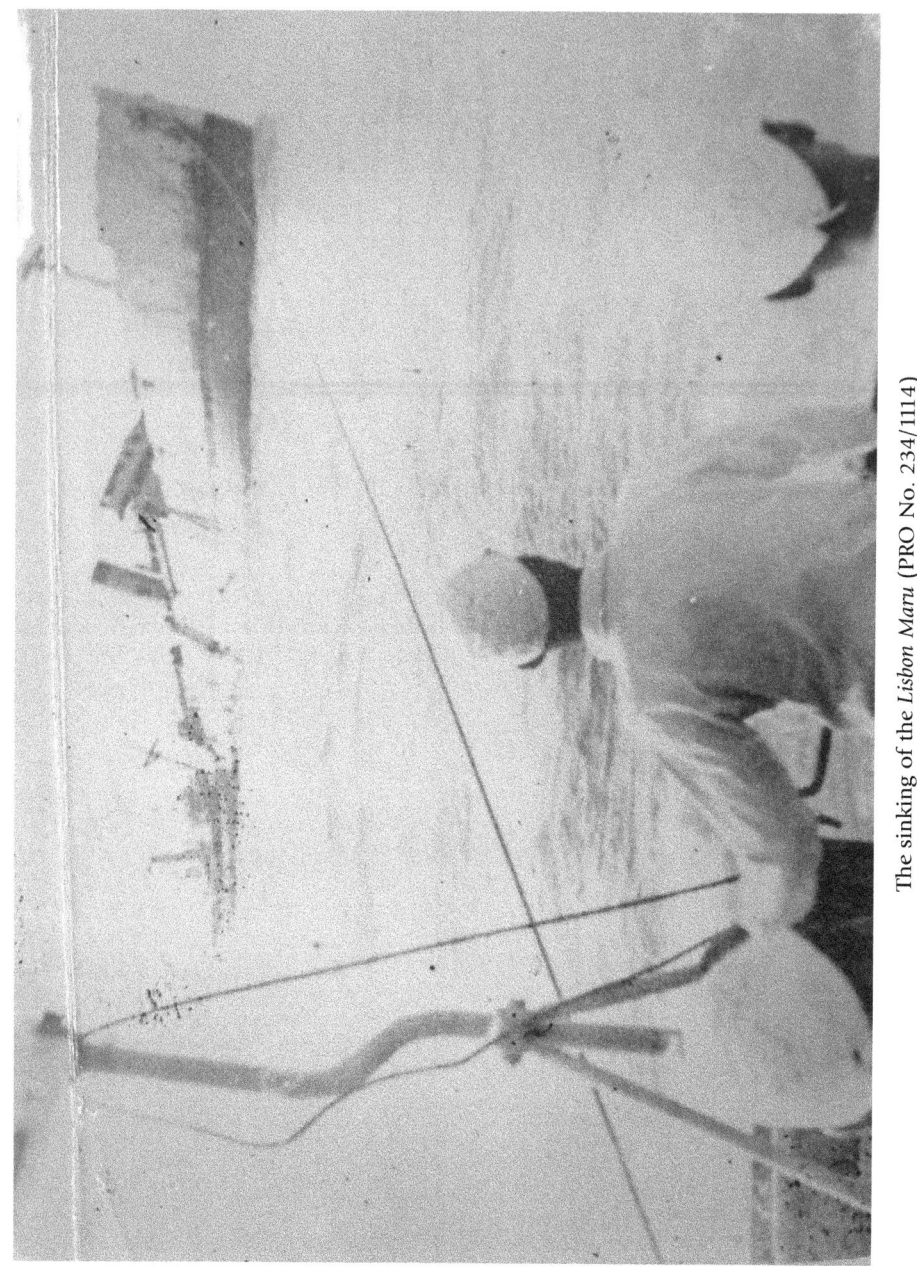

The sinking of the *Lisbon Maru* (PRO No. 234/1114)

Drawing of the sinking of the *Lisbon Maru* (W. C. Johnson)

U. S. S. GROUPER (SS214)

ROME SAYS U.S. SUBMARINE SANK JAPANESE SHIP:

Rome, October 7. (AP)--Radio Rome broadcast a Tokyo announcement today saying that an American submarine, October 1, sank a Japanese vessel in the South China sea.

The broadcast added that there were about 1,800 English and Australian prisoners aboard the vessel enroute to Japan, but that many hundred were saved by two Japanese vessels which hastened to the scene.

Other survivors were able to reach neighboring islands, it was added.

(London heard a Domei (Japanese) report from a Shanghai broadcast from Tokyo indentifying the ship as a 7,152 ton army transport called the Lisbon Maru.)

Wire release on the sinking of the *Lisbon Maru* picked up by the *Grouper*

Some of those lost in the sinking of the *Lisbon Maru*

Some of those lost in the camps

Some of those who survived the war

Lisbon Maru survivors landing at Moji, 10 October 1942. Pollock 2nd from right (Royal Engineers Museum, Chatham)

Tel. No.— MAYfair 9400 Ext.

Any further communication on this subject should be addressed to:—
The Under-Secretary of State,
The War Office
(as opposite),
and the following number quoted.

THE WAR OFFICE,
(Cas. PW),
Curzon Street House,
Curzon Street,
LONDON, W.1.

49094(Cas. PW).

Your Reference...................

September, 1945.

Madam,

I am directed to inform you with regret, that an official report has been received to the effect that No. 6213420, Private S.A. Atkins, Middlesex Regiment, who has been released from Japanese hands, is at present on board a hospital ship in the Far East, suffering from chronic amoebic dysentery and beri-beri and has been placed on the seriously ill list.

The Department has cabled to the appropriate authorities for reports to be rendered on your husband's condition and you are assured that you will be kept informed of all further reports which are received.

I am to convey to you the sincere sympathy of the Department in the anxiety and distress which this news must inevitably cause, especially in view of Private Atkin's release from captivity.

I am, Madam,
Your obedient Servant,

Mrs. M.E. Atkins,
School Road,
Finstock,
Charlesbury, Oxfordshire.

Formal notice of survival of Samuel Atkins (Barbara Tindle)

No. CASL/Div.III/1
(If replying, please quote above No.)

Army Form B. 104—82A.

R.A. (C.A. & S.L.) & C.M.P. Record Office,
Savoy Hotel, West Hill Road,
Bournemouth. Hants.

10th August 1945.

Madam,

It is my painful duty to inform you that, no further news having been received relative to (No.) 1410996 (Rank) W.O.I. (Name) Charles Frederick BROOKS (Regiment) Royal Artillery who has been missing since 1/2 October 1942, the Army Council have been regretfully constrained to conclude that he is dead, and that his death took place on the 1/2 October 1942. (or since).

I am to express the sympathy and regret of the Army Council at the soldier's death in his Country's service.

I am,

Madam,

Your obedient Servant,

(signature)
V.C.O.
for Colonel
Officer in Charge of Records.

Mrs. Brooks,
9. Limes Road,
Buckland,
Dover. Kent.

[P.T.O.]

Formal notice of death of Charles Frederick Brooks (Ron Brooks)

Liberation at Hirohata camp (Wallace Hastings, between US flag and flag pcle)

Welcome Home

Gallant defenders of Hong Kong
Manitoba Salutes You

Train Reception Committee
Greater Winnipeg Co-ordinating Board

Canadian repatriation card (Dennis Morley)

Garfield Kvalheim and Jack Etiemble in front of a Mark 14 torpedo: The 'circular' (Ja-k Etiemble)

The 1998 reunion, from left to right: Nobby Hunt, Jim Fallace, Reg Westwood, Garfield Kvalheim, Dan O'Hanlon (Garfield Kvalheim)

9

Survival and Death: 3 and 4 October

> The never-surfeited sea
> Has caused to belch up you, and on this island
> Where man doth not inhabit
>
> *The Tempest*, Act 3, Scene 3
>
> Be not afeared, the isle is full of noises,
> Sounds, and sweet airs, that give delight and hurt not.
>
> *The Tempest*, Act 3, Scene 2

Away from the rescue ships and the islands, hundreds of hopeless and abandoned men had already drowned. Hundreds more were still drifting away to the open sea, in ones or twos in the water, or clinging to whatever wreckage they could.

Amongst them, Bill Spooner was sharing a makeshift raft with Micky Myles, Royal Scots, and two unknown survivors. The latter had been in a poor way ever since he dragged them out of the water. "All the rest of that first day that we were adrift on the raft, Micky, the other two chaps and I, drifted about on the sea, towards the shore, out to sea again. Soon exposure, hunger, and thirst dulled our senses. Then the rains came, buckets of it hurtling down on our bare skins (we had discarded our sodden clothing long since — they were an encumbrance). All the protection that we had were small strips of cloth around our dangly bits. Such modesty!"

"The weather turned stormy, huge waves came lunging at the raft hitting our stomachs, dependant on which way the raft was facing at the time. Ironically, we were in a shipping lane, but not one ship tried to save us — doubtless the Japanese had warned them all off."

The waters off Shanghai were always busy with shipping, but spotting heads or even makeshift rafts from freighters was no easy task in stormy weather, even if their captains were willing to stop.

"The first to drown was the chap sitting behind me on the raft, who started to drink the seawater. I tried to stop him drinking it, but he resisted and even convinced me that it would stop our bodies dehydrating. I started to drink also, but Micky forcibly restrained me from doing it. The chap who had started it had already jumped off the raft. I vaguely remember turning my head and looking at a rear corner of the raft, the other chap was lying across it, his head in the sea, lolling from side to side, his feet also. I watched him, fascinated, my head moving in time with his. I was beyond being shocked — that came later. Micky took over, he gently pushed the dead man into water".

Spooner and Myles were lucky. After forty-eight hours in the water (during which so many of their comrades had been dispersed over tens of square miles of sea, putting them beyond all hope of rescue), Chinese fishermen somehow found them and took them to an island. A lucky handful like these reached land well after the other survivors had been picked up. "I woke up in heaven, an old, angelic Chinese, sans wings, dressed in traditional Chinese peasant's clothes, black trousers, black blouse, her grey hair plaited in the customary pigtail. She was feeding me a warm sweet liquid from a china bowl, with a china spoon. Then I blanked out again."

Two other men were even luckier. Frank Miles, Manager of the Hong Kong American Club, and Private McGillivray[178] of the Royal Scots had managed to find spaces on a large raft with ten other men. When they were picked up, on the fifth morning after the disaster, they were the only two men still alive.

But these few men who survived days in the water were the exceptions; most of those not picked up by the Japanese patrol boats had either reached the islands by the time darkness fell on 2 October, or would drown.

Jim Fallace: "The following day [3 October] I, together with about eighty others who had arrived on this island, were taken by sampans to the main island of Tsing Pan. Here we were given a bowl of rice in the temple and some Chinese gave us old garments, which were naturally much appreciated. It was then estimated that about 200[179] had landed."

Inglis remembered the flotilla that ferried these men early next day: "From out of the morning mist came first one sampan, followed quickly by about ten more. Came a spontaneous cheer and the Tommies, some helped by others, went down to the water's edge to await the arrival of the sampans. With a show of superb seamanship, the leading craft was brought close against the rocky shore, its occupant keeping it off the rocks with a long bamboo boat hook, indicating at the same time that he could take but six men because of the heavy seas ... One after the other the sampans came in and, loading their human cargo, pulled out and around again."

Once on Qingbang Dao they rejoined their comrades. All simply felt lucky to be alive. Wet, battered, exhausted, sick, and hungry, many had slept in the temple overnight, and awoke on the morning of 3 October still dreaming of food.

Alf Taylor, that dawn: "The temple was full of men still sleeping. The outhouses were full of men, and the haystacks also. I learned later that the villagers had rescued about 300 men and fed them all as they came in one by one."

*   *   *

Meanwhile, out at sea, the *Grouper* was still in the area. Still looking for prey, she had moved to a position covering the sea-lanes between Taiwan and the northeast.

3 October 1110	Arrived patrol station during night. Sighted smoke. Ran at full speeds on normal approach but could get no closer than 6000 yards to target (5000 ton freighter). When she went "hull down" surfaced. Intended to go round her and assume new attack position ahead during daylight. Found we had bit off more than we could chew. With excellent visibility it's a long way round. Finally decided to stay forward of targets beam until night. Unfortunately the night turned out to be exceptionally dark with target in densest portion of horizon. Attempted to locate target for 3 hours. Finally desisted and headed back for patrol line. Again we had figured a good patrol spot but missed out by a few thousand yards. Will trail next time instead of attempting to go around.

*   *   *

Inglis: "The Chinese inhabitants of the Islands were absolutely and utterly magnificent to the shipwrecked survivors. They gave up all their food and spare clothes unselfishly ... We were all seated around a wood fire eating bowls of steaming rice when one of the Middies held his bowl up and said to a venerable-looking chap dressed in a black padded jacket, black baggy pants, wearing a mandarin-type hat on his head and steel-rimmed glasses tied behind his greying hair with string. Holding up the bowl of steaming rice, the Middy turned to this person and in a mixture of English, Pidgin English, and Chinese said loudly: 'This good. This very hot. Plenty good.' 'Yes', came the answer, 'and it will do us a power of good!" 'Cor', gasped the Middy, 'you speak good English. Are you the King of the Island?' 'I am not', snorted the figure, "I am Lieutenant W. Clarkson, Royal Engineers.' Hearty spontaneous laughter all round, including 'our Willy' who later on was to be a tower of strength".

However, for these men stranded on the islands, there was little choice. They could not live on the hospitality of the locals forever, and many needed medical attention. While twenty-four hours of freedom in friendly company had been welcomed, it also had to come to an end.

Signalman Taylor: "With no prospects, it was decided that the only thing we could do was to send smoke signals, which the Japanese picked up. By early afternoon they arrived in some small craft to take us off the island ... The arrival of the Japanese, who were marines by their badges, meant much shouting, jostling and confusion."

Fisherman Shen Agui: "The Japanese were very brutal when they arrived, blowing whistles and with fixed bayonets. The British had no option but to surrender."

Taylor again: "One team searched all the houses, prodding bayonets into haystacks, turned the whole place inside out, rounding us up. They then escorted us onto the beach where we boarded small rowing boats before being taken on the vessels in the bay ... A more bedraggled lot of skeletons you never saw. Once on board we were squeezed onto the deck. During the afternoon we received a few tins of hot water but no food."

But three exceptional and experienced men, Arthur 'Bill' Evans, William Johnstone, and Jim Fallace[180] — Old China Hands — decided that they had no interest in being captured by the Japanese again and sent back to POW camp, and instead talked the local fishermen into aiding them. The village elder, Woo Tung-Ling, despite the obvious and serious risks, decided to hide them in the village and lead the Japanese off the scent.[181]

Fallace: "[When the Japanese boats arrived] three of us who had previously arranged with the fishermen to hide us and to assist [us] to escape were taken to the other end of the island where we lay in hiding in the rocks from dawn to dusk. At nightfall we were taken to a fisherman's hut where we were given a meal of hot potatoes and were allowed to sleep on the ground of his hut."

The three men went to ground, hiding out when the Japanese came and recaptured their comrades, in the hope that they would be able to make it to free China and the British authorities there.

The Zhoushan Archipelago had many small islands, and the survivors were still dotted amongst them in ones or twos, or larger groups. On 3 and 4 October the Japanese spent many hours gathering the *Lisbon Maru*'s POWs from these small rocky outcrops, and the larger land masses on which Chinese fishermen had already concentrated many of them.

Some were less fortunate than others. Gareth, speaking of his father Royal Marine Henry Llewellyn-Williams: "When he was dying of stomach cancer in 1980 my father told me something of his escape from the *Lisbon Maru*. He was a strong swimmer and managed to swim to an island. His legs were cut badly on the rocks that surrounded the island. There were several small islands in the area. The one he landed on was populated by a couple of dozen islanders who showed great kindness to him and dressed his wounds, gave him food and found him some clothes.

A day or so later a small Japanese patrol boat called at the island. They were making a tally of the number of survivors with a view to arranging to transport them on to prison camps. There were three or four men on the boat and no room for my father (who was the only survivor on that particular island) so to stop him escaping (as if there was anywhere he could escape to) two of the Japanese soldiers held my father while the third systematically broke each of my father's toes with his rifle butt.

After the Japanese soldiers left, the islanders gave my father some sort of alcohol to drink while they bandaged his feet. A larger boat with a number of other POWs on board called some hours later. The Japanese guards threatened to shoot the islanders who were trying to carry my father on to the boat so he had to hobble on to the boat unaided."

Those who the Japanese picked up from the sea were luckier. They were fed and generally well treated on the Japanese boats. Many of the veterans recall hot condensed milk and biscuits being handed out on the decks.

Frank Bennett, on a Japanese patrol boat with some twenty survivors: "Some of the group were naval personnel who considered that a Jap sailor was a cut above a Jap soldier. This evidently derived from the fact that the Japanese Navy in years gone by had been taught what they knew by the British Navy, and over the years a lot of British tradition had rubbed off."

CSM Soden, on being picked up by a Japanese craft: "We were welcomed aboard by that most loved Commanding Officer of my Regiment — Colonel Stewart. The Jap officers on board treated us very well, stating that our Navy had trained them. They gave full military honours to those who died, and fed us well."

Bandsman Arthur Alsey, who had been one of the first picked up by the Japanese on the 2nd, was still on the same Japanese patrol boat with about seventy-five others: "Still in vicinity of sinking. Beautiful sunny day. Got piece of stick and whittled away for two hours to make a spoon. Barley tea at 10.30. Enjoyed the clean air. Chatted with crew, some good lads — one calls me Schubert and sings several airs. My tongue swells up, makes biscuit chewing a misery. A fair amount of fags from crew who don't mix with army Japs aboard."

However, at nighttime on these vessels it was a different story. There was a cold wind, and no shelter. Shanghai was considerably further north than Hong Kong, and autumn was coming quickly.

By midday on 4 October, most men were on the Japanese patrol boats, having either been picked up from the sea or 'rescued' from their sanctuary on the islands.

Robert Wright: "Nearly all of us had the minimum of clothing, and it was bitterly cold on deck. Under such conditions sleep was impossible, and the nights following upon our rescue were an ordeal."

The winds were rising and seas were breaking at deck level. Cold spray soaked these poorly clad men.

Bennett: "There were apertures in the side of the craft for excess sea water washed on deck to run off again. At this time, the wind was blowing through them and we were getting the full force of it. We huddled together tightly like a herd of sheep. God! It was cold. All that could be heard was the chattering of teeth. It was decided that at intervals the bods on the inside changed places with those on the outside, so giving everyone a chance for a warm-up. It was during one of those changeovers that it was discovered that one of our number had died. Just couldn't stand up to the exposure. He was laid on deck, and we carried on swapping places and trying to stop our teeth chattering. That was the coldest night of my life."

Bennett continued: "We pointed to the dead body and [the Japanese sailor] went off, only to return with another sailor and between them they put the body over the side. There was much discussion between the two, then off they went. About a half hour later, one returned with a tray of some sort on which were rice-balls and the other with a pot of steaming green tea. It was like manna from heaven."

Taylor was with those picked up from the islands: "The ship sailed in a convoy after dusk and the wind became cutting and chilling although we huddled together for warmth. At about midnight the first man died. We made such a fuss that the whole ship's company was mobilized, thinking that they had to quell a mutiny. When the Japanese eventually discovered that only a POW had died, they quite heartlessly tossed the body overboard without a hint of humanity."

Lynneberg also recalled the cold: "On the day the *Lisbon Maru* sank we were lucky for the sun was shining and it dried and warmed us. But for the following two days it was cold, wet and windy — so cold was it that three or four who were too weak to move about at night and keep themselves warm were found frozen stiff in the morning. The other two lads and myself took turns in sharing my shirt — we would cuddle together rub each other's back — in fact we tried practically all possible promotions of circulation to try and keep ourselves warm."

Robert Wright: "In fairness it must be said that, due to the intense cold, some of the more sick men were allowed to sleep in the coal bunkers, but there was insufficient room for all the prisoners below deck."

But this did not help the men who had already died on these craft. Wright recalled two: Private William Steele of the Middlesex and ERA Lees, Royal Navy.[182]

Wright: "Tall, gaunt, and likeable, [Steele] was the most inoffensive of men. Though not of my company, I had grown to like him, not least of all because of his passionate wish that there should be peace among his fellow men. [Lees], regardless of the agony he was suffering, had humorously christened his withering legs Hitler and Mussolini, to inspire fun and laughter in his fellow sufferers."

*   *   *

Shivering, and becoming sicker by the minute, these cold, soaked, and shocked survivors neared Shanghai.

10
Shanghai: 5 and 6 October

> Irreparable is the loss, and patience
> Says it is past her cure.
>
> *The Tempest*, Act 5, Scene 1

Those men who the Japanese patrol boats had plucked from the sea were the first to land. These smaller craft took the POWs straight to the mainland, and they disembarked at the Railway Wharf of the Wusong Flats, on the Huangpu River halfway between Shanghai and Wusong.

Frank Bennett was on one of these craft: "The vessel pulled in and a gang-plank was lowered on to the quay-side and there, in evidence, were Nip soldiers. We moved forward to the top of the gangway and after thanking the ship's company for what they had done for us, proceeded to leave the ship. I must say that whilst we were on board we were not ill treated, screamed at, harangued or in any way made to feel inferior. There may have been some truth in what the matelots had said about British tradition rubbing off on the Japanese navy."

But all that was about to change. Here on the dockside they were handed back to the Japanese army.

CSM Soden: "On leaving the ship we noticed how quickly the mood changed when the army took over. My coat was ripped off me, leaving me naked once more except for the eighteen inch by six inch piece of loin cloth."

Next to arrive were the surviving prisoners picked up from the islands. They were generally in worse shape.

Bennett: "There was a new influx of survivors. These were the people who had made for the islands when the *Lisbon Maru* went down, and what a state the poor sods were in. Some had suffered injuries, and all had tales to tell."

Now their captors formed all the POWs up on the waterfront. Lieutenant Wada Hideo, together with the infamous interpreter Niimori, berated them. Shanghai, in October, is never the warmest place to be; the prisoners were stripped of all the thick Chinese clothing the islanders had given them, leaving some naked and all underdressed.

Jack Etiemble, for example: "I had gone overboard dressed in shirt shorts and gym shoes, when I was eventually picked up I was down to my underpants, and a lot of others had taken off everything. On arrival in Shanghai we were met by the interpreter Niimori who had been responsible for the POWs in the *Lisbon Maru*. His very friendly greeting was 'none of you should be here, you were all meant to die like rats in a trap'. Very friendly person!"

Dennis Morley was less diplomatic: "The bastard of an interpreter made life hell for us."

RSM Challis: "Most of them were only wearing loincloths. Niimori ordered us to hand over these remnants of clothing; I ignored the order whereupon Niimori kicked me in the testicles."[183]

The men lined up in the cold winds of the wharf were horrified by their fewness in number; they had been halved. Until this point, it had been possible to think that 'the others' were on other islands, or had been picked up by other patrol boats. Now the truth was clear; men searched for their comrades in vain.

Hamilton: "Of the 50 POWs in Group No. 20, 26 men, including CQMS Henderson, were no longer there. Less than half of Howell's group remained, and this was the common pattern."

James Miller: "Most of the survivors were completely naked and were suffering from exposure and all were completely exhausted and ravenously hungry. To make matters worse, we were sitting on the cold stone of the quay. No attempt was made to supply us with warm clothing or a blanket to wrap ourselves in. There must have been about 800 survivors out of the 1,800 who boarded the ship. We were encircled by machine-gun crews and we dared not talk to one another at the risk of getting a beating. Later that day, we were all packed into the hold of a Chinese junk, under armed guard to await further orders. The armed guard could not have been more brutal, they took this opportunity to rob anybody who had a watch on their wrist or rings on their fingers.

You had to give or suffer a beating or a blow from a rifle butt. In the condition that we were in, we did not argue."

All the survivors remembered the vessels on board which they spent their first night in Shanghai. While uncomfortable, at least they provided some shelter from the wind.

Wallace Hastings: "By now the time was late evening and we were crowded into open junks which were moored at the quay side, which provided standing room only. Early on, someone discovered that these craft had at some time carried a cargo of rice and grains of this could be found between the floor timbers. We took turns at bending down to recover these.

The following morning we were 'unloaded' and paraded on the quay side, where a short while after we were provided with clothing. This was in the form of a buttoned tunic and a form of pantaloon which tied at the ankle, black or dark brown in colour and made of a corduroy material. Canvas and rubber boots with a separate toe were also produced."

William Poulter: "Every article of clothing that was issued to us was covered with lice eggs. After the issue of clothing we were again sprayed and then put back on board ship. We were then given a meal of rice and what appeared to be onion soup. We needed it, especially the soup; it warmed us up a bit."

James Miller: "By next morning [October 6], a few of the prisoners had perished from exposure, or had simply given up and let their life slip away … The Japs were now running around again, shouting out orders, in a state of agitation. We were bustled and pushed out of the junk's hold, back on to the quay."

A second day at the Wusong dockyards was eating away at the men's resistance. By this time, the hidden viruses that were transmitted in the foetid air of the *Lisbon Maru's* holds had visibly taken hold of many of the men lined up and shivering on the cold concrete in the autumn air.

Surgeon-Lieutenant Jackson feared that many men were not fit enough to face a second shipment, transferring them to Japan; their only chance of life would be to stay in Shanghai.

Robert Wright: "On the Wusong wharf, Surgeon-Lieutenant Jackson of the Royal Navy performed miracles. I can see him now, seated on a wooden box, his Vandyke beard aflow in the breeze, the gold braid on his sleeve gleaming in the pale sunshine, as he strove to sort out the sick from the very sick, and arguing with Nomura[184] about who was fit to travel and who ought to be allowed to remain behind."

Those who remained behind were truly sick. CERA George Williams would die there on 7 October, Acting Yeoman of Signals Robert Symons on 12 October, CPO James Todd on 14 October, SBA Gwynfor Thomas on 15 October, Motor Mechanic Douglas Horder on 16 October, all of bacillary dysentery. Signalman Joseph Watts, Sergeant William Campbell RE, Lance Corporal Ronald Cane, Boom Skipper Stanford Bailey, WO Charles Heath RE, WO Eric Butcher HKRNVR, Sapper Edward Stone, Sergeant John Fergus Royal Scots, Corporal Donald Grant, and Corporal Ronald Reeves of the 1st Middlesex would follow them within days or weeks. They would bury sixteen urns of ashes in a single common grave at Wusong. The Japanese would not allow the Red Cross to visit their camp until January 1943.

*   *   *

For the more than eight hundred men already dead, such matters were academic. But their families would not learn of their fates for several months, and in many cases would still be receiving their letters long after their passing. The Brooks family was no exception.

Charles Frederick Brooks
Hong Kong P. of War Camp S. (undated)

My Dearest Em,
It is a few months now since I wrote you letting you know that I was quite fit and well and I am pleased to say that I am still the same. I sincerely hope that yourself and the boys are enjoying the best of health and not worrying too much. We will be together again soon I hope.
I shall be leaving the Colony in a few days time and will write again as soon as possible. I trust that all at home are in the best of health and I must leave you to let them know how I am, as I can only write a limited number of letters.
Both Geoff and Ron must both be pukka Aussies by now and keep you fully occupied I should imagine. Has Geoff altered I wonder? He should be a great help to you just now.
Well Dear, I must close now having reached the allotted number of words. So cheerio, sweetheart, all my love to yourself and the boys, and keep smiling.
                    Ever your loving Hubby
                    Charlie

Many such letters brought false hopes. Most families sent them to the Colonial Office, on 2 Park Street, London W.1 as 'proof' that their boys were still alive. The Colonial Office soon evolved a standard reply, formally ending all such hopes:

> As regards the letter which you have received from your son I am to say that both the War office and this department have been advised of many such letters having arrived, and that in every case where they bore a date it was prior to the sinking of the 'Lisbon Maru'. In the circumstances it would seem that the whole of the mail in question was collected from Hong Kong before the departure of that vessel, and that the receipt of these letters cannot unfortunately be taken to mean that the writers are safe if they have already been reported missing by the Japanese.
>
> In the circumstances explained in this letter the Secretary of State fears that he can extend no hope for the survival of your son ...

11 Back at Sea: 7 to 9 October

> Let them be hunted soundly. At this hour
> Lies at my mercy all my enemies.
>
> *The Tempest*, Act 4, Scene 1

On board the *Grouper*, the submariners gasped in the foul air. Submerged since attacking the *Lisbon Maru*, they were now struggling to breathe in an atmosphere heavy in carbon dioxide and water vapour.

It was now some time since they had heard the last depth charge, and there was no sound of maritime engines in the waters above; Rob Roy McGregor gave the order to surface.

Garfield Kvalheim was in the Control Room on the trim manifold when the order came through. This compartment also contained the controls for forcing air back into the ballast tanks and thus pushing out the water, causing the boat to again become buoyant enough to rise to the surface. McGregor ordered that done. Once more, the submarine broke through the waves of the East China Sea.

At the after end of the Control Room was the Radio Room containing *Grouper's* communications equipment, including their 'code machine' — arguably the most secure communication device of its period. However, the *Grouper's* crew did not need their sophisticated high-security data encryption device to read the most important message they picked up that day. While surfaced, they received a signal in plain text.

Kvalheim: "We picked up a newscast from Rome stating that an American Submarine had sunk the *Lisbon Maru* carrying British and Australian POWs. Needless to say, there was nothing but silence when we received the news."

ROME SAYS U.S. SUBMARINE SANK JAPANESE SHIP:

Rome, October 7. (AP) — Radio Rome broadcast a Tokyo announcement today saying that an American submarine, October 1, sank a Japanese vessel in the South China Sea.

The broadcast added that there were about 1,800 English and Australian prisoners aboard the vessel enroute to Japan, but that many hundred were saved by two Japanese vessels which hastened to the scene.

Other survivors were able to reach neighboring islands, it was added.

(London heard a Domei (Japanese) report from a Shanghai broadcast from Tokyo identifying the ship as a 7,152 ton army transport called the Lisbon Maru.)

Fortunately, the *Grouper* had only two more days of her patrol left. They would be steaming for home on the ninth.

However, the same shocking information about the sinking had already reached the POW and Internment Camps in Hong Kong.

Barbara Redwood — who had served with Hong Kong's Air Raid Precautions (ARP) during the fighting — did not know it then, but she was familiar with several of the young men aboard, including Arthur Alsey and Harry Hale, friends of Barbara and her sisters. On 8 October, she wrote in her diary in Stanley: "Rather worrying news that a ship *Lisbon Maru* carrying British and Australian prisoners of war had left a southern port and was torpedoed by American subs. Some were able to swim to a nearby island, others were rescued, and a few drowned, and every one very worried about their men, but rumour is that Nakazawa[185] has given his word that no soldiers have left Hong Kong yet."

Sergeant Millington, HKVDC, in Sham Shui Po POW Camp, Friday, 9 October 1942, was of course in no doubt that there were Hong Kong prisoners on board: "We had news today from the Chinese foreman at Kai Tak,[186] that the ship which took the last draft to Japan was torpedoed south of Shanghai, and that there were only 300 survivors."

Jean Mathers, also in Stanley and wife of a POW officer,[187] heard the details a few days later: "There seemed no end to this dreadful time of disasters. News came through that some 2000 men from the POW camps had been loaded on the *Lisbon Maru* to work in the coal mines, on the docks and railways in Japan. Nearing Shanghai the ship was torpedoed. Most of the men were battened down below decks, so for them there was no hope. A few managed to swim to some islands off Shanghai whilst the rest of the survivors were re-shipped to Japan. This was a crippling mental blow to us all, and the terror was heightened by lack of authentic details ... No names of any of the work force were ever released. The agony of not knowing whether members of our families, or friends, were passengers, was relieved only by infrequent messages getting through to the camp officers."

Painfully, for the wives of soldiers, there was a way to find out whether their husbands had boarded the ship, but not whether they survived. At Stanley, they received a small allotment of money from their husbands on a regular basis, and saw their husbands' signatures when they paraded to receive the funds. Topsy Man, wife of Captain Man of the Middlesex, reported: "I had been told there was money for me, and it was with tremendous relief that I joined the queue of wives and saw their joy and relief when they recognised the precious signature. It came to my turn and I was given a great deal more money than usual, but all I wanted to see was that signature. It wasn't there. I knew then that he was on the ill-fated ship."

Meanwhile, in Shanghai, utterly unaware that their fate was being discussed in the outside world, the survivors were scratching from the lice in their newly issued Japanese corduroy clothes, underwear, and heelless socks. In the evening, they were loaded onto the *Shinsei Maru* for transportation to Japan. Fear, hunger, and cold dominated their thoughts.

William Poulter: "What I wouldn't have given for a nice big juicy steak with all the trimmings, still it only made one hungrier to think about food. In the evening we were given a meal consisting of fish, rice, pumpkin and sweet potatoes, all boiled up together like pigswill. To you it may sound revolting, and it looked it, but to us it was food. This was our first meal for six days. I for one enjoyed it."

James Miller: "Orders came through, that we were to embark that night on another Japan bound ship. Apprehension and near panic surfaced among the prisoners. We did not like running the gauntlet of American submarines a second time, but being prisoners we had no option."

Arthur Alsey: "We all go aboard at 7 pm on *Washington Maru*[188] down below the Jap troops. The stench is terrific, but we sleep fairly well. The ship is filthy from top to bottom. I thought the Japs were very particular!"

Wallace Hastings: "She was a rusty and thoroughly dilapidated hulk which looked unlikely to survive any time at sea. Only one memory remains of an incident before she got under way. Someone had managed to filch a large tub of what was called soya butter. This was shared around and spiced up our next meal of rice and watery stew."

Lieutenant Bucke of the Signals went further in his condemnation of the vessel: "Registered at Fuchu, dirtiest ship ever seen. Rat infested, inches of dirt, cobwebs, no air circulation; laden with Japanese troops and war material."[189]

However, there was one advantage. Martin Weedon: "Though the conditions were appalling, and we were quartered in the lowest tiers of the holds where the ventilation was terrible, the majority of us were only too glad to reach a spot where at least it was warm."

CQMS Poulter agreed: "After we had eaten we were again paraded, counted, sprayed with disinfectant and then marched onboard the *Washington* or the *Shinsei Maru*. Here we got a type of Japanese bed, just a bare board but no blankets. At least we are out of that raw cold wind, and at long last I had found my brother,[190] and so to sleep."

This time they were lucky; the *Grouper*, which could so easily have taken up station off Shanghai again and put one of her remaining seventeen torpedoes through the *Shinsei Maru*'s thin, rusty sides, was coming to the end of her patrol, far to the south near Taiwan.

By now, almost every man was sick through malnutrition, cold, and exhaustion. Dysentery was rife. Queues had to be controlled.

"It was both amusing and deplorable to hear the NCO call from the top of the gangway: 'One for a piss, two for a shit'."

Poulter, one of the senior NCOs on board: "During the night one of the men that was sleeping above me, and was suffering from very bad diarrhoea, had an accident. I received all of it on my chest, so now I had lost my singlet. I, like Queen Victoria, was not amused! Sanitary conditions on this boat were very bad and now many of the men were suffering from very bad diarrhoea and shock. It's the same old story. You line up to go to the latrine and come back and line up again for the next trip."

Many men, of course, were in no condition to await an empty stall. Captain Cuthbertson of the Royal Scots tried to give solace to men, who were already dehydrated and were now dying of dysentery, by reading them Robert Louis Stevenson's "Virginibus Puerisque".

> I care not that one listen if he lives
> For aught but life's romance, nor puts above

> All life's necessities the need to love,
> Nor counts his greatest wealth what Beauty gives.
> But sometime on an afternoon in spring,
> When dandelions dot the fields with gold,
> And under rustling shade a few weeks old
> 'Tis sweet to stroll and hear the bluebirds sing,
> Do you, blond head, whom beauty and the power
> Of being young and winsome have prepared
> For life's last privilege that really pays,
> Make the companion of an idle hour
> These relics of the time when I too fared
> Across the sweet fifth lustrum of my days ...

But literature and good will were not enough to save mortally sick men; they started dying. Lieutenant Kenneth "Chippie" Young, Signal Officer of the Middlesex Regiment died first and was buried at sea; four more would follow before the voyage ended.

Hamilton was with Young: "Occupying the bed-space between Captain Cuthbertson and myself was a Middlesex officer who was suffering from diphtheria. He could neither eat nor drink, but obtained some small relief when we took turns in dipping chopsticks in water and letting it drip into his mouth. When he died the Japanese permitted a burial ceremony on deck by Colonel Stewart, after which his body was slid into the sea. Having obtained photographs of the ceremony, the Japanese merely threw overboard the bodies of those who died later."[191]

The next to die after Lieutenant Young, Drake of the HKRNVR, was buried at sea the same day, 9 October.[192]

While the majority of survivors were on their way to Moji, Spooner, Myles, and a number of other POWs who were rescued from the sea later than most, finally arrived at Wusong. Here they found the sick who had been abandoned there waiting for them, under the command of Sergeant Overy and tended by a number of medics.[193]

*   *   *

They — like all those still breathing — thanked their lucky stars that they were still alive, but few realized just how damning the hours shut up with the mortally sick on board the sinking vessel had been.

12 Japan: 10 October

> All torment, trouble, wonder, and amazement
> Inhabits here. Some heavenly power guide us
> Out of this fearful country!
>
> *The Tempest*, Act 5, Scene 1

The *Shinsei Maru* arrived at the port of Moji, gateway to Japan's inland sea, at noon on 10 October. Three more men, Francis Cassin of HMS *Thracian*, Michael Mulcahy of HMS *Tamar* (though attached to HMS *Cicala*), and Murdo Stewart of the NZRNVR, had already been buried at sea that morning.[194] This sea voyage had helped no one's health.

Sensing a Public Relations opportunity — and most especially the opportunity to try to drive a wedge between the Allies — the Japanese government moved swiftly. Newspaper reporters waiting on the dock tried to quiz the men about the 'dastardly American attack'. Frozen and shivering, the POWs were hardly prepared for the media, though they could not avoid the attentions of the photographers.

William Poulter: "As soon as we were tied up we were boarded by a crowd of newspaper reporters who started asking questions, of both the officers and men, about the sinking of the *Lisbon Maru*. Very few of the men gave them a decent answer. They were trying to get us to agree that the Jap sailors were very brave in rescuing us, and that the submarine meant to kill us all. We were not falling for that one!"

One of the photographs taken that afternoon, of emaciated and bearded POWs looking thirty years older than they actually were, would shortly appear in the Japanese magazine *Samura* (Volume 4, Number

11), with a devilish caricature of Franklin D. Roosevelt haunting its corner.[195]

Whatever the POWs actually said, Domei swiftly broadcast their 'interviews'. The BBC Monitoring Service picked up the transmission, read out in English:

"Commander S. J. Horswell, the highest naval officer amongst the survivors, and formerly attached to the British garrison at Hongkong, declared emphatically 'The treatment accorded to him and his subordinates was the best they could hope for', adding: 'Japanese officers and men were very good to us — very good indeed. I swear this is the truth.' When told that Japanese internees in Britain and elsewhere were treated as criminals the British officer stated: 'All I can is [sic] that it is only just that British officials should treat them as good [sic] as we have been treated.' Asked about the ability and gallantry of Japanese forces during the siege of Hongkong, Commander Horswell answered: 'Very strong, efficient and brave. Moreover I can say definitely that they fought cleanly[196] and with sportsmanship.' [Asked what he wanted most] 'I wish the war would come to an end so that I could go back home and see my wife. If I ever had the chance, I would like to broadcast to the people at home and in the USA that they knew only the Japan of yesterday and this was the sole reason for the unfortunate rupture over Pacific issues.' "

"Lieutenant Charles D. W. Brown, 49, of the Royal Signals Corps, said that the Japanese must be very efficient since they captured Hongkong in two weeks. 'To tell you the truth I cannot tell you about my experiences, because the battle ended all too soon — in fact before I knew what it was all about.' However Brown went on to say: 'Bombs dropped by Japanese air units found their mark with deadly accuracy, blasting only military establishments. Practically none of [sic] civilian houses were damaged.' Referring to life in prison camp ... Hongkong, he said ... was excellent, considering everything. Talking of his experiences ... said he wanted to thank the Japanese for doing everything possible for the prisoners. He declared: 'Their attitude was most generous.' "

"Short, chubby, Lieutenant Pollock from Sydney, Australia, confessed he was very much impressed by the traditional Japanese spirit of Bushido. He said it was the happiest moment of his life when he was rescued by the Japanese just as he was about to go down, disclosing that Japanese soldiers immediately gave him a glass of hot water, thick slices of bread, enough blankets to warm up his icy body. He said: 'The same warm, kindly treatment was accorded to every rescued man. It can't be anything else but a manifestation of the true Japanese spirit.' Asked what he thought about the future of the war, Lieutenant Pollock grinned: 'I don't care a hoot about Churchill, Roosevelt, or honourable Chiang Kai Shek. With me love comes first.' He asked that a personal message be sent to Mrs Pollock, Buckingham Flats, 149 Beach Road, North Bondi, Sydney, informing her as well as Jeff, Jessica and Barbara that he is well treated and happy."

But the propaganda did not stop there. "Lt. Col. Stuart [sic], 48 years old, the highest ranking officer among the British war prisoners declared they entered the war to fight for Britain and its ally, America. No words can express his chagrin over the fact that so many of his comrades are no longer with him because of the thoughtlessness and reckless conduct of an American submarine, Stuart said."

Probably the only accurate reporting of any of the above 'quotes' was the address of Pollock's family.

Coolly, Lloyds of London, in their weekly casualty report[197] recorded: "*Lisbon Maru* — London, Oct. 10. — Tokyo Radio reported to-day that survivors of the Japanese transport *Lisbon Maru* arrived this morning at Moji. Among the survivors were an unspecified number of British prisoners."

After disembarking, the men queued up for a medical examination, which consisted of a glass tube being shoved up the rectum. The Japanese were most amused by Private Green's tattoo across his buttocks; 'I see you as you see me'.

Apart from this superficial inspection, there was little other activity that afternoon. Wright: "We were on the wharf most of the day. I was allowed to go and clean myself at a water tap, and that made me feel much better, although I had to throw away my underwear, which left me more exposed than ever to the cold wind."

That evening, at seven o'clock, a train steamed into the wharf and all British POWs boarded; they were bound for camps in both Kobe and Osaka.[198] The carriages were comfortable and the food was good. Even though some of the worst cases had already been taken to hospital, many other men were also seriously ill. They sickened rapidly on the journey.

Poulter was on that train, though fitter than most: "I scrounged a couple of fags off our sentry and he thinks it's very funny to see one cigarette being passed round at least six men. Later in the evening, we stopped at a place to get a drink of hot water and took on some boxes that contained food for the trip. Each of us was given a small box with food in. The sentry calls it 'Bento'. The food it contains consisted of Rice and Barley, some small fish, Seaweed, salted Plum, Bamboo Shoots and pickled Turnip. It all tastes very unusual to our palate but we are very hungry, so down the hatch it goes. I am suffering from a mild attack of diarrhoea, it's possibly due to a lot of the China Sea I swallowed when being towed by that tug or maybe I caught a chill hanging about on the dockside."

The train stopped shortly at Kokura,[199] where a party of thirty-six of the sickest men left were dropped off. Twenty-one of these would die.

Alf Hunt was in that group: "After landing at Moji I was taken off the train en route to Osaka with about thirty other cases of dysentery and diphtheria and put in the annex of a Jap military hospital somewhere between Hiroshima and Osaka. There were only ten of us came out alive after five weeks.[200] We were then taken by train to the Stadium Hospital in Osaka. In it were all the sick from the two camps, Osaka and Kobe. I was there for about a month in which many men died. The doctor in charge was a navy doctor called Jackson and he did a marvellous job and saved many lives. I was then sent to the No. 1 camp in Osaka."

Wallace Hastings was one of the medics allocated to serve in this hospital: "I and several others were sent to Osaka Stadium Hospital for POWs under the supervision of Surgeon Lieutenant Jackson RNVR. Other staff assigned to the Stadium Hospital included Thomas McCready LSBA, Ken Baggs, LSBA, and possibly other Sick Berth ratings the names of whom I cannot recall. Also assigned were other ratings for duty as cooks and assistant ward orderlies. These were drawn from any of the service personnel and names in my recollection are: John Quinn Royal Marines, Harry Pelham Royal Engineers, Ken Hagger A.B., Jack Hughieson Telegraphist RN, James Kelleher Leading Stoker RN. There were others whose names I cannot recall. There was also a civilian named Mr Gibbs.[201] The hospital was an area beneath a sports stadium the outside of which we never saw. It consisted of straight walkway of somewhere between sixty and one hundred yards in length."

This makeshift hospital would save many men; it would also witness the last moments of many more.

The train's second stop, at Hiroshima, saw fifty-one more sick men disembark. At the third stop, Kobe, a party of some five hundred Royal Scots and Middlesex left the train and started marching to their camp. Steaming through the night once more, the train disembarked the remaining 326 men at its final halt in Osaka. Here, too, they marched to barracks in the middle of the town. Nine of their number were immediately taken to hospital.

Hamilton: "We were a pretty sorry lot on arrival at Osaka. There were about 350 of us, including seven officers. There were three Royal Navy officers, of whom Lieutenant Pollock was our senior officer. Of the four Army officers one had been Distribution Manager of the Daily Mail, and one was Ginger Howell who had opened the hatch for our escape."

At half past one in the afternoon of 11 October, the Kobe group arrived at their destination. Their new camp commandant, Morimoto, introduced himself and ordered them to sign a pledge not to escape.

Robert Wright: "This was farcical, for our resistance was now so low we lacked the strength and spirit to try and make a breakout … The new camp was made up of two red-brick warehouses with iron bars and shutters, and wooden slats across the windows. A grim looking place, it turned out, ironically, to have belonged, before the war, to a British shipping company".

Wright's colleague Wilson could hardly stand. He slept on one side of Wright, Jack Daly[202] (who was also very sick) on the other. After the exertions of the day Wright slept soundly on the hard wooden floor, the soundest sleep he recalled in his life. His two chums slept too.

They never woke. At dawn, Wright found both of them dead.

Poulter, that morning: "We all had to go to part of the burial service. This was held in an open field just across the road from Kobe House, and it was a lousy show as far as we were concerned. The Jap Officer, who was in charge of the POW camps in the Kobe area, gave us some drill instructions in Japanese and how to bow. I got a rifle butt in the back for not bowing low enough; I'd love to drill him, the old bastard. I spent a very bad night with diarrhoea and was losing a lot of blood."

* * *

Belatedly, on 12 October, BAAG agent seventy-five reported to Lieutenant Colonel Lindsay Ride in Guilin:

RIDE KWEILIN
DOUGGIE SEVENTYFIVE DATED 20/10 STOP QUOTE GEORGE NEWS DATE TWELFTH STOP ONE EIGHT ONE SIX PRISONERS ON BOARD TRANSPORT LISBON MARU TORPEDOED STOP ABOUT NINE HUNDRED SURVIVORS NINE ONE SIX MISSING STOP SURVIVORS REACHED MOJI STOP FOLLOWING SAFE COMMANDER HORSWELL LIEUTENANT COLONEL JACKSON CAPTAIN HOUGHTON LIEUTENANT BROWN LIEUTENANT POLLUCK MISSING INCLUDE LIEUTENANT WOOD MAJOR SUGAR WALKER MAJOR W WRENBROOK MAJOR M GREENWOOD STOP FIRST ATTACK TOOK PLACE SEVEN ACK EMMA FIRST OCTOBER STOP SIX TORPEDOES LAUNCHED NUMBER TWO HIT STERN UNQUOTE STOP OUR INFORMATION SIX HUNDRED FROM ALFS TWELVE HUNDRED POINTERS STOP[203]

DUGGIE

But for the Hong Kong POWs, finally on dry land again at Kobe and Osaka POW camps, in hospitals at Moji, Hiroshima, Kokura, and Osaka, the real test was still to come.

13 Prisoners of War: Japan, 1942 to 1943

> They fell together all, as by consent;
> They dropped as by a thunder-stroke.
>
> *The Tempest*, Act 2, Scene 1

And then they dropped like flies. Eight hundred and twenty-eight men had been lost in the ship or the waters round it, and a further six had died on the way to Japan; these were not fit men. All had survived nine months on a diet that would have horrified modern mankind, in both its miniscule volume and its lack of basic nutrients — vitamins at the forefront. Many had also been wounded in the battle of Hong Kong and had never had the bed rest and the nutritional supplements that today would be considered vital.

The shock of their experience, the stress of the sinking and the escape, the diseases that had been carried on board the *Lisbon Maru* and spread through the foetid atmosphere of its holds; the exhaustion and malnutrition, the inadequate clothing and the cold weather; all had taken their toll.

On 10 October, three men died, then eight on 11 October. Then a steady trickle; three men this day, six men that, until — by the end of that month — eighty-three had been lost since they arrived in Japan just three weeks earlier. November was slightly better with only twenty-three deaths, and December too, with only sixteen, but the decline in these numbers was Darwin's doing; only the strongest were left.

The shock was also still sinking in back in Hong Kong. Barbara Redwood's diary, 12 October:

> Dreadful headlines in Jap. newspaper — the *Lisbon Maru*, which went down on 1st October, was full of Hong Kong troops; supposedly 1,800 troops on board and 900 saved. Old Horswell (late P. D. O. Dockyard) saved and made statements, among which that Major M. Greenwood was among the missing — rank could be mixed up — feel so sorry for Mrs. Greenwood. Also a Lieut. Wood missing — I don't know if that's Joanie's husband — dreadful doubts for her. Don't really think Topper or Sid[204] or Arthur would be classed as technicians (which we understood earlier were the folk meant) — but it's an awful doubt in everyone's mind …
>
> Oct. 13th. Not feeling so comfortably sure that our men are alright because today's paper tells of other prisoners who had arrived in Japan and were broadcasting. Fears that this was just a batch that were sunk. i.e., the boys may have been among them …

The sinking of the *Lisbon Maru* had been just the start. A further two hundred of the survivors of the sinking would be dead before 1942 ground to a painful end.

The Osaka group took stock of their surroundings and had a surprise; they were to be interviewed on the radio.

Hamilton recounts: "Shortly after we arrived in Osaka some of us were informed that we would be permitted to broadcast messages to our families, and that we could include information about how the 'wicked' Americans had sunk the 'unarmed' POW ship and how grateful we were to the 'gallant' Nipponese for saving our lives. The radio people who spoke to us seemed indeed to believe their own propaganda. We of course declined. They then said that the broadcasts could contain personal message only. After some anxious discussions about whether this would be contrary to King's Regulations we concluded that there could be no objection; and we informed the men that if there were repercussions after the war we would inform the authorities that we had so advised them. (In fact no objections were raised.) On the 29th October 1942 we recorded messages giving our names and the names and addresses of our next of kin, with brief personal messages. These messages were picked up by the BBC Monitoring Service, and within a few days the Colonial Office and the War Organisation of the British Red Cross Society and Order of St John of Jerusalem transmitted word to my parents. This up-to-date news must have come as some relief, as reports had appeared in the British press that many Hong Kong prisoners, including the Royal Scots, had been drowned on the *Lisbon Maru*. My father later received about 40 letters from individuals in Australia and New Zealand who had heard the broadcast. He passed this information to relatives and friends."

> **LOST TROOPSHIP**
> Survivors to Broadcast
> - Tokio Report
>
> Tokio radio is to broadcast more than 60 short talks by survivors of the troopship *Lisbon Maru*, stated to have been sunk on October 1 by a United States submarine in the China Sea with British prisoners of war on board, it is announced. The broadcasts begin on Monday, and will last for about a month.
> Among those who will speak are Lieutenant Cyril Edward Bucke (32), of the Royal Corps of Signals, 3, Kitchener Road, Ipswich, Suffolk; Lieutenant Charles Brown (49), Royal Corps of Signals, Windermere Road Gloucester; Lieutenant James Spencer Badger (37) of the Hong Kong Garrison, 14, Muriau Walk, Caernarvon, North Wales; Petty Officer Joseph Millican, (26), formerly of HMS Tamar, 59, Dallas Street, Preston, Lancashire; and Sergeant James Stevenson (25), of the Royal Scots, Aberdeen. All these men were captured at Hong Kong. – Reuter

A transcript of one such recording survives: that of Stoker Petty Officer Jeremia Casey:

"This is Stoker J. Casey of the Royal Navy speaking. Anyone hearing this message please convey it to Mrs Casey, Union House, County Cork, Eire ... After being captured in Hong Kong we were kept nine months there, where we were treated well. We were removed on 27th September to Japan. The ship unfortunately met a submarine which caused a great loss of life among us. I was picked up by the Japanese navy and fortunately arrived in Japan where I was treated very well."[205]

James Miller described Osaka thus: "The camp itself was just an enclosed compound, off the main street. It had one entrance, a cookhouse, storehouse, sick bay, prisoner's living quarters. Washing facilities were a pipe with a few taps (cold water) and toilet facilities was a hole in the ground. There were about one hundred of us in this camp. There were several seamen from the Merchant Navy already occupying one part of the building; they must have been captured recently. The war news we heard from them was all bad."

Hamilton was also at Osaka: "The Japanese Colonel Murata who was in charge of all POW camps in the Osaka and Kobe area called us together and made a speech, the first of many. We would be well looked after and treated in the honourable tradition of Bushido. We must look after our health, keep ourselves clean and rub ourselves down with a towel (we had no soap, towels or toothbrushes.) We must bow to, or salute, all Japanese officers, NCOs, and sentries. We must learn to count in Japanese, and roll call would be conducted in that language. Working parties would be under command of British NCOs who would give orders in Japanese, or rather Nipponese which was the word to use in future. Disobedience or questioning of orders would be severely punished, and for a long list of serious offences the penalty was death."

The Kobe group encountered a surprise of a different kind. Their camp consisted of two large red-brick warehouses — formerly go-downs owned by none other than Hong Kong's Butterfield & Swire — with iron bars and shutters and wooden slats across all the windows.

However, on arrival in this camp, the survivors were in a shocking state. One floor of a warehouse was declared a hospital, and approximately a third of the camp's strength of five hundred was admitted under the charge of Staff Sergeant Ross. In normal circumstances, all the men would have been deemed worthy of admission.

Captain Martin Weedon: "Crammed in anyhow for first night, and pleasantly surprised to receive five blankets each — thin, but far more than we expected."

Soden, like Weedon, at Kobe: "The early days were the sad ones as so many died through lack of proper medical treatment. We were all paraded in the park opposite our camp for the first funeral, and a proper coffin was provided. Later, when more died, their bodies were just squeezed into an apple barrel. I shall never forget the smell when these poor souls were kept just outside the camp hospital waiting to be collected for cremation. I still get a lump in my throat when I hear the song 'Roll out the barrel'."

Weedon's early hope soon faded as the diphtheria epidemic really took hold, just as it was doing back in Hong Kong at Sham Shui Po POW camp; deaths were to dominate his diary for the next two months: "12th October: Naval Warrant officer died during night[206] ... 12th–17th October: Difficult to write about this period. A really grim time. Over eighty hospital cases — mostly dysentery — and almost whole camp suffering from acute diarrhoea, chills, and shock. ... Lorry load of worst cases taken away, crammed like sardines into an open lorry, to supposed hospital. Heard later that several subsequently died, including Cuthbertson (Royal Scots), Ptes. Ferris (Mx.), Jones (Mx.),[207] Fountain (R.E.), Cpl Taylor (R.E.). Two more deaths here. Went out with latter two when taken away for cremation. Bodies put into wooden barrels and taken away in hearse. Drove to crematorium on hillside above Kobe and witnessed barrels being put in furnace. Returned next day to collect ashes which will be kept and returned to the relatives after the war. Gruesome business watching them pick out with chopsticks some of the choicer charcoal remains."

"W. O. McFarlane (R.N.) died on 17th, Sgt. Booth (R. S.) on 18th, and apparently several more dead of those who left here recently ... 20th October: Another party of sick taken away to Osaka. Possibility of better conditions there. Colonel [Stewart] and Innis both went — Colonel looking desperately ill and trying not to show it."

Poulter was one of those taken to hospital on 20 October: "We were put into open lorries and the trip took two and a half-hours with no stops on the way. This was fatal to the men suffering from very bad diarrhoea and consequently there were very many messy pairs of pants on arrival. I was lucky, but only just. I can't say that I saw much of the journey, as my thoughts were concentrated elsewhere! Hospital? It was under the stands or terraces of the Osaka Stadium or Ochinioka.[208] It was a trifle better than [what we had] left in two respects. One is that we had a real doctor, and it was much lighter and a bit more room. The doctor was Surgeon Lieutenant Jackson. So far he had no medical supplies, but we were living in hope."

Morale was taking a battering from this onslaught of diseases.

Howell: "Within the next three years in various camps I thrice woke up in the morning with a seemingly unharmed corpse next to me, apparently because the night before it had remarked, 'This will last for years and I can't go on!'"

The same day came another blast from the Japanese propaganda machine:

> *Survivors of Lisbon Maru at Moji voice indignation at U.S. action. Gallantry of Japanese who rescued British War Prisoners described in eye-witness accounts of disaster caused by cowardly American submarines.*
>
> Carrying an undisclosed number of British War prisoners who narrowly escaped death, thanks to gallantry of Japanese stalwarts when the army transport *Lisbon Maru* with 1800 British War Prisoners on board was sunk in the East China Sea by a cowardly American submarine, an undisclosed ship arrived at Moji at 2 p.m. Saturday 10/10/42. Our country, compatriots, look at the facts! These surviving British War Prisoners shouted from the housetops, with clenched fists, their eyes glistening with impressive wrath over the brutal callousness of the American forces which left their forces to die in the open sea.
>
> With one voice and in the highest terms these surviving British prisoners referred to the strength and warm-heartedness of the Imperial Forces, and lauded the gallantry of the Japanese mariners.
>
> Following the quarantine, the British War Prisoners were transferred to a train which left Moji at 7 p.m. Sub-Lieut. Hideo Wada [sic], Commander of the transportation of the war prisoners, who directed the rescue atop the mast of the sinking *Lisbon Maru*, described the scene of the disaster as follows:
>
> "We must rescue the British War Prisoners, was the first and foremost thought which leaped into our minds when the ship met the disaster. It was just the hour for the roll-call of prisoners, somewhat taken aback, they were about to stampede. 'Don't worry, Japanese planes and warships will come to your rescue,' we told them. The commotion died down. It was encouraging to note that they had come to have such trust in the Imperial Forces during a brief War Prisoners' camp life.
>
> All the Japanese, of course, were prepared to share a common fate with the British War Prisoners. That is why we

all put on lifebuoys all at the one time. The fact that we were able to rescue the majority of the British War Prisoners was due to my subordinates and to the prisoners' obedience to the Commander; the prisoners' reliance on us, and the brave action of the Navy men in the face of the enemy.

The gunners who were on board the ship and who rendered distinguished service included — Corporal Ryoya Moji of Takagicho, Arka-Saka-Ku [sic], Tokyo. In response to volleys of questions posed by the Press, the actual sinking of the ship was described in the following vein:

"It was just about 10.30 a.m. that I happened to discover the sixth torpedo discharged by the submarine rushing towards our vessel. 'If it scores a direct hit on our ship it will shatter her to pieces,' we were informed by our squad leader, Corporal Moji — he then gave us the order to fire at the torpedo which was rushing towards our ship from a distance of 1200 meters. Surprised beyond words, but faithful to the order, we charged our cannon with a shell, aimed at the torpedo, and fired. We then looked ahead of us and discovered that we had scored a direct hit. During drills there is a slim chance of hitting such a fast-moving objective, but Providence was undoubtedly with us at the time."

Rushing out of his cabin in spite of a high fever, directing his view in its operation against the American submarine, and when his ship was going down, remaining on the bridge until the last of his prisoners was transferred to the lifeboats, Shigeru Tsuneda,[209] Captain of the *Lisbon Maru*, has drawn much praise for his courageous action. Arriving at Moji, Captain Tsuneda said, "I am sorry I have caused so much trouble," and gave the following account of the sinking:

"I rushed up on the bridge immediately on hearing the warning that we were being attacked by an American submarine. As soon as I got to the bridge a torpedo came tearing through the water towards us — I thought that the end had come and closed my eyes. But this first shot was a dud and did not explode. The second torpedo came at us, then a third — we avoided these by manoeuvring, but a fourth and a fifth cut across the seas towards us. The fourth torpedo, which was shot at us from the front, hit us on the starboard side. I ordered the ship to be turned to starboard in order to avoid the fifth torpedo, but by this time part of the engine-room and starboard stern were shipping water; then the after hatches started to be threatened by water. I decided that we could do no more, and sent out requests for help. The first torpedo came at us at 7.10 a.m. and it was five minutes later that the fourth torpedo hit us. The fifth shot passed us from the starboard to port; as the sixth was bearing in upon us our courageous gunners hit it at a distance of 1200 metres. But it was already too late. We tried to prevent the ship from sinking by sealing the boiler rooms, but because the walls burst soon after we were hit, the ship could no longer move. The water kept rising and finally the ship sank."[210]

And then, on the twenty-first came the news that the Middlesex had been dreading: Stewart — their commander and the most respected officer aboard the *Lisbon Maru* — was dead.

Martin Weedon: "Worst blow we've had, and news thoroughly depressed whole camp. If ever a man gave his life for others it was the Colonel, who has worn himself out in his efforts to get things done to put these ghastly conditions right, and refused to admit his own sickness. We shall feel his loss sadly in many ways. News of RSM Goodfellow's (R.S.) death at Osaka."[211]

Bill Poulter had been at the hospital with Stewart: "Colonel Stewart died at 6 am October 21st 1942. I was with him when he died. Four men of the Middlesex Regiment and one man from the Royal Engineers helped me put him in his coffin and carry him out to the hearse. It was the only military honours that we could pay him. He was not beaten to death as it was rumoured; in fact no Jap laid a hand on him."[212]

That same month, the East Asian Residents' Association in Sydney sent out a letter offering shaky assurance to their members: "It does not of course follow that because Tokyo says that 800/900 were drowned that anything like that number lost their lives. It may well be propaganda on Tokyo's part aimed at discouraging American submarine operations in the China Sea." This was a false hope; the number of dead had risen well beyond the count of those drowned, and it would rise further still.

By the end of that month, and into the next, other diseases came to the forefront. Weedon again, 24 November: "Diphtheria outbreak apparently over, and only three dysentery cases. Most serious complaint is beri-beri. About 20 percent of camp suffering from it — many unable to get to sleep owing to pain in feet. My ankles very tender and pellagra still troublesome. One of our men in desperate condition with beri-beri spreading over whole body. Putting up a wonderfully brave fight. If only we could get more food for him."[213]

The beri beri came under control to a degree. Weedon: "11th December. After repeated applications succeeded in getting supply of yeast tablets and small issue of sugar and flour in order to brew liquid yeast for beri-beri cases."

However, malnutrition remained a constant threat. Weedon once more: "13th December. Only half rations, as non-working day. No bread at midday — only a bowl of thin vegetable soup. Only half bowl of rice in the evening. Everyone desperately hungry."

By December, three months after the sinking, Weedon and the other POWs had forgotten about Fallace, Johnstone, and Arthur Evans — the three men who had been with them on the islands of the Zhoushan Archipelago but had not been seen since. In fact, they probably assumed they were dead.

Nothing could have been further from the truth; these three men had escaped and were on their way back to the United Kingdom.

Fallace: "[We remained on the island] for six days until the 8th October when two men who were afterwards known to be guerrillas took us by sampan to the mainland, via Chekiang, Kiangsi, Fukien, Kwangtung, Hunan."

The three men had formed an effective team, all having been — in one way or another — associated with the Hong Kong Royal Naval Volunteer Reserve.

Arthur Evans had been about to go on leave when the Japanese attack came, and was caught in Hong Kong. Although ranked as a 'Seaman Gunner', he was not really a member of the HKRNVR. He had done ARP work during most of the fighting in Hong Kong and when he was no longer needed in this role, worked at Aberdeen as a truck driver with the Naval Volunteers for the last two days before the surrender. He was taken with them to North Point for internment and was accordingly treated as a Seaman Gunner. When he finally reached British authorities in free China after his escape from the *Lisbon Maru*, the administrators despaired of categorizing him: "He has had no naval training and is really a civilian. I do not know how he should be treated as regards pay for the period he was a prisoner of war."[214]

William Johnstone had joined the Minewatching Branch of the HKRNVR in July 1941 and was a Warrant Officer. "Based in Aberdeen during the Hong Kong fighting, his pay was HK$15.80 per day including all allowances. He did not receive any pay for December 1941 but was given HK$20 in camp. He has had no seagoing training or experience."

Jim Fallace had also joined the Minewatching Branch of the HKRNVR (a few months earlier, in February 1941), and was also a Warrant Officer. Despite having been a marine in the Great War, he was also recorded as having: "no seagoing training or experience. His rate of pay was HK$13.20 per day. He also received no December pay but had HK$20 in camp". However, the British authorities in China were more comfortable with Fallace than the other two escapees: "With his police experience and 13 years service in the Royal Marines he should be useful to the Military. He is a First Class Small Arms Instructor."

Evans, Johnstone, and Fallace finally arrived at Chungking on 5 December after their long trip through China. They were the only survivors from the *Lisbon Maru* to avoid the POW camps in Japan. Their arrival in Chungking led to the first eyewitness reports of the sinking being sent back to the UK and the families of the POWs (who had been waiting since October for further news). Reuters, Associated Press, and other agencies covered the story, and as well as appearing in many newspapers, it was reported by Lloyds:

Lloyds of London: "*Lisbon Maru* — Chungking, Dec. 22. — The British Embassy here told to-day[215] the first full story of the torpedoing of the Japanese prison ship off the Chekiang coast three months ago when hundreds of British prisoners of war from Hongkong lost their lives. The facts have reached Chungking from three Britons who were onboard the vessel. As internees in the Shamshuipo Camp, Kowloon, they left HongKong on Sept. 27 on board a Japanese cargo vessel with 2000 officers and men, both naval and military. All the prisoners were accommodated in the holds. The torpedoing occurred on the morning of Oct. 1. That evening the hatch boards were closed. Later someone removed the tarpaulins from the hatches, enabling the prisoners to force their way into the deck. The stern of the vessel was then submerged, resting on the bottom, with her bow high out of the water. The Japanese then abandoned the vessel. Hundreds of men jumped into the sea and started swimming towards five or six Japanese auxiliary vessels. Suddenly the vessel sank so that only the crosstrees of the mast remained above water. The auxiliaries picked up a few men, but made no effort to save the vast majority of those in the water. The three men said that after three hours in the water they were picked up by Chinese fishermen, who put them ashore."[216]

JAPANESE PRISON SHIP TORPEDOED

Survivors' Horror Story

WASHINGTON, Wed, AAP

The British Embassy at Chungking has quoted a Japanese news despatch from Hong Kong indicating that more than half of 1,816 British and Canadian prisoners were lost when a Japanese prison ship travelling from Hong Kong to Shanghai was torpedoed off the China coast. Nine hundred survivors were taken to Moji, in south-western Japan.

A gruesome story of their experiences aboard the ship has been related by Warrant-officers J.C. Fallace, W.C. Johnstone, and A.J.W. Evans, of British American Tobacco Co, and other survivors, who were picked up by Chinese fishermen and eventually reached free China.

They said that they and British naval and military officers of the Hong Kong garrison were crammed into the hold, with no provision for the sick, although many prisoners were suffering from dysentery, beri-beri, and diphtheria when the ship left Hong Kong on September 29. When the vessel was torpedoed (but not sunk) on October 1, they were forced to remain below all day without food and water.

A United Press message from Robert Martin, in West China, says survivors, whose identities cannot be revealed, but whose accuracy is unquestionable, stated that a nightmare began when the ship was torpedoed. The Japanese closed all hatch covers with tarpaulins, leaving no air inlets. Hour by hour the hold became more and more unbearable. There were no latrines, and the stench was overpowering. Several men died. Next morning the ship seemed to be settling down. There was no sound on deck, and stronger men decided to try to escape. They forced their way through the hatch and saw the prison ship being towed. No Japanese had been left aboard. Then the Japanese began to cast off the tow, and the prison ship lurched and began to founder.

Prisoners, although they lacked lifebelts, jumped overboard amid machinegun fire from several Japanese vessels cruising around the ship. Some continued firing at swimming prisoners, many of whom were so weak they were drowned immediately. The Japanese later picked up some prisoners, but they did not lower boats.

For those left in the camps, Christmas 1942 brought little joy.

Poulter: "Christmas day. One year had gone since we had to surrender, and what a year that had been. No Robin to wake me up and show me his presents, woe is me. At 4 pm we all got together and had a little singsong but I couldn't take it any more when Topper Brown sang 'The Little Boy that Santa Claus forgot' it reminded me too much of Doff and Robin. It hadn't been too bad a day really at least the Japs left us alone, but I hoped that this is my last Christmas in Japan, but some how I didn't think so. The cooks had been saving little bits of our rations in an effort to make this a decent day for us, so we had nothing to thank these little sods for."

As Poulter recorded in his diary, the menu for Christmas day 1942 read:

Breakfast	Rice and a bit of salmon from the Red Cross parcel with beans and coffee.
Lunch	Rice and orange juice, helped out with the Red Cross parcel
Dinner	Half a bowl of soup
	A vegetable pasty. Two slices of fried potato
	One dumpling with carrots in.
	One small pancake with jam
	One bowl of tea

* * *

After the initial losses of 1942, the death rates in the POW camps slowed. Following this settling in period, the Kobe POWs were sent to work in the docks in groups of twenty. The work was hard and dangerous, but at least it offered some variety and — vitally — the opportunity to follow the age-old dockers' craft of pilfering. All sorts of foodstuffs made their way back to camp.

CSM Soden: "When I was unloading from a cold-storage depot, one of the lads hid a large frozen fish between his legs; it was held in place by string. This caused much amusement among the guards who searched him. Feeling the fish they mistook it for his penis, shouting: 'Oki Jimpo', meaning 'big cock' ... It was always our ambition to smuggle extra food into our camp in Kobe, especially as the officers and the sick received half rations as they did not work. If we were caught we were severely beaten and made to stand outside the guard room for hours."[217]

It was no different for the men at Osaka. By now, everyone realized that the only protection against sickness was food, thus risks were worth taking. The risk of starvation outweighed the risk of a beating.

James Miller at Osaka: "Next day, fifteen of us were assigned to work on unloading a ship, anchored in the harbour, the remaining men were assigned to various steelworks. The weeks passed slowly, our position was hopeless, we had no recreation facilities, the food was not sufficient to keep us in good health and there was complete boredom, nothing, but work and sleep. The realisation came to us, that to survive and also help our sick mates, we would have to resort to stealing anything that could help us to survive. We knew we were taking our lives in our hands, the punishment would be severe, if we were caught. We became expert in the art of stealing and concealing, anything, that would help us to stay alive. Sugar, fruit, tinned food, clothes and especially any sort of medicine or medical items, that we could lay our hands on, were brought back to the camp."

Even for those proven survivors who managed to make it alive into 1943, the years in Japanese Prisoner of War Camps were brutal. Men worked daily in the dockyards and shipyards — hard physical labour supported by a diet that was quite inadequate and still lacking in vitamins. When men fell sick, their rations were halved. The Japanese logic was simple: the sick could not work, therefore they were not adding value, and therefore there was no point in wasting food on them.

Not surprisingly, deaths continued as New Year 1943 arrived. Weedon: "January 24th. Yet another of our men died during night. Nothing left of him but skin and bone. His thigh nowhere thicker than normal man's forearm. Makes 29th known death in the regiment since *Lisbon Maru*."[218]

By now, news of individual losses from the sinking was getting to the victims' families.

War Office Welfare Officer, Melbourne — 8 January 1943

Dear Mrs. Brooks,

It is with deep regret that I have to advise you that notification has been received that your husband, 1410996 W.O.I. C.F. Brooks, R.A., is now officially reported as Missing at Sea following sinking of the Lisbon Maru.

I am asking the Australian Red Cross Society to arrange for this notification to be delivered personally, and to advise me when this has been done.

Please let me know if there is anything I can do for you, and meanwhile accept my sincere sympathy.

Yours Sincerely

The War Office — 12 January 1943

Madam,

With regard to the information already communicated to you by the War Office Welfare Officer, Melbourne, and with reference to War Office letter of 14th July, 1942, I am directed to inform you, with regret, that a report received from the Japanese authorities states that your husband, No.1410996, Warrant Officer Class 1 C.F. Brooks, Royal Artillery, who was on board the Japanese ship "Lisbon Maru" when that vessel was sunk, is missing.

Every endeavour is being made to obtain further details relative to this regrettable occurrence and any information which is received will be communicated to you without delay.

I am to express sympathy in the anxiety which this notification must inevitably occasion you.

> I am, Madam,
> Your obedient Servant

Housing Commission, Victoria — 12 January 1943

Dear Mrs. Brooks,

I have just learned with great regret that you have been notified that your husband is missing at sea.

I should like to express the very sincere sympathy which the Commission and its staff feels for you and your sons in your trouble.

> Yours sincerely

Ron Brooks: "I don't know when my mother first learned of the tragedy. Amongst her possessions is a newspaper cutting reporting the incident, published just before Christmas and official letters dated January 8th and 12th 1943 stating that my father was 'missing at sea'. My mother did not receive notification that my father was presumed dead until August 1945 when we had returned to England. However, I do remember that my mother's financial situation changed significantly in 1943. I can only assume that she no longer received the full salary of my father (as a prisoner of war) but that it was perhaps reduced to that of a war widow.

Anyway, from that time my mother had to seek ways of maintaining her income. My mother had taken in lodgers in our flat for short periods. I remember another lady evacuee with a small daughter and at another time a young man from Tasmania in the [Royal] Australian Air Force. In March 1943, she went to work full time as a sales assistant in the millinery department of Manton's Department store in Melbourne city (I have the reference she received on leaving on 9th February 1945). Geoff and I became 'latch-key' kids. Sometimes, by arrangement, I went to the flat next door after school where the lady made me a cup of cocoa, and played with her daughter Judith until my mother returned home from work."

Local newspapers all over the United Kingdom also covered reports of these losses, though they remain grimly hopeful. From the 22 January 1943 edition of the Eastwood & Kimberley Advertiser:[219]

JACKSDALE
OFFICER MISSING
(photo)

W. A. BARLOW

Mr. Bert Bromley, Jacksdale Street, Jacksdale, has received news from his daughter-in-law, Mrs. Barlow, of Old Windsor, Berks, that her husband, Warrant Officer William Arthur Barlow, R.A., is posted as missing. The official document states previously reported a prisoner of war at Hong Kong, now reported by the Japanese authorities as missing, following the sinking of the "S.S. Lisbon Maru," a Japanese vessel which was transporting British prisoners of war to Japan.

Mr. Barlow joined the Colours at 18 years of age. As a scholar he attended Jacksdale Council Schools, and later was employed at Codnor Park Forge. He was a thorough

> sportsman and had passed out as a
> boxing instructor. He was also a
> sprinter of no mean ability.
>
> Mr. Barlow was an expert swimmer
> and it is felt that there is still every
> possibility that he is safe and sound.

The British government, meanwhile, was inundated with inquiries from those who had had family members on board. Working from the lists passed by the Japanese from Sham Shui Po, lists of those who boarded the *Lisbon Maru*, and information from the three survivors, they did the best they could. Sometimes, though, the game of Chinese whispers as handwritten or poorly typed documents were copied and copied again, made identification of individuals almost impossible. For example:

> We have no file for a man of that name, but we have a record of a Sergeant Andrew Brotehrton who was serving in the Hong Kong Naval Police, and whom we had assumed to be the 'Sgt. Andrew Btoyhrtdyon' reported as a prisoner of war in S.B.2119. By coincidence we have just heard from the Red Cross that the sister of one Andrew Brotherston has just written to ask for news of her brother, so it would seem that there may be two men of similar name and that some further enquiry might not be out of place."[20]

Back in the camps, the men had little idea of what news was getting home to relatives, whether parents and extended family in the UK, or wives and children evacuated to Australia. Worried though they were, food was still the primary focus of survival.

Weedon on 13 February 1943: "Struck lucky with RSM Challis' party to Mitsubishi Takahama. Unloading beans off ship with godowns fill of sugar, tinned salmon, sardines, tea, etc. Sat in small hut on dockside with fire, and brewed endless cups of tea with unlimited sugar given to us by coolies. Also had good feed of salmon and sardines. Got caught making off with tin of herrings and got a couple of clouts on the ear. No harm done, and made up for it later! Came back completely gorged — first good feed I've had for many months". But next day: "Another death — Private Root. Poor old Mids."

On 17 February, Cheesewright, who had done so well in the defence of Repulse Bay in Hong Kong, died 'delirious and in great pain'.[221]

Alf Hunt: "In Osaka we had three parties working at Nakatani (Mitsubishi), Maeda, and Kanamoto, all dock working companies. At Nakatani we unloaded or loaded rice, beans, sugar, salt, pig iron, soda nitrate, wool, cotton, tobacco, copra and all kinds of goods. About a hundred were in these parties. Also there were parties working in timber yards, cement works, iron foundries and different factories."

Jack Etiemble: "Work in Osaka was very varied, steel works, iron foundry, cement works and docks. Most of the time I was working at various docks or unloading ships, our two main aims were (1) to pinch as much foodstuff as possible to help us stay alive, (2) do as much sabotage as possible, for example if we were loading or unloading sugar or rice, if no Jap was looking it was dipped into the sea before loading into railway wagon or barge. On one occasion, we were unloading a cargo of iron ingots into a barge, our sentry had gone off to play cards, so we just loaded the ingots all at one end, and eventually the barge sank. Someone found our sentry and told him we had finished, he said this was quick so he was told to come and look, all he could see was the bubbles from the sunken barge, we said it must have been a hole. He could not disagree as he was supposed to be watching us. Work finished early that day!"

Squads of fifteen men worked on a ship. James Miller described how, when a ship load of sugar was being off-loaded, each man made bags made of any spare cloth that could be found, and hung them round any part of his body where they could be hidden. For three days, they brought back as much as they could. On the fourth day, the Japanese discovered what was happening, but as the Camp Commandant only delivered a stern lecture and the men were still left working on the ship, they decided to make one more effort to get as much as they could.

Miller remembered that last day: "Bags of all sizes and shapes were filled and tied to arms, legs, round the waist, and worn like a scarf, prior to finishing that day. After that day's work, we were marched back to the camp, we must have looked a queer lot, with bulges all over our bodies. We were halted at the camp entrance and counted by the guard, who reported all correct to the Camp Commandant. On the order 'dismiss', we made a rush for the entrance, to get in fast. A loud shout of 'halt, back on parade' was heard. We were shoved into line, and made to stand at attention; this was in the main street, in full view of the public. The Commandant was approaching us, holding aloft a bag of sugar, which had loosened and fallen off someone's leg. He demanded to know who had dropped it, nobody would confess, which was expected. On a negative answer, he gave the order that everyone must strip. To the Commandant's surprise, clothes and sugar bags were dropping all around us. The public stared in amazement at us and the amount of sugar lying revealed. After stripping, we were brought to attention, the Commandant came forward and began looking at the loot, in front of each person, and he seemed to be more amused than angry. On confronting one of them, he bent down to pick up one of the bags which had interested him. It was a long slim bag, which obviously had been tied around a waist. The Commandant swung the bag at the man's face, he ducked, and the bag wrapped itself around the face of the Jap Guard who was standing behind, it was comical."

As Miller pointed out, the Japanese guards were perfectly happy for this pilfering to continue, as long as every now and then they could raid the POWs' illicit stores and make off with them.

On another occasion, Miller and comrades were unloading pig-iron and sabotaged the winch so that when it lowered the off-loaded pig-iron onto the waiting barge, the load would fall out of control. The plan worked perfectly, and the Japanese guards shouted at the POWs to come out of the hold and give assistance.

Miller: "We came up, out of the hold and made tracks for the ship's dining hall where we were to receive instructions. We started a hunt to see what we could pilfer. One of the lads spotted a small larder, we found a large, dried, rock salmon and a fair sized ham, and this was a prized find, now we had to figure out how to get it into the camp. Recently, the Japs had started to search all work parties returning to the camp, as so much pilfering was taking place, so we would have to be very careful in taking our prized items into the camp. It was decided that the salmon would be tied to the tab of a man's jacket and allowed to hang down his back, another man would wrap the ham up in his jacket and carry his jacket over his arm. This was part of the plan; the other part would be enacted when it came to the search at the camp. On arrival at the camp, we halted and were then counted, then reported all correct. The guard came forward and started the search. Just then, a man further down the line dropped in a dead faint, the guard on seeing him drop, pointed to the man next to him, you pick him up and take him to the sick bay. Our scheme had worked perfectly, the ham and the salmon, were safely in the camp."

Camp life continued much unchanged throughout the war. The philosophy remained: grab what foodstuffs you could, and sabotage any Japanese equipment in your path. In the face of the twin spectres of boredom and hunger, men looked for any little variety to raise their spirits.

Hamilton: "Occasionally the officers were taken to a near-by field for exercise ... One day we persuaded a friendly sentry to let us enter a shop and buy some pickled seaweed and tomato sauce. The Japanese were continuing to pay us. The guard changed each week. The following week we stopped outside the shop and indicated to our escort that we were going inside. He indicated that this was forbidden. We expressed surprise. The shopkeeper knows us; ask him. The shopkeeper agreed. The escort let us in ... after a few weeks we had a chain of shops that welcomed us as regular customers ... Alas, we were seen coming out of a shop by an NCO from the camp staff, and our walks through the town came to an end."

*   *   *

However, in the outside world, unknown to the prisoners, on 20 March 1943 a war of words had begun through neutral Switzerland, protesting against their treatment. Axis and Allies were trading insults. The loss of life on the *Lisbon Maru* would neither be easily forgotten, nor forgiven.

*   *   *

Weedon, just three days after this distant dispute began, noted his own trading relationship with the Axis powers: "Another little present of tobacco, given to the men by German sailors from raider now in dry dock. German sailors are very decent to our men."

Poulter, the following day: "Joe Bindon,[222] who was lying next to me, was dying and he knew it, but refused to keep quiet about it. He had kept me awake all the previous night by trying to get out of bed and fight the Jap Medical Orderly. He died at 2.40 pm and at the finish he was quiet. He was at one time a good athlete and sportsman, and I say that in the true sense of the word"

Weedon, 29.4.43: "The Emperor's (and my) birthday. Non-working day. Up at 5.15 for bath — getting quite used now to early rising. Had succession of presents — tablet of soap from Chris, tobacco from Ewan and Challis,[223] peanuts from one man, sweets from another, and (terrific!) a tin of cherries from two more. The men really are a nice crowd, and many have shown up wonderfully under these conditions. Inspection by camp commandant and staff during morning, all reeking of drink! Big issue from ration store for Emperor's birthday — bully (one tin per man), M. & V.[224] (one between two), dried fruit. Chris and I had celebration lunch of M. & V. and cherries — magnificent meal! Fruit and gruel in evening. Quite a social gathering after supper — several of the men up to see us and a concert from the Harmony Trio in Americans' quarter next door. A wonderful birthday — the best day, I think, since our captivity."

Equally good for morale was the arrival of letters. Sam Atkins had already succeeded in getting a letter out to his family, telling them he was moving to another camp. Now he received one in return.

30/4/43   135 Derington Road
                Tooting, S.W. 17
                London, E

DEAR SAM
        JUST A CARD FROM US ALL AT
HOME. WE ARE ALL WELL, TRUSTING YOU
ARE. MARIE AND CHILDREN ARE WELL
DAD AND BOY SEND THERE BEST WISHES
HARRY CAME YESTERDAY TO SEE ME.
CISS, ARTHUR, TON ARE WELL. DOLL AND
CHILDREN WELL, (L – remainder of line censored)
BOY DON'T YOU THINK I PRINT WELL. HOPE TO
HEAR FROM YOU SOON, ALL
LOVE, MUM +[225]

With the unpredictable and irregular mail service, Sam's 'reply' was probably sent before he had received the previous letter from his family:

IMPERIAL NIPPONESE ARMY 25th June, 1943.

Dear Marie,
   I hope that you and the children are in good health. I am quite all right and in fairly good health. Please write to me and send me a photograph of you and the children. Give Anne and Barbara a kiss for me.

   Lots of Love,

   SAMUEL ARTHUR ATKINS

But many families had still heard nothing from fathers, sons, and husbands who had been on board the *Lisbon Maru*. The British government still could not provide authoritative information in most cases. Arthur "Bill" Evans, one of the three escapees, found himself inundated with letters from those desperate for news of friends and relatives missing on the ill-fated freighter, asking for any details he could give them:

From P.W. Grant, Mostyn Hall, Penrith, Cumberland, father of Donald Grant, Royal Engineers (who had, in fact, died of bacillary dysentery at Wusong, Shanghai, just nine days after the sinking):

> He was on the *Lisbon Maru*, according to the Japs, he was alleged picked up by them out of the water. They stated he died of illness along with 14 out of the 79 survivors they picked up. There is just the slightest chance you might know him seeing as he reached land. Of course we heard they machine gunned them in the water and I presume he died of wounds.

From Miss Winifred Hosford, Bertrand School, 10/11 Eccles Street, Dublin, sister of Petty Officer Telegraphist Robert Hosford, Royal Navy, who had been lost on the day of the sinking:

> Six months later I heard he was a prisoner, and then nothing further until the Japanese reported him missing after the sinking of the *Lisbon Maru*.

And from Mr J. A. Jupp, Crumbleholm, Long Preston, Skipton, Yorkshire. Father of Warrant Officer John Edmund Jupp, HKRNVR, who had died in Osaka on 12 October, ten days after the sinking:

I was in London a week after I got your message and called at the Colonial Office (Enquiries and Casualties Department) where I saw a Mrs Harrop.[226] She informed me that no word of any sort had come from Tokio with regard to those prisoners of war missing from the *Lisbon Maru,* and this in spite of repeated requests for information from the authorities here. The C.O. has promised to let us know if and when they hear anything from Tokio.

*   *   *

In the camps, caring for the sick was never an easy task. Aside from the dangers of infection, and the lack of basic medical equipment, drugs, and foodstuffs, there was always the chance of running foul of the Japanese guards, especially when risks were taken.

Hamilton: "Another trial was the omnipresent bug. Fleas were with us night and day ... My record catch was over fifty. A more revolting creature was the bed-bug which lived in the cracks in the wood and would sally forth at night. They could be quite large, half the size of one's little fingernail, and gave off a smell when squished ... Then there were the mosquitoes ... Finally there were lice which lived and laid eggs in the seams of clothing."

The British prisoners considered pilfering from Japanese ships, and stealing from the Japanese guards, legitimate activities, but stealing from fellow POWs was a different matter. But sometimes men broke their own code: "[James Clark] did tell us of the tale where he had a pet chicken that he looked after for ages, taking it to the docks in the morning, and smuggling it back in the evening. One day he found it missing from the post he would tie it to. When he got back to the camp in the evening, he could smell cooked chicken. He was told that because the men were so hungry, they had stolen his chicken to eat, but they had the good grace to keep back a leg for him. He refused to eat it. He said that through all that happened to him, starvation, torture and abuse, that was the only thing that ever made him cry during captivity."[227]

One way or another, food was always the main focus, whether it was provided or had to be 'liberated'.

Hamilton: "Before they became expert they would break open a case of (say) tuna fish and steal a few tins. The broken case would then be discovered and they would be beaten. Later, they would take a case to a secluded corner, remove all the tins and hide them, fill the empty case with bricks, and replace it with the original consignment for shipment. The tins would then be gradually smuggled into camp."

Miller: "About a month later we received a very pleasant surprise, we were told to line up for a Red Cross issue. This was the first and last time we would ever receive anything from the Red Cross. One parcel was issued to every ten men, to be shared amongst them.[228] The men decided that night, to give all the parcels that were issued to the men in the sick bay. It would do them more good than us. The Japs were very surprised at our action. There was a sad sequel to this event. During the night, two of our lads had broken into the camp store, to see if there were any more Red Cross parcels, they were caught in the act. The next day we found out they had been handed over to the Kempei (Military Police), they never returned to our camp, we feared the worst had happened to them."

Miller again: "It was round about this time, that the three of us were transferred to a hospital as cooks. The hospital was a space under a stadium, fitted with two raised wooden platforms. There was no bedding; sanitation was non existent, no medicine and no medical equipment whatsoever. The staff was four Jap medical orderlies, who never attended any of the prisoners. We had a surgeon lieutenant from the Royal Navy. This man performed miracles, with razor blades and sharpened ordinary kitchen knives. He would do operations on men's feet and bodies with these implements. A lot of the patients had gangrene, so the doctor was flat out, operating on these patients. The Japs were firm believers in the fact, that when a man was sick or injured, he was of no use to them, therefore, his rations were cut in half. This was practically a death sentence to the patients as the rations were hardly sufficient to keep a healthy man alive. The three of us, as the days passed, tried our hardest to get extra rations of rice from the Jap quartermaster, but we usually ended up by getting a blow on the face for our trouble. The men were dying off like flies. We three and the doctor were really worried at this tragic loss of life due to the refusal of the Japs to give us medical supplies. It was a terrifying experience watching men dying and not being able to help them in any way."

Leading Sick Berth Attendant Wallace Hastings had been working at that hospital from the start: "Patients were brought from nearby British occupied POW camps in Osaka and Kobe and the hospital rapidly filled and remained so until we left. With limited facilities and medical supplies, it was difficult to provide adequate treatment to them. Most were suffering from deficiency diseases together with various illnesses and the poor diet severely retarded recovery.

Meals consisted of rice gruel for breakfast, three small slightly sweet bread rolls for lunch and for supper, boiled rice and a watery soup made from a swede-like vegetable called daikon. Occasionally there was an issue of pickled seaweed and more rarely a portion of salted fish. A further extra on a rota basis was a portion of the burnt rice which adheres to the sides of the cauldron in which it is cooked.

Duties were organised in shifts and night duty was very popular among staff for the following reason. The food store which was supervised by the Japanese quartermaster was enclosed with a bamboo fence structure through which could be seen the sacks of rice. Some devious person devised a method of tapping these using a length of cane which was hollowed out and sharpened to a point. Pushing through the fence into the rice sack which was not tightly woven, lowering the other end and with a twisting action a steady flow of grain trickled into a waiting receptacle.

This was cooked on the stove during our shift using American issue aluminium water bottles (where these came from I do not know) and as these were used as hot water bottle for the patients the guards were never suspicious on seeing several atop the stove. I was on duty one night with Harry Pelham who raided the store as usual but instead of tapping into a rice bag, dug into soya beans and we decided to cook these in the same manner. A short while later the guard came in to stand with his back to the stove for a warm when to our dismay the beans started to boil and pop out of the bottle onto the top of the stove. With great speed of thought, Harry grabbed the bottle with his cap and dashed off to the patient area where it was thrust beneath the blanket of one very surprised sufferer!

I regret that I cannot remember the names of any patients in the hospital. Treatment given was very basic; dressing of wounds from injury; bedsores which were an inevitable complication and general nursing care for those with other illnesses. Wet and dry beri beri was suffered by all including staff. The dry beri beri causes severe nerve pain in the lower limbs especially the feet and ankles. Some relief can be obtained by cooling, and I can vividly remember one patient who, to achieve this walked outside in the snow. Some days later his toes turned black and gangrene set in necessitating the removal of all of them on both feet. This was done by Dr. Jackson without anaesthetic, the tissue was without sensitivity by now and was, therefore, of no consequence. The rest of his feet were affected and severe sepsis set in. They were cleaned and bandaged. Healing was very slow. Some time later on removal of the bandages for re-dressing his feet were covered with maggots. On seeing this, Dr. Jackson told me to leave them, re-apply a clean bandage and review in a few days time. Later inspection found that the sepsis had completely gone. With further care, the patient recovered sufficiently to walk again albeit with difficulty having no toe joints. His name is lost to me but he was soldier of Scottish origin.

There were many deaths. Disposal of bodies was by cremation arranged by the Japanese. Before collection we had to put the body into empty daikon tubs which were like large half barrels, placing them in a sitting position with legs drawn up to the chest and head bowed forward. Following cremation, the ashes were returned to the hospital."

While the prisoners were grateful for any medical care afforded them, the hospitals themselves were dreaded places. Weedon: "One [pneumonia patient] back from Osaka with note from Dr. Jackson. Have had 24 deaths in 174 days. Figures speak for themselves."

Food was the only preventative medicine they had, but it was always in short supply. Hamilton kept ducks at Osaka, Man and Weedon kept rabbits[229] in Kobe. Although all these were intended for the Japanese war effort, the POWs managed to at least benefit from sharing the animals' feed.

Poulter, noted in his diary on 2 October, the first anniversary of the sinking: "One year ago we were sailing merrily (?) along when crash, we had copped it! It's the day we started our swim to Japan, October 2nd. What a swim that turned out to be, anyhow some of us are still alive and that gives us some hope. When I sit and think about it, it doesn't seem as though it has happen to us, and yet I'm afraid it has. Today we were all potential film stars. A Japanese Propaganda Film Unit came and filmed us at work. Nearly all the men contrived to have two fingers a la Churchill. They took a close up of Challis directing the crane and one of me driving it. They also took one of Darkie Smith. I wonder what they will use it for?"

Most surviving POWs in Japan were by now managing some sort of communication with home. Sam wrote:

> Postmarked: Tooting, 12:45 PM 18 Nov 1943, S.W.17
> IMPERIAL NIPPONESE ARMY
> I am interned at the Prisoner of War Camp, Kobe Sub Camp.
>
> My health is usual.
>
> I am working for pay.
>
> Please see that Marie and Children are taken care of.
>
> My love to you <u>Le-y</u>

Christmas 1943 found the POWs in a better state than the previous year. Weedon, after a midday meal including smuggled wine and beer: "After lunch to concert party — first in one building, then this. Did new Oliver Wakefield[230] act, well received and encored both times ... Easily the best concert we've had. Evening meal of fried fish, and opened our tin of peaches. Thoroughly gorged by unaccustomed eating. More singing and impromptu numbers after supper and allowed extension of lights till 9 p.m. and allowed to smoke after evening Tenko. Really wonderful to see the spirits among the men. Morale sky high and unbelievable difference between this and last year's Xmas, when men were dying like flies and still a bit shattered by *Lisbon Maru*."

14 Prisoners of War: Japan, 1944 to 1945

> Imprisoned thou didst painfully remain
> A dozen years; within which space she died
> And left thee there, where thou didst vent thy groans
> As fast as mill-wheels strike.
>
> *The Tempest*, Act 1, Scene 2

However, less than a month into 1944, Weedon's memories of 'sky high morale' were forgotten. In the cold of January he noted: "Heated row in mess over question of giving cigarettes to cooks. How glad most of us will be never to see each other again. We really have got a motley crew."

The final two years of war passed with much of the same routine as the previous. Rations were no better, but fewer men died, and they lived for rumours of D-Day and the fighting in the Pacific islands.

Weedon, 7 June 1944: "In evening heard from Nip paper that Second Front started. This time it seems to be true." And again, on 19 July: "Unconfirmed rumours of the fall of Saipan, probably accounts for yesterday's excitement."[231]

It was a frustrating period for the Prisoners of War. Through snippets of news they had no doubt that the Allies were winning the war in the Far East as well as the European Theatre, but all they could do was wait. But in this time of hope, the Japanese shut down Surgeon Lieutenant Jackson's makeshift but life-saving hospital.

Jackson: "From October 1942, to July 1944 I endeavoured, against orders, to maintain clinical notes to cover about 700 admissions and 202 deaths. In March 1944, however, my quarters were raided by Japanese officials who confiscated every scrap of paper and arrested my writer, G. H. Bignal, and myself. We were taken to the guard room of Osaka main hospital, where we were interrogated all next day. As a result, the hospital staff was broken up and the hospital was closed four months later. I was dispatched to a 'punishment' camp in Kameoka."

Wallace Hastings also remembered the hospital's end: "Routinely we had snap inspections with no warning and on one such occasion which was in 1944, during the searching of the doctor's office some Japanese newspapers were found, showing maps of the far eastern theatre of war indicating the movements of Allied and Japanese ships. Their discovery caused an uproar among the Japanese officers present. For some reason they believed that the staff were involved in a conspiracy and the result of this we were informed that all staff would be individually dispersed to other camps. We were told to pack our belongings and the following day I was taken in the company of one armed guard by rail to Hirohata Camp near Himeji. I arrived to find that it was peopled by about four hundred American servicemen from the Philippine war zone and one Australian airman."

Towards the end of 1944, both in the camps and at home those affected remembered the second anniversary of the disaster. Wright: "The second anniversary of the sinking of the 'Lisbon Maru' was a reminder that our imprisonment at Kobe had lasted two years. It seemed more like an age. We attended a memorial service for those who had lost their lives in the disaster and I read Kipling's 'The Light That Failed'. Our interpreter, who was a Christian, attended the service. He proved to be the best of those who filled this position."

Now, two years after the deaths of those lost on the *Lisbon Maru*, the next of kin were receiving the first letters changing 'Missing at Sea' to 'Presumed Killed'. Despite the lack of bodies and proof, the unacceptable had to be accepted; hope had run out. From the Portadown News, 7 October 1944: "News has reached Portadown of the death by enemy action in Far Eastern waters in October 1942, of L/Bdr. Samuel John Boyce, son of the late Mr. and Mrs. Isaiah Boyce, Bridge Street, Portadown. It is known that he was captured in Hong Kong and was on a Jap prison ship."

And from 20 October 1944 in the Eastwood & Kimberley[232] Advertiser:

JACKSDALE SERGT.-MAJOR PRESUMED LOST.

(photo)

SERGT.-MAJOR W.A. BARLOW

Mr. Bert. Bromley, Jacksdale Street Jacksdale, has just received a communication from his daughter-in-law Mrs. Barlow, in residence at Old Windsor, stating that her husband, William Arthur Barlow, warrant officer, second class, battery sergt.-major, of the R.A., must be presumed killed in action at sea, while a prisoner of war, October 1st/2nd; 1942.

Mrs. Barlow has had notification from the War Office, Liverpool, that after careful review of all the available evidence, conclusion has been arrived at that all hope of the survival of her husband must be abandoned, and that there can be no longer any alternative but to presume that he must have been lost when the ship "Lisbon Maru", on which he was being conveyed as a prisoner of war from Hong Kong to Japan, was sunk.

Mr. Barlow, who was a stepson of Mr. Bert. Bromley, was well-known in Jacksdale and Ironville area, prior to joining the Forces at the age of 18 years. He was a scholar at Jacksdale Council Schools, and afterwards was employed at Codnor Park Forge. He volunteered for the R.A. and passed out as a boxing instructor, and was a sprinter of repute. As he was also an expert swimmer, it was felt that he might possibly have got away.

Families in Australia also had to make plans for a fatherless future. Ron Brooks: "It would have been in 1944 that my mother must have had to face decisions about our long-term future. My mother was the eldest child of a family of five. Her mother had died when she was 21 and she had acted as housekeeper for the family until she met and married my father in 1927. My father had been serving with the British Army stationed in Queenstown, near Cork. My mother's father and three of her four brothers still lived in Southern Ireland. Her eldest brother, Addie, was in the army in Italy having survived Dunkirk and the North Africa campaigns. I know that she was in regular correspondence with her youngest brother Arthur as he sometimes included a letter to Geoff and me. My mother had been a surrogate mother to him.

My paternal grandfather lived in Dover. He had been a regular soldier in the R.A. My father had three brothers and a sister living in England. I don't know how much any of these influenced her decision to return to Britain. I have very vague memories of her discussing the subject with Geoff and I rather think that he was against it. I don't know what had happened to the friends my mother had when first in St Kilda but they no longer seemed to be around. She made one good friend from her workplace who was very kind to me. (I think the name of this lady's son is on the Sai Wan memorial. He had been recently conscripted into the RAAF at that time.)

I think that my mother must have felt very lonely, unsupported and far from home. I also wonder if she had some intimation about her health. I can never remember her being ill when we were in Australia. I assume that the army offered her free passage back to Britain and that it was an offer she dare not refuse in case it was not made again."

The final New Year of the war came quietly.

From S. Atkins, Pte No 58

14 JAN. 1945

MY DEAREST MARIE,
ONCE AGAIN I AM
ALLOWED TO WRITE TO YOU. HERE WE
ARE ENTERING ANOTHER YEAR AND
I HOPE THAT THIS IS THE YEAR OF
PEACE SO I CAN BE WITH YOU
AGAIN. THE WAITING HAS BEEN SO

> LONG THESE LAST FOUR YEARS WHEN I
> LEFT YOU. I CANNOT IMAGINE WHAT ANNE
> AND BARBARA LOOK LIKE NOW AS I HAVE
> NOT ANY PHOTOS OF THEM. IS EVERYTHING AT
> HOME ALRIGHT? AND EVERYBODY, BEING I CAN
> ONLY WRITE TO YOU YOU MUST TELL ME ALL
> THE NEWS. MY HEALTH IS FAIRLY GOOD, BUT
> I HAVE BRONCHITIS BAD THIS WINTER.
> GIVE MY LOVE TO EVERYBODY, ESPECIALLY ANNE
> AND BARBARA. HOPING I AM SOON WITH YOU
> ONCE MORE.
> I AM YOUR LOVING HUSBAND
> LENY

But just two days after Atkins sent his hopeful letter, another instance of friendly fire occurred. Far away, in Stanley Civilian Internment camp in Hong Kong, Bungalow 'C' was one of the buildings that housed the internees. Twice during the fighting for the Colony, the invading Japanese and the defending Garrison had fought over it to the death, and now a bomb dropped by a United States Navy aircraft aiming for a Japanese lighter off shore made a direct hit. The resulting explosion killed fourteen civilian prisoners.[233]

Amazingly, news of this accident reached the POWs in Japan on the 24th. Weedon: "Nasty story of bombing of internment camp at H.K., several British men and women killed."

In Japan, as Allied forces closed in, the POWs were also being bombed. Poulter: "On February 1st, we had another Air Raid Alarm. This reminds me of the *Lisbon Maru*, the doors are shut and bolted, the iron shutters outside the windows are shut and the lights are out. This sort of gives one the feeling of being trapped and in fact it is very wearing on the nerves."

*   *   *

Wright: "We were cheered by the news from the Pacific, although the initial Jap versions were designed to discourage us. They claimed to have shot up many American planes over Taiwan, and to have sunk twenty aircraft carriers and five battleships in a big naval engagement. They then admitted heavy casualties and damage to ground installations. Still claiming that Taiwan had been a victory, they announced the loss of four rear admirals and hinted that all was not well around Taiwan. I concluded that they had received a severe mauling."

Everyone knew that the two wars, in Europe and the Far East, were coming to an end. Some families evacuated to Australia, decided to return to the UK. No one considered the German U-Boat menace serious any more. Times had changed.

Ron Brooks: "We sailed from Sydney in March 1945 on the MV *Stirling Castle*, formerly of the Union Castle line on the South Africa run from the UK. There were many troops on board and other families like us. It was a great adventure for Geoff and myself. The voyage took a long while; I seem to remember six weeks but I can't be sure when we left Sydney.

The ship went first to Wellington where it docked for three days. The children were taken in army trucks to a picnic site and plied with ice cream. The ship took a southerly route across the South Pacific to the Panama Canal to avoid Japanese submarines. From Panama to Bermuda where we waited to join up with a convoy for the journey across the Atlantic. We docked in Liverpool on 11th May 1945. There were many memorable incidents. The engine of the ship broke down. It was becalmed for several days in the South Pacific rolling in a long oily swell whilst the engineers ominously banged away down below. A mother, who shared a cabin close to ours with her son (about my age), died. There was a burial at sea. The coffin slid out from under a Union Jack and plunged into the ocean. A soldier volunteered to share the cabin with the boy who was now on his own. The broadcast [announcing VE Day] was put out over the ships Tannoy and there was much celebrating.

I have never understood why my mother didn't go straight to her family in Ireland.[234] It was a land of relative plenty; no food-rationing etc. Instead we went to Dover, very much knocked about in the war and stayed at first in a small terrace house with my Grandfather who I remember as a very strict gentleman, used to living by himself. This was not at all suited to two young tearaways who hadn't been at school for a couple of months. We were introduced to 'ITMA' on his radio. We arrived in time for the street party to celebrate the end of the war in Europe. However, my main memory was how dull, grey and worn out everything and everyone seemed to be. I don't think we lived very long with my Grandfather. My mother bought a house (I think they were very cheap in Dover at that time) at Crabble Hill, on the busy main road from Canterbury into Dover."

For those still alive in the camps, American air raids on Japan were a new threat that increased as the war wore on.

Wright in Kobe, on 17 March 1945: "They poured thousands of incendiaries on to the city and followed with 500 pound oil bombs. To the noise of the hellish baptism was added the clamour of guns as Kobe's defenders opened fire on their enemies ... I risked a look from the window and saw a scene that awed me. Flares lingered over the city, and countless drums of incendiaries were pouring from the skies on to a town that was already in flames. Wherever I looked, there were fires, and the H.E. bombs were adding to the devastation."[235]

Poulter described the same raid: "St Patrick's Day, March 17th and about 1.50 am the general alarm sounded and then the local alarm and we could hear the sound of planes overhead. Without any orders from the Japs every man got up and packed his kit ready to go. All this took place in the dark, but as we use most of our clothes as a pillow there was very little confusion. We lay on our bed spaces chatting and all this time we were in the dark. Round about 4 am we noticed a red glow through the cracks in the shutters, this could only mean that the fires were quite near us.

Over the PA system came the order: 'Outside everybody and take all you can carry'. We trooped out and as we went I noticed that the Navy HQ was well alight, some cad has dropped an oil bomb on it! Later I learned that they had scored a direct hit on the gun.

We showed the Japs what control really meant. We marched to our Air raid Shelter, formed up in sections, and then sat down quietly waiting. I noticed that we were completely ringed with fire, but fortunately for us the wind was in our favour. The raid finished at 6 am, but we were kept in our shelter till noon. At times it was impossible to see the sun for smoke and when you did see it, it was like the red ball that they use on their flag, or as we call it the 'Poached Egg'.

Several Jap families came on to the field and they looked as though they had had a rough time. I took a chance and spoke to one of the civilians, he glanced around furtively, gave me a cigarette and said 'korewa pikki' which means, 'this is no good!' I agreed with him, I couldn't see any thing funny in it."

Miller in Osaka: "There came the day when we heard the sound of lots of aeroplane engines droning overhead. We could not tell whose, they could have been Japanese. Shortly afterwards we heard the thump of bombs in the dock area and planes over Osaka. We were overjoyed and boy, did we let the Japs know it, we now knew that the Japs were losing the war. We were confined to the camp for a week and were not prepared for the sight that beheld us, when we were eventually allowed out to work. Everywhere was devastation, the city was flattened and this was after only one air raid. The docks were in ruins with warehouses gutted and rubble everywhere. It was decided that the prisoners would start cleaning up the warehouse rubble … We did not see any heavy bombing of Osaka after this; it was not needed, that was our reasoning. Everywhere was devastation and ruin. The population of Osaka were in complete shock, but their morale was still high. Shipping was almost at a standstill, no longer were we being detailed to work on the docks or ships. The various factories now got our labour. Time was passing very slowly, work seemed to be taking its toll of our health and food rations were cut. It was well into 1944 when word came through that a squad of 40 men would be shifted to another camp called 'Notogawa', and I would be in that squad."

Hamilton recalled: "Sometimes a trick would recoil on us. It became the practice after raids by B29s for the man numbered 29 on roll call to shout out his number in a particularly triumphant voice. They got away with this for some time before the Japanese noticed."

Jack Etiemble experienced that recoil himself: "When in the camp, after the first couple of air raids we noted that at each roll call, the person who was no. 29 was being taken outside and being given a beating. On asking why we were told, Americans bomb with B29, if your number is 29 you get beaten. Can you imagine the jockeying for numbers that took place on subsequent roll calls!"

For the last time, POWs were allowed to broadcast messages home via radio.

Cas/108/570   Infantry Record Office,
                                Stanwell Road School,
                                    ASHFORD,
Middlesex.
                                    13th June, 1945.
Mrs. M. E. Atkins,
School Road,
FINSTOCK,
Nr. Charlebury, Oxon.

Madam,

   I am directed to inform you that the following item relating to a Prisoner of War was included in a broadcast from Tokyo on 19th May, 1945 which was apparently sent by No. 6213420 Private Samuel Arthur ATKINS, The Middlesex Regiment.

Message: "My dearest —— Have received cards from you and mother. I am well as can be expected, and hope that all is well at home. Remember me to everyone, especially the ————. Your loving husband, Sam."

   You are asked not to mention this broadcast report when corresponding with the Soldier.

   I am,
      Madam,
         Your obedient servant.

The feeling that the end was just round the corner was palpable. Most men were simply frustrated with the delay, though others were still dying.

Poulter: "Pte. Andrews of the Middlesex Regiment died on the night of 30/31st of July. He appears to have died quietly in his sleep and his was the third death since we came here.[236] After his body was cremated, I took his ashes and kept them."

Weedon, on 5 August: "This period is proving easily the worst we've had as POWs, at any rate mentally. We're so near and yet so far, and everyone is desperately impatient."

But unknown to the POWs, the 'old war' of tanks, battleships, and aircraft like the B29, and the 'new war' represented by nuclear weapons, were to meet at the island of Tinian in August 1945. From that dot in the Pacific Ocean, the B29s took the nuclear bombs to Hiroshima and Nagasaki. Suddenly the war was quickly racing to an unforeseen end. However, for many, it was far too late.

R.A. (C.A. & S.L.) & C.M.P. Records — 10 August 1945

Dear Madam,

<u>1410996 W.O.I. Brooks C.F.</u>

It is with the deepest regret that I enclose the notification of the death of your husband.

There is little that I can say to comfort you in your bereavement, but I would like to convey to you a personal expression of sympathy in the sad loss that you have sustained.

Yours faithfully

Army Form B. 104-82A. — 10 August 1945

Madam,

It is my painful duty to inform you that, no further news having been received relative to (No.) <u>1410996</u> (Rank) <u>W.O.I.</u> (Name) <u>Charles Frederick BROOKS</u> (Regiment) <u>Royal Artillery</u> who has been missing since <u>1/2 October 1942.</u> (or since).

I am to express the sympathy and regret of the Army Council at the soldier's death in his Country's service.

I am,
Madam,
Your obedient Servant

NOTE

If Death Certificates are required for Life Insurance and similar purposes, application should be made to the following address:- "The Under-Secretary of State, War Office (Effects), Bluecoat School, Wavertree, Liverpool, 15."

If any articles of private property left by the deceased are found, they will be forwarded to the Officer in Charge of Records, but some time will probably elapse before their receipt, and when received they will be disposed of when authority is received from the Effects Branch, who will also communicate with you in due course concerning any amount that may be found to be due to the late soldier's estate.

Some delay in these matters is inevitable, particularly where death occurs abroad.

Royal Artillery Association — 22 August 1945

Dear Madam,

The committee of the Royal Artillery Association have learned with much regret of the death of your husband and I am asked to convey to you their very deep sympathy in your loss.

Should you be in need of some temporary assistance now or at any time in the future, please let me know and I will arrange for representative to interview you.

In the meantime, if I can help or advise in any way, perhaps you will kindly write to me, otherwise please do not trouble to answer this letter.

Yours truly[237]

On 11 August 1945, just two days after Nagasaki was hit by a Plutonium bomb — the cruel and unnecessary destruction that followed the reasoned and vital reduction of Hiroshima — Battery Sergeant Major Thomas William George Banham, 12 Coastal Regiment, Royal Artillery, died. Buried in Yokohama now, he was the last of the *Lisbon Maru* survivors to be lost before Japan's surrender. His cause of death is unrecorded; the records of the Commonwealth War Graves Commission do not even list his next of kin.

15 Liberation

In the camps, the situation was rapidly becoming chaotic. Ross Lynneberg was one of those sent to another POW camp, Notogawa, after the bombing of Osaka. "Then while out working near the camp one day a B29 went over and later we heard an explosion and saw a column of smoke rise skyward with a large mushroom top.[238] I thought good work, for it seemed as if the bomber must have hit an ammunition factory and this gave us another three days in camp before returning to work. One afternoon on our return to camp from a working party there was a strange Jap officer asking if anyone knew anything about radiation poisoning — we had never heard of it."

Wright was working in the Minatagawa goods yard when he and his fellow prisoners were herded into their hut and locked in. They looked out of a small window and saw: "The coolies were bowing low over their radios, the office girls were weeping and wailing. The whole city was silent, listening to the news."

The Japanese people were listening, for the first time, to the voice of their Emperor. It was noon on 15 August 1945: "… But now the war has lasted four years. Despite the best that has been done by everyone — the gallant fighting of the military and naval forces, the diligence and assiduity of Our servants of the States, and the devoted service of Our one hundred million people — the war situation has developed not necessarily to Japan's advantage, while the general trends of the world have all turned against her interest."

James Miller was also at Notogawa: "Rumours started circulating from an unknown source, that all prisoners were to be killed in the event of an invasion on Japan. We believed these rumours to be true[239] and vowed that none of us would give up life cheaply. We had suffered too much, what with degradation, slavery, starvation, disease and the threat that any day could be our last. I do not think that any civilised person could believe, just how sadistic, inhuman and utterly bestial the Japanese military were. We started hiding anything that could be used as a weapon. One morning in late August 1945, we woke up to find that there were no guards in the camp, the Japs quarters were deserted. We were unsure what was happening, so we just took it as a normal day. Later on that day, as some of us were standing, talking, outside the camp gate, we noticed a figure coming up the road. It looked like a soldier, but not a Jap soldier, but who? As he approached us, he was heard to say: 'Is this Notogawa, prisoner of war camp?' We answered, yes it is, but who are you? 'I am an Australian Officer, who has been given the task of evacuating you to Kobe. The war is over.' We could not believe him at first."

Hamilton: "Gradually and cautiously, for we were still in the middle of a hostile people, we took control of the camp. Everything we asked for was granted. No work, increased rations. So we asked for the keys of the food store, the clothing store and the hut containing the Red Cross parcels and medicine, and they were handed over. There were all the medicines which could have saved so many lives."

Like all the men in the remote camps, Lynneberg wanted to be back in a major centre like Osaka or Kobe or Yokohama where an early evacuation might be possible. "News was now circulating in the camp that we would be moving out in a few days, so coupled with the knowledge that travel was to be restricted next day to visits to Kyoto and Notogawa, another lad and myself loaded up a couple of bags with food and at 11 pm went down to the station where we had to wait just on six hours for a train we could board. Several trains passed through without stopping — others that stopped were crowded with demobilized soldiers and civilians returning to their homes in the cities. Eventually we boarded a train and reached Osaka and took a tram to the area where our camp had been. Unfortunately the tram could not go the full distance so when we alighted we were lost due to the fact that all the familiar buildings were just rubble strewn across side streets hiding them completely. We finally found the remains of our camp surrounded by water and razed to the ground. From here we went in search of one of the few buildings left standing in which those of our original camp lads not moved inland were living.

After our being sent to the lake area Osaka was raided many times — on those occasions heavy explosive bombs were used to destroy the few buildings which had withstood the fire raids some months earlier. While visiting our old camp we and many visitors were rounded up by our own people and told that there was a general order that all prisoners of war to return to their camps by 10 am next day or they would be arrested and court martialled so that night my companion and I left for Notogawa. There was a little excitement locating the right train for our return journey because the first part was by electric and the last section with steam engine. It was during this last leg that I fell asleep waking sometime later to see the station name in Japanese as well as English (most names having been painted out). This really woke me for we were many stations past where we were to alight and the train was so crowded that by the time we reached the exit the train was in motion and we had to jump.

We were now faced with how we were to get home and where to sleep and get food for the night. I then remembered there was a prison camp near this station so we were able to locate it, stay the night, returning to our own camp just on 10 o'clock to find it in an uproar as we were to leave that day for the station, and then on to Yokohama where we'd pick up air transport and fly to Manila."

But for the Atkins family, liberation was to bring an emotional rollercoaster ride. First came the news they had been waiting to hear for nearly four years. Sam was alive and well, free and coming home:

Early Sept 1945?

From Sir Edward Wilshaw, K.C.M.G.
Chairman[240]

    Electra House
        Victoria Embankment
            LONDON W.C.2

Dear Sir or Madam,
    It is a great pleasure to me to be able to send you the enclosed copy of a telegram from your relative who is now liberated from the Japanese

    In order to relieve your anxiety at the earliest possible moment this message had been transmitted free of charge by Cable and Wireless Ltd. From the Far East, and by the Post Office, in co-operation with the War Office.

In the same way we shall be happy to send your reply free, if you will write it – using about 12 words in addition to the address – on the enclosed form and hand it in at your local Cable and Wireless Office or any Post Office where telegrams are normally accepted.

Will you please insert on the reply-paid form the address given in the enclosed telegram and sign it with your surname.

With best wishes
I remain,
Yours sincerely

Chairman

P&M   MRS M E ATKINS 135 DERINGTON RD
TOOTING S W 17 SAFE ALLIED HANDS, HOPE TO BE HOME SOON, WRITING. ADDRESS LETTERS AND TELEGRAMS TO:- LIBERATED P.O.W. C/O AUSTRALIAN ARMY BASE POST OFFICE MELBOURNE AUSTRALIA. S ATKINS

But then, almost immediately, that assurance was taken from them. They had no idea how sick Sam was. CQMS Poulter had noted in his diary, at Nomachi soon after the Japanese surrender: "Pte. Atkins left here for Tokyo by air, he should do, and he is just a bundle of bones and certainly would not last a long journey." Sam was dying:

Tel. No.- MAYfair 9400, Ext.
    Any further communication on
this subject should be addressed
to:-
The Under-Secretary of State,
    The War Office
    (as opposite)
and the following number quoted.
49894 (Cas./P.W.).
Your Reference _____

THE WAR OFFICE
(Cas. PW),
Curzon Street House,
    Curzon Street,
    LONDON, W.1.

14 September, 1945

Madam,

    I am directed to inform you with regret, that an official report has been received to the effect that No. 6213420, Private S.A. Atkins, Middlesex Regiment, who has been released from Japanese hands, is at present on board a hospital ship in the Far East, suffering from chronic amoebic dysentery and beri-beri and has been placed on the seriously ill list.

    The Department has cabled to the appropriate authorities for reports to be rendered on your husband's condition and you are assured that you will be kept informed of all further reports which are received.

    I am to convey to you the sincere sympathy of the Department in the anxiety and distress which this news must inevitably cause, especially in view of Private Atkin's release from captivity.

            I am Madam.
                Your obedient Servant

Mrs. M.E. Atkins,
    School Road,
        Finstock,
            Charlesbury, Oxfordshire.

Then, just four days later, the authorities delivered fresh news.[241] Sam was getting better:

Tel. No.- MAYfair 9400, Ext.
 Any further communication on
on this subject should be
addressed to:-
The Under-Secretary of State,
 The War Office
 (as opposite)
and the following number quoted.
49894 (Cas./P.W.).

THE WAR OFFICE
Cas./P.W.,
Curzon Street House,
Curzon Street,
LONDON, W.1.

18 September, 1945

Madam,

 With reference to War Office letter of 14th September, 1945, I am directed to inform you that a further report has been received in the Department which states that your husband's condition shows a slight improvement.

 I am, Madam,
  Your obedient Servant

The belated official notification of Sam's release from POW camp, finally received a week later, must have added almost comic relief:

Telephone; MAYFAIR 9400
Your Ref._____
W.O. Ref. SS/330/120/216
 (Cas.P.W.)

THE WAR OFFICE
CURZON STREET HOUSE
CURZON STREET,
LONDON, W.1.

25.9.45

Madam,
 I am directed to inform you with pleasure that official information has been received that your   HUSBAND
 6213420 PTE S.A. ATKINS, THE MIDDLESEX
 REGIMENT
previously a prisoner of war in Japanese hands, has been recovered and is now with the Allied Forces.

 The repatriation of recovered prisoners of war is being given highest priority, but it will be appreciated that some time must elapse before they reach the United Kingdom. Information of a general character regarding those recovered prisoners, including their movements before they reach home, will be given from time to time on the wireless and will be published in the press.

    I am, Madam,
       Your obedient Servant

But no one could relax. Just two days after this letter — and many others like it — was sent stating that the POWs were safe, a story of a new tragedy started to break.

Alf 'Nobby' Hunt sets the scene with his account of the airlift to Okinawa: "About ten days after the war finished (the guards had previously left) the camp was bombarded by B29s dropping supplies in 40 gallon drums, many of which came adrift from their parachutes. It was more dangerous than the actual bombing. We estimated that there were enough supplies for about five thousand men and there were only about eight hundred in the camp.[242]

We went by train to Yokohama and then flew down to Okinawa and went into tents. One night we caught the tail end of a typhoon and it carried most of the tents away."

Jack Etiemble travelled with Alf Hunt: "About three weeks after the war had ended some Americans came down from Yokohama to arrange for our repatriation, these included a female press reporter, who took lots of snaps and was amazed at our living conditions (bear in mind our camp had been destroyed by bombing). Once again we had lost everything and we were living in what I imagine was the top section of what had been a grain store. It was so low in most of the area that even I at 5' 6 could not stand upright. We were sent by train to Yokohama, got deloused and reclothed, then most of us flew to Okinawa in B24s."

From Okinawa, the next stage was a second flight, heading further south to Nielson Field, Manila.

Significantly, Alf Hunt noted: "I did hear rumours about men being lost on the way home but nothing definite", and Etiemble recalled: "a bit scary sitting on the bomb doors! I believe on one of the planes the bomb doors opened and 22 POWs fell to their deaths."[243]

The stories were true. More tragedy had come, in the shape of a plane crash whilst the USAAF was flying men back from POW camps to Allied soil. Twelve men who had survived the fighting in Hong Kong, followed by three years and eight months of starvation in Japanese POW camps (and in nine cases, the *Lisbon Maru* as well), were lost.

From the *Lisbon Maru*:
    John Clarke, Royal Artillery
    James Clapperton, Royal Scots
    Sidney Fred Gilham, Middlesex Regiment
    Gerald Gollege, HKSRA[244]
    Desmond Harrington, Hong Kong Signals Company
    William Richard James, Royal Artillery
    Thomas Patrick King, Middlesex Regiment
    Ernest Arthur Pargeter, Middlesex Regiment
    Charles Henry Price, Hong Kong Signals Company

From other Hong Kong transportations:
    Sydney Francis Bates, Royal Artillery
    John Burke, Middlesex Regiment
    William Doxford, Hong Kong Volunteer Defence Corps

Wright, a close friend of two of those on board, remembered it well: "We were roused at dawn, and I remembered another dawn — the one we had awakened to when we embarked on the *Lisbon Maru*. There was some confusion in the darkness. The Americans did not single us out in sections or in groups. All we were required to do was line up in two rows and march to the planes. Pat King, Viner, Shore, Pope, and I, remained together as we jostled and bustled together. After quite some time we marched to the waiting aircraft, carrying rather more kit than usual. It was so dark that we could barely see the silhouettes of the machines.

Twenty men were allotted to each plane, and the Americans were naturally not concerned about who made up the different parties, which explains why Pat King and Bill Pope became separated from the rest of us. Viner, Shore and I took the first plane, while Pat King and Pope were in the next one."

It was an uncomfortable journey, and Wright landed in Manila at four o'clock that afternoon. While waiting in a train, they, like Alf Hunt, heard a rumour that two of the planes had crashed.

Wright: "We knew then that we had lost our two friends, and the timing and circumstances of their death appealed to us as being particularly bitter and ironic. Fate could not have been more cruel. How could it be that these two boys who had survived so much, sustained by the thought of release and home, should perish now, in the very hour of their victory and while on their way to their loved ones? To have won through by such high courage, such determination and such endurance, and then to die where none of these qualities were of the least avail, that seemed to us to be a very bitter thing."

Taffy Evans recalled the incident very clearly, which was hardly surprising as he was one of those who parachuted from the plane, B-24J #44-40666, "Les Miserables", as it crashed into the sea that day fifty miles south west of Taiwan:[245] "In Japan we were issued chest chutes, told to put them on, then boarded the plane. Some time later, the plane took off. Suddenly we were told that we would have to (as he put it) ditch the plane, so get ready to jump."

The *South China Morning Post*[246] for Thursday 27 September 1945 carried a front-page story under the headline 'AIR DISASTER'. It went on to tell how on 15 September[247] twelve American Consolidated B24 Liberators were transporting POWs from Okinawa to Manila when, east of Taiwan, one of them had a mechanical failure and had to ditch in the ocean. The crew issued parachutes and told the POWs to jump, but the POWs were in no condition to follow the instructions. The first man to jump failed to pull the ripcord, and some of those who followed opened their parachutes in the plane itself.

By pure luck the destroyer *Ursa* was in the sea below the aircraft. Acting as an escort on an aircraft carrier, she had been forced off course by a typhoon. While the other Liberators circled round, the *Ursa* picked up all the survivors. She managed to rescue eight[248] of the twenty passengers and the Liberator's crew. She then took these survivors to Taiwan where they were taken aboard the *Maunganui*[249] which had arrived from Hong Kong.[250]

*   *   *

For the majority of men, the initial repatriation was anything but tragic. Most remembered the treatment given to them by Americans and Canadians as the kindest they ever received.

Jack Etiemble: "On to Manila by B24s. Eventually embarked on the

Admiral Hughes manned by the U.S. Coastguards. Headed for San Francisco, then as we had some Canadian ex POWs on board the destination changed to Vancouver. We recuperated there for about a month, then by train right across Canada. They even stopped the train at Banff for one hour so that we could take in the beautiful scenery. Down on the Prairie they stopped the train again as a train was coming the other way with Canadian Soldiers returning from U.K. They wanted us to be aware of what to expect in U.K after all the bombing."

Alf Hunt: "At Manila, we boarded the American transport, *Joseph T. Dickman* (APA 13) and went to Pearl Harbour and then on to San Francisco. There we were on an island quite close to Alcatraz. One could see the convicts walking around. From there we went by train on the Santa Fe route via Phoenix Arizona up to New York, but there was a dock strike on there and we carried on up to Halifax in Nova Scotia and then to Southampton on the Queen Elizabeth, the last trip she did as a trooper, arriving home after seven years in the Far East, on bonfire night."

Poulter travelled down to Manila in a series of vessels, the American Hospital ship *Rescue*, the USS *Gosselin*, HMAS *Warramunga*, USS *Monitor*, and finally the USS *Oconto*: " 'Pug' Barron and myself decided to go into Manila to have a look round. We got to the gate and two Military Policemen stopped us and told us that we could not go. We stood and argued with them for a while when two officers in a jeep came along. They stopped and asked us what was the matter and we explained that we were two 'Limeys' on our way home from Japan, and that we would like to look at Manila. That put a different complexion on the matter. The two MPs said, 'why the heck didn't you tell us that?' the two officers gave us a lift into Manila. It's really embarrassing when these Yanks find out that you have been a prisoner of the Japs, they just cannot do enough for you."

Miller also travelled from Yokohama to Manila by ship, the USS *Goodhue*.[251] Sailing across the Pacific on the same vessel, he landed at Victoria, British Columbia: "The transit camp was well organised and the food and medical attention was first class. We were allowed out of the camp to visit the city of Victoria and to mingle with the population. The Canadian people took us to heart; we were invited to that many parties and to the local pubs. There was one glaring weakness to this round of pleasures. We had not many thoughts about it until it struck home; we had no money with which to pay for our share of the festivities. This fact was made known to the Officer-in-Charge of the camp, who arranged for an advance payment to all prisoners. Guess what, we all received C$5 (five dollars) what an insult! What could we do with that amount, we protested, but our protests fell on deaf ears. After three days, the first batch to leave for home was announced. We were to cross over to Vancouver by ferry and pick up the train, which was to take us all the way across Canada to the port of Halifax by 'Canadian Pacific Railway', at last we were on the way home. The train was fitted out with sleeping berths and we got into them immediately we boarded the train. You must remember, we tired very easily and we were still not strong enough to exert ourselves. Halifax was a long, tiring journey, by train from Vancouver. At every whistle-stop, hordes of Canadians boarded the train to feed us and bring us fresh fruit, cigarettes, chocolate, and the usual cup of hot tea. As usual, the hospitality and kindness was staggering."

Poulter was with the first men to arrive at Vancouver: "I landed with the first party and was promptly collared by a lady reporter, a smashing piece of work! She got on the train with me and we sat chatting, she was so interested that she only just managed to get off the train before we really got moving. Her main interest was in the two white boxes that I was carrying. When she heard that they contained the ashes of two men of my regiment, she wanted to know the why, where and how."[252]

Eventually arriving at the end of the line on the east coast, it was time for the final leg of the journey. Etiemble: "Finally got on board the *Ile de France* heading back to U.K. Believe it or not, first meal on board, *rice*. A delegation went to the Skipper and told him what to do with the rice; he explained he was doing what the British Government had ordered. He was told (very politely) if he put rice on again he would be thrown overboard. Arrived in Southampton, good reception; dockers on strike. Good old UK."

The Canadians and Americans had treated the returning POWs as royalty, and the former had accepted them into their families. Now that they were back in British hands, the survivors found the restrictions and pettiness[253] hard to accept. One wag scrawled on a bulkhead: "Hong Kong POWs: Captured by the Japanese, December 1941. Liberated by the Americans, September 1945. Recaptured by the British, October 1945."

And so, on that dull note, it ended. After eighteen days of pitched battle in Hong Kong, nine months of captivity there, eight days on the *Lisbon Maru*, the sinking, and two years and ten months as POWs in Japan, the fortunate few were finally home.

Fourteen thousand men and women had defended Hong Kong from Japanese attack. Some 1,560 of them died in the battle, and the remainder (minus a few escapees and evaders) became POWs. One thousand, eight hundred and thirty-four of them had boarded the *Lisbon Maru*, and the remaining 761 of these were free at last.[254]

Some just felt lucky to be alive. Atkins, now largely recovered from his chronic amoebic dysentery and beri-beri:

Telegram
CABLE AND WIRELESS 5 OCT 1945
   WZB329G   AUK   4
PWM MRS M E ATKINS C/O/ 135 DERINGTON RD
   TOOTING LN

ARRIVED SAFELY NEW ZEALAND BEING WELL CARED
FOR ADDRESS LETTERS TELEGRAMS TO EXPOW
CARE CPO AUCKLANDNZ =
   LENY ATKINS

Some saw opportunities. New Zealander Lynneberg had hoped to fly home from Yokohama, but had instead been put on a troopship that took him to Manila: "After a day at anchor we were sent ashore to a camp specially prepared for us with further kitting out and another medical examination before being drafted to the HMS *Implacable* — sister ship to the HMS *Indefatigable*. We then headed for Vancouver, then overland to the Atlantic and on to the UK.

On this draft were two other NZ lads who didn't want to go to the UK. I told them the chance for a trip like this was a once in a life time opportunity so they joined the draft but became homesick before reaching Pearl Harbour where they went ashore and rang their parents saying they were being sent to UK against their wishes. Wellington Navy Office must have been made aware of these NZ ratings going in the wrong direction with the result all NZ ratings had to report their presence. The outcome was these two lads were given a good telling off — while to me they apologised for having to send me back saying no New Zealanders were to go to the UK as there was no transport to return them to NZ — we would therefore stay on board and work our return passage to Sydney. As it turned out I had to do watchkeeping in a wireless telegraph (w/t) office while they travelled like tourists and I was messed with the w/t ratings being allocated a berth in a mess backing on to the anchor chain flat at the forward part of the vessel. On this occasion we were experiencing very rough conditions, no one being allowed on the flight deck which was 65 feet above sea level, for the waves were breaking on the deck and rolling along and over the rear end. That night when I slung my hammock, I asked the only other occupant where the rest of the mess were and he replied that when they had a rough sea like that on a previous occasion the bulkhead had collapsed and a couple of the boys were drowned by the in-rushing seas."

Lynneberg eventually returned home, via Canada, Hawaii, Japan, Hong Kong, Indonesia, Manila, Borneo, and Australia.

He was one of the lucky ones. Going home was one thing; adjusting was another.

Let a son and a daughter explain.

*   *   *

Son Gareth: "My father Henry Llewellyn-Williams was a Lance Corporal in the Royal Marines (HMS *Tamar*). He was twenty-nine years old in October 1942. He rarely spoke of his experiences on the *Lisbon Maru* and as a prisoner of war in Osaka. After the war he spent six months in a rehabilitation camp near Vancouver BC. When he returned to the UK he lived with his parents at Aberdare and he was still so traumatised that for the next two years or so he would only venture out at night. He couldn't cope even with living in the house so he made a den for himself in the garden shed.

Eventually his father persuaded him to write everything down and bought him an old typewriter. Shortly after he finished his account, he burned it. According to my grandfather (who never read it himself) my father did not want anyone else to have to live through what he had, even second-hand."

*   *   *

Daughter Hilary:[255]

MY FATHER SWIMMING

1

In the cold sea his body
slid like a warm knife,
softened the water's slab
coming up buttery
and sleek, with the green
tumbling and rolling off his skin.

His arms flung out to grasp
one handful then another
of solid swell, held all
in a broad embrace
face buried in the foam
blinded with salt. He loved
the pressure of its tongue,
a pearl flicker running over him

like light. And lifting
his head broke the air
into splinters that spun and shone:
sky and land one swinging bright
transparency. No sound
but the red drum of his heart –
all senses drowned
save touch: the sun's hand
smoothing his back and the surface
of the sea. He'd forgotten me

but I was there too, perched
in the rocks stacked like houses
or smoothskinned animals
flushed with heat, sparked with mica;
glad to be high and dry and watching him.

They called it *The Tank*:
this scoop in the cove
granite walled, where the sea funnelled
and boomed, then lingered

pushing at rafts of weed.
Beyond, the Atlantic roared
and fell on the land.
Down here the currents
spread their webbed fingers, tugged
their nets. He felt the cords
loosen, and kicked free.

2

My father's affair with the sea
almost broke my mother:
always dragging us to some shore or other
some windswept headland
our faces whipped with spray.
His eyes the same blue-grey, the same distance.

Twenty years before, in the war –
a ship of prisoners, torpedoed
blew apart, spilled its guts, oil,
dying men, their captors.
My father swam all day
all night. His life fell away
with the ship, left him clean
of past and future, just a swimming creature
lost in the vast glitter,
the ocean's mirror
hung in deep space, swaying.

The friend he tried to save
stopped moving, became dead
weight, and slipped down.
My father would not drown,
the sea loved him.
He lay back, and rocked
like flotsam, cradled in brine.
Swimming to live, floating
an imprint on his cells
that one day would be mine.

At dawn he reached an island.
Fishermen hauled him in
gently, and turned him over.

This was his great adventure.
He never spoke of the captivity
that ground him to a shell:
a five stone man, still walking,
still believing that the sea saved him
for coming home somehow.

3

He never taught us to swim.
We taught ourselves, after school
in the public pool
floundering around the shallow end.
The water seared my eyes
with chlorine stink, I disliked it,
the yammering din, the big kids
shoving, barrelling in.

The sea was wild. It swept
my feet from under me, it thundered
over my head, filling my mouth with iron
the taste of blood; it slammed
against me with the weight of the whole world.

But to reach down with my feet
into a void: that was fear
of a different order, feeling death
close over me. So I watched my father
swimming with held breath,
his body blurred
to a paperweight feather
in a sea solid as glass;
until he rose, expanding
toward the surface, smashed through it,
took flesh again, and laughed.

It was the land that killed him.
The long, dry years
grew dense inside him
to an end that was ordinary –
landlocked, and slow.
The tide inched back and left
nothing but a shell, a carapace.

> That shrunken face
> in the coffin was not him:
>
> he was off somewhere, away
> swimming perhaps, with long
> and easy strokes, carried
> out to a shoreless space
> where I cannot follow.

But a handful of men knew they could never adjust, and never went home at all. For these few men, the events had been too traumatizing. At the last minute, they discovered that after these experiences they could not face their families again.

* * *

These lost men survived, but could never go home; the damage to their families was just as great as it would be to those whose loved ones had been killed.[256]

16 Reunion

> This gallant which thou seest
> Was in the wreck, and but he's something stained
> With grief – that's beauty's canker – thou mighst call him
> A goodly person. He hath lost his fellows,
> And strays about to find 'em.
>
> *The Tempest*, Act 1 Scene 2

And now another American submarine, the *Bullhead*, steams into our story. She made her first patrol in the South China Sea from the latter part of March to the end of April 1945. She failed to make any enemy contacts, but on 31 March and again on 24 April *Bullhead* bombarded Pratas Island with her five-inch gun. She also rescued three airmen from a downed Boeing B-29 SuperFortress following an air strike on the China coast. In May and June 1945 *Bullhead* patrolled the Gulf of Siam and the South China Sea during her second patrol. Here she sank four small vessels, and damaged three more, all in gun actions.

What relevance does *Bullhead* have to the story of the *Lisbon Maru*? It is Holt. We last saw Lieutenant Edward R. Holt junior on the *Grouper* as torpedo officer on the day the submarine torpedoed the *Lisbon Maru*, but he had fought a long war.

In 1945, as a Lieutenant Commander, the United States Navy transferred him to Australia where he took command of USS *Bullhead*. Departing Fremantle for her third war patrol, *Bullhead*, with Holt as her captain, steamed for her assigned area on 31 July 1945. She was to patrol in the Java Sea. Two more American submarines, *Capitaine* and *Puffer*, were also to patrol the area, as were the British submarines *Taciturn* and *Thorough*. *Bullhead* arrived in position in the Java Sea on 6 August, with *Capitaine* following. On 12 August, *Capitaine* ordered *Bullhead* to take position the following day with her and *Puffer*. There was no reply. After waiting three days, *Capitaine* reported that she had been unable to contact *Bullhead* since arriving in the area. *Bullhead*, the last American submarine of the war to be lost with all hands — eighty-four officers and men in all — was gone.[257]

In time, *Bullhead's* loss would lead to a very unusual meeting.

*   *   *

For the POWs, liberation had been a shock, but there had never been any hatred of the Americans based on the fact that it was an American submarine that had sunk the *Lisbon Maru*. On the contrary, most men were very pleased to see that the Allies were striking back one way or another.

"On one thing everyone is agreed", Hamilton had said. "The submarine commander who sent the torpedo into the ship and sank it was simply doing his duty. As far as he knew, and as far as the Japs allowed him to know, the vessel was a troop carrier. It was armed fore and aft, and there were no visible markings to show that it was carrying prisoners of war. The American Navy was fully justified in sinking it."

But the survivors now faced the challenge of rebuilding their lives, and for some it was almost too much to ask. Some of the youngest men had no adult experience other than surviving the camps. When they had finally achieved that aim, they had nothing to replace it with.

None found the home-coming easy, and most suffered from ill health all their lives, but the majority coped one way or another. There was little choice; while there was tacit understanding that their fathers' war — the Great War — had led to a rash of suicides and mental disorders, Post Traumatic Stress Disorder had not yet been recognized. Many returning American submariners also found readjustment a challenge, some refusing to talk about their war years.[258]

But one of those returning submariners — Garfield Kvalheim, and one of the ex-POWs — Jack Etiemble, would eventually come together and share their experiences.

Jack Etiemble, one of the few survivors from the Royal Artillery in the *Lisbon Maru's* third hold, continued his Army service when he returned to the UK. Soon the Army posted him to Dover where he met his wife-to-be Ruth.

"Early in 1946 my Regiment was moved to Dover Castle, and one morning I had to speak to the NAAFI Manageress and while I was waiting to see her, a lovely looking girl walked by, we eyed each other but apart from saying hello nothing else was said. After that, I used to spend my spare time in the canteen, but I was too nervous to make the first approach. A while later the Regiment held a dance in the Gymnasium, I was stood at the bar having a drink with my mate when the band announced a Ladies excuse me dance. Ruth then came and asked me to dance and I refused, I got an icy glare and she left. My mate then said: 'You are mad, you have been wanting to get to know her, and when she made the first move you refused instead of telling her that you couldn't dance.' He told her the next day, and luckily I was forgiven. I apologised, and then we started going out together until we were married."

They were married on 19 December 1946, five years to the day since the heaviest fighting had taken place on the Hong Kong battlefields. After almost ten years in the UK, Jack's next posting was to, of all places, Japan.

"My feelings about going to Japan again were rather mixed. Firstly, I did not like the idea of leaving my family but at the same time — as fighting was still taking place in North Korea and I did not want to be branded a coward — I decided to go. I was posted to J.R.B.D.[259] Hiro just outside Kure. On arrival I was shown where my bunk was, picked up my kitbag and walked in. An elderly Japanese lady was sweeping the floor, she muttered something about another British soldier arriving, I answered her in Japanese, she nearly dropped her broom. 'How can you speak Japanese you have only just got off the ship?' I explained that I had been there before, she asked when, I told her as a POW at Osaka. 'Number 2 Camp?' she asked; I replied yes. Apparently she had been living close to Number 2 Camp when the whole area was flattened during a US air raid. She then dashed away and told the others, and when I walked into the mess for a meal it did not matter who was sitting there, a waitress would come and bow. This did not go well with some of those senior to me, but they were told Jacksan must be Number 1! Unfortunately I was not able to get to see Osaka, and only managed to see Hiroshima."

Following this, Jack had postings in Singapore, Malaya, Germany, and Bahrain. During this period, Jack and Ruth raised five children, four girls and a boy. His final posting was to Northern Ireland where he eventually requested discharge in 1974. After that, he continued to work for the British Army until December 1977, and then migrated to Australia.

Garfield Kvalheim, whose 25th birthday present had been Edward Holt's sketch of the *Lisbon Maru* — which he had just helped to sink — served another six hard War Patrols on the *Grouper*.

"On one of our patrols we took a very hard and long pounding from depth charges — silent running — no ventilation and very hot. Two sailors showed signs of 'losing it' and were transferred from sub duty."

Kvalheim had no such problems however, and stayed with the submarine until her eighth patrol. Then the authorities transferred him to help put the latest American submarine, *Entemedor* (SS-340) into commission. They were on the new boat's first War Patrol when the war ended.

He married his sweetheart Gertrude, on 31 December 1945 and they brought up two boys, Richard and Larry, and one girl, Camille.

After the war, he served on several further submarines (*Tilefish, Drum, Carp, SeaLion, Bashaw,* and *Barbaro*) and finished his twenty-year naval service on shore duty in Tacoma from 1955 to 1957. Before being finally discharged, he was contacted by a government recruiter for a job overseas. In mysterious conditions he was sent to Washington DC for an interview. The interview went well, and when he was told that he had been accepted he was also informed that his new employer was the CIA, and that his first assignment would be Taiwan.

They sold their house and set off on a new adventure, living in Taiwan for nearly ten years and travelling on missions covering the whole Far East. Even today, all Gar will say about his role with the CIA is that "it involved a lot of surveillance". From Taiwan, he was transferred to Vietnam where he served for three years. Officially, in those days, dependents were not allowed "in country". However, both his sons were also serving in Vietnam, Richard in the Army and Larry in the Navy.

During this period, Gar rented a flat in Happy Valley, Hong Kong, across the water from where the British POWs had been ferried to the *Lisbon Maru* some twenty-five years earlier. He was able to make trips to Hong Kong every month and fell in love with the city.

Gar: "When I was assigned to Vietnam our normal tour was eighteen months. At the end of that tour I was given thirty days leave and was assigned another eighteen-month tour (I must have done a Hell of a good job!) While I was on leave I told my former wife that I was planning to find a place in Hong Kong so she could come out and I could visit about every month. That sounded great to her. While working in Vietnam, the hours were long and seven days a week. I could not draw overtime pay but instead was credited with compensatory time off. This was used instead of annual leave. I had many days to my credit. On my way back from home leave, I stopped in Hong Kong and tried to get some leads on a place to lease. I had contacts with friends in the Agency working in Hong Kong and later was given a lead on an apartment building being built in Happy Valley. To shorten the story, I leased a flat on the third floor overlooking the tramline and in the distance was the racetrack. We really loved Hong Kong. I was able to travel to Hong Kong every month for five to ten days which gave me an opportunity to see much of Hong Kong and meet many interesting people. One in particular, the owner of the Ocean Bar in Wanchai who would give me his membership card to the racetrack and I would place bets for him. Through our friends in the Agency my wife was able to get a job as a secretary with the Consulate in Hong Kong."

Finally, he then served two years in Iran, followed by a short assignment in Virginia, and wound up his career with two years in California with the U2 Program, retiring at the end of 1974.

After retirement, Gertrude and Gar settled down near the town of Gig Harbor, Washington.[260] When Gertrude passed away in 1977, Gar put their house up for sale. It was listed with a realtor where a lady by the name of Fran worked. Fran and Gar seemed to hit it off and were married in 1981. Fran was a widow with one daughter — her former husband, John, had passed away in 1975.

However, Gar had never forgotten that signal, picked up in October 1942 aboard the *Grouper*, stating that they had sunk a ship carrying British and Australian Prisoners of War. The American submariner veterans ('Subvets') had remained a tight-knit bunch, and one day around the end of 1983, Gar read an article in *Blow and Vent*,[261] a newsletter published monthly by his Subvets Local Chapter (the Admiral Lockwood Chapter, Seattle, Washington) about the loss of the USS *Bullhead*.

This piqued his interest, as he was very well aware that the *Bullhead* had been the last American submarine lost with all hands in the Second World War, and that its captain had been none other than his old friend Edward R. Holt. Gar immediately wrote to *Blow and Vent* with the details, which were reported thus:

Blow and Vent:

At least one of our members found my article on Radm[262] Griffith, skipper of the BULLHEAD, of interest. The following was sent to Merril Edson from G.M. Kvalheim, Gig Harbor, Wa.

"I read, with much interest, the article in the December Blow & Vent about the saga of a sub skipper's grief (Walter T. Griffith, skipper of the BULLHEAD). I have a short story which fills in a little bit more on the BULLHEAD.

On October 1, 1942, while I was serving on the GROUPER patrolling off the China Coast, we spotted a ship coming out of Amoy. After a little maneuvering, we closed and scored a hit aft and she went dead in the water. In a very short time we were being harassed by two planes, but, after a short working over we were able to maneuver around and get in a stern shot which hit amidships. The skipper on the periscope commented that personnel were jumping over the side all over the place and figured it must be a transport. By this time the patrol boats were out and, needless to say, we had one Hell of a time getting out of there.

The torpedo officer on board the GROUPER was Lt. E.R. Holt, Jr. and a fine free hand artist. Since October 1st was my birthday, he drew a silhouette of the ship we sank with rising sun in background and signed it with birthday greetings.

The point of the story is, Lt. Holt, later Lt. Cdr. E.R. Holt, Jr., relieved Capt. Walter T. Griffith on the BULLHEAD, which, we all know, was the last boat lost.

The ship that we sank on Oct. 1st was identified as the *Lisbon Maru* and was carrying English and Australian prisoners-of-war enroute to Japan. As I relive this story, I can't help but wonder, and I have many times, if there might be a survivor or two from that ship wandering around Australia? Does anyone have any contacts down under?"

Another US Submarine veteran, Jack Kidder read this article with interest. Kidder had kept in touch with his Second World War girlfriend in Perth, Australia, and sent the article to her. She in turn passed it on to a feature writer, Bill Bailey, of the *West Australian*. Bailey found the idea interesting, that a submariner whose craft had been responsible for the death of so many POWs would want to get in touch with any who survived and he published the following article in response:

Bill Bailey: 26 March 1984[263]

"There may be a certain reluctance on the part of many former servicemen to get in touch with an American submariner who is seeking to renew his links with the past. The one experience they have in common is the time his submarine sank their ship in the South China Sea.

Val Kvalheim, of Gig Harbour, Washington, says "I was in the USS *Grouper* and on my birthday, October 1, 1942, we contacted a Japanese ship coming out of Amoy.

"We fired one torpedo which hit her in the stern and she went dead in the water. The skipper observed many men abandoning the ship and figured she was carrying troops and was being used as a transport."

"We turned and fired a stern shot, which finished her off. It took two days to get back to normal, because we were really harassed. When we were able to stay top-side to charge the batteries we picked up this news report."

The report quoted a Tokyo radio announcement that a U.S. submarine had sunk a Japanese ship and said it was carrying about 1800 English and Australian prisoners who were on their way to Japan. Many hundreds, it said, were saved by two other Japanese ships and some prisoners were able to reach neighbouring islands.

Says Mr Kvalheim: "Who knows, some of these survivors may have gotten back to Australia and still be around. It would sure be something if I could make contact with a few of them."

It might be one reunion where the survivors would be trying hard to forget where they first met.

In fact, of course, no Australians (beyond, possibly, one or two who had joined British regular units) had been on board. Logically, this article would be expected to have remained uncommented on. However, as luck would have it, Jack Etiemble had not migrated to one of Australia's big concentrations of immigrants, Sydney or Melbourne, but to Western Australia. Not only that, but he saw the article and was keen to respond. To the credit of the US Postal Service, they delivered his letter to Gar despite the fact that it was simply addressed to "G. Kvalheim, Gig Harbour, Washington":

Jack Etiemble, 16 April 1984

> 84 Lagoon Drive
> Yanchep 6035
> W. Australia
> 16/4/84

Dear Val:

I read with interest your letter which was published in the West Australian on the 26th of March.

On October 1, 1942, I was one of the 1800 British prisoners of war being transported from Hong Kong to Japan on the *Lisbon Maru*. I, with most of my regiment, the Royal Artillery, were in No. 3 hold, which happened to be next to the engine room where the second torpedo hit. A large crack appeared in the bulkhead and water started pouring in. Most of the Jap soldiers in the decks above took to the life boats. The others battened down all the POWs' holds, a hand pump and four candles were passed down to my hold and we were told to keep the ship afloat.

It is very hard to describe conditions in the hold, no food, no drinking water and no fresh air. Four men at a time were manning the pump, but as the situation worsened, men were fainting through exhaustion and the water kept gaining.

We kept the ship afloat for 27 hours, but, by then, it was listing badly. Luckily, a POW had managed to break out from another hold and he undid the battens on our hold. As he did this he was shot by one of the guards. We started scrambling out of the hold and sliding down the deck into the water. Japanese patrol and tugboats were circling the stricken Lisbon Maru, and the gallant Japs decided to have fun by shooting POW's who swam towards them. Also, making out you were going to be rescued, picking you out of the water and when your face was level with the deck, kicking you and then pushing you under the water.

I was one of the lucky ones. I managed to evade being shot and after swimming for six hours, was finally picked up and transported to Shanghai where we were lined up and told by the interpreter that we should have all drowned like rats.

Out of the 1800 POWs that set out from Hong Kong, about 900 died on the Lisbon Maru and many more died in camps in Osaka and Kobe. It so happens, that both of these prison camps were bombed and burned out by U.S. bombers. I reckon the good ol' USA must have had something against those "Limey" POW's from Hong Kong!!

Regards to you and any other crew members of the USS GROUPER

Sincerely yours,
Jack Etiemble

They had made contact. In 1986, Val and Fran travelled to Australia to meet Jack and his wife Ruth.

Kvalheim: "After corresponding with Jack Etiemble for about two years I decided it was time to make a trip down under and meet up with Jack and Ruth. Besides, I wanted to stop in Brisbane and look over the New Farm Wharf from where we operated during the war. Fran and I flew to Sydney and enjoyed seeing the sights, a beautiful city, for several days and then flew on to Perth to meet Jack and Ruth. After checking into our hotel in Perth, I contacted Jack and we made plans to meet at the hotel the following day. Fran and I waited in the lobby near the entrance and in a short time Jack and Ruth came walking in. Since Jack had sent us a photo, there was no doubt who they were. It was like meeting old friends. Jack said something like: 'This is a bit different than our last meeting at opposite ends of a torpedo.'

After the usual chit-chat, we discussed his experiences on the *Lisbon Maru*. Also about them being picked up after the sinking and transported on to Japan in fishing packets crammed in like sardines — half of them standing and half sitting then exchanging positions. Some were very sick — some with dysentery. I am sure you have read the horror stories as this was one of the worst atrocities of the war. He also told me when on the *Lisbon Maru* he heard or felt a definite thud (I surmised it could have been one of our duds). He also later felt and heard a large explosion and a large crack appeared on the bulkhead of the adjacent compartment. I told him about our making contact with the *Lisbon Maru* and had to make an 'end around' and submerged before dawn and waited for them. We discussed his life in prison camp — some tales humorous and some very sad. Also, the fire-bombing of Tokyo and Osaka — they thought the Allies were going to wipe them out. He also explained that after the war he returned to Jersey [where he had lived pre-war] and everything became much too expensive to live there. That was why he took a job in Australia. Also, their daughter lived there with her family.

We all chatted a bit over a pint and Jack informed me he had contacted the newspaper as to our meeting. In a short time a reporter and photographer showed up. Incidentally, the photographer was the son of an American submarine veteran who had married an Australian girl and was living in Perth. Sadly, his father had been killed in an automobile accident a few weeks prior to our visit. Jack and Ruth took us on a grand tour for a week to all the points of interest in the area. We had a wonderful time with them. Among other things, we saw the Submarine Memorial and also the Americas Cup was on display at the Royal Yacht Club. That was the year America lost to the Aussies. We wished that we had planned to stay in Perth longer, but, after seven days we left our new friends and took the Indian Pacific Train back to Sydney — three days and three nights on the train crossing the Nullabar which was not too exciting. After a few more days in beautiful Sydney, we flew to Brisbane and I saw my old stomping grounds. We took the bus from Brisbane down the 'Gold Coast' and visited the old bar where I had been on R and R so many years ago. What a surprise to see it was still standing and still the same old bar."

But this was far from being the only reunion.

"After meeting Jack I read an article in Naval Proceedings (the Navy Periodical), written by Dan O'Hanlon saying he had been a POW on the *Lisbon Maru* and did anyone know the name of the submarine that sank her. I wrote to Dan answering his request and also informing him that Fran and I had met Jack and his wife in Perth. He replied thanking me for Jack's address and said he had not seen Jack since the war. He also sent me the addresses of Nobby Hunt and Reg Westwood. We all exchanged letters. Then, at the conference in Bournemouth in 1995, we all met. We had a grand time."

In 1995, Val and Fran were invited to attend the conference of the British Far East POWs in Bournemouth, England. There they met some twenty survivors of the *Lisbon Maru*: "We had a grand time and also met the Lord Mayor and his wife. It was the first meeting we had with Dan O'Hanlon, Reg Westwood, Nobby Hunt and their wives. Jack Etiemble was also present at the conference. It was like an old class reunion."

In 1997 Dan and Nobby and their wives met again at Reg Westwood's home in Westbank, Canada: "My wife and I met them there and we had another reunion. When we left for home we brought Dan and his wife, Pat, with us and they stayed with us for about a week. In 1998 we had another reunion in Portsmouth, England. Dan, Reg, Nobby, Jim Fallace (then 95, he had served in the Royal Marines in WWI) and myself and our wives. We stayed at the Royal Sailors' Home Club. We had all become very good friends by that time.

To answer your question about meeting the survivors. I was a bit apprehensive but they all showed absolutely no animosity towards me or the U.S. They were all happy to see the U.S. had advanced that far in the war in the Pacific. Dan O'Hanlon said, 'As I was swimming around I was wondering if you chaps had ham and eggs for breakfast!' I assured him we had been at battle stations all day — no breakfast!"

*   *   *

Thus the torpedo had been a 'circular' after all, though those at either end of its short and brutal journey did not meet till forty years or more after it was fired. One of the saddest episodes of the war had finally ended, and it had ended in reunion and friendship.

*   *   *

Those onboard the *Lisbon Maru* were prisoners who had committed no crimes, and liberation could never free them of the memories of the sinking, the deaths, the starvation, the disease, and the wasted years of their youth. None of that could be undone; there is no such thing as closure. The closest we can come to offering them freedom, is simply to tell their story.

> As you from crimes would pardoned be,
> Let your indulgence set me free.
>
> **Being the last two lines of**
> **William Shakespeare's *The Tempest*,**
> **Act 5, Scene 1**

17 Epilogue

> Sir, he may live.
> I saw him beat the surges under him
> And ride upon their backs; he trod the water,
> Whose enmity he flung aside, and breasted
> The surge most swoll'n that met him; his bold head
> 'Bove the contentious waves he kept, and oared
> Himself with his good arms in lusty stroke
> To th' shore, that o'er his wave-worn basis bowed,
> As stooping to relive him. I not doubt
> He came alive to land.
>
> The Tempest, Act 2, Scene 1

And there the story of the *Lisbon Maru* ends. Yet life continued for the survivors, and the families of those who had perished. Without the glue of war, they spread out from Australia to Canada, from Hong Kong to New Zealand, the Philippines, South Africa, and every part of the United Kingdom.

Let the pages of this epilogue pull their stories back together.

We followed Master Gunner Charles Brooks, from capture to drowning, and his family from evacuation from Hong Kong to the end of the war. They, by mid-1945, were now back in the UK where they received this letter from Lieutenant Colonel Richard Penfold, the commanding officer of Brook's unit, 12 Coastal Regiment, Royal Artillery:

Fleet, Hants, 27.11.45

Dear Mrs Brooks,

At this late date I am writing to tell you how grieved I was to hear of your husband's death in the sinking of the "Lisbon Maru" — and to offer you my deepest sympathy in your great loss.

I recently got back from Hong Kong and applied to Records for your address which it took some time to obtain.

We were told by the Japanese in Oct 1942 that the Lisbon Maru had been sunk — but we could get no details out of them. It was only after we took charge on 17th Aug this year that we managed to get a list of those who sailed and those who were lost; I was sad to see your husband's name among them. I met some of my men in Manila, and those who had sailed in that ship confirmed that your husband was unfortunately among the missing.

It is a great sorrow to me that such a valuable member of the Regiment and one who I knew so well should have been lost in this way after surviving the fighting in Hong Kong, where he had, as you would expect, done his job well and thoroughly. It is bad luck too that he should be taken when he was so near to getting his commission which of course he was recommended for.

There seems to have been no need for any casualties in the sinking, as the ship remained afloat for at least 27 hours after it was torpedoed — all the Japs were got off — but our men — particularly the RA were kept battened down in the holds. When eventually some got out it was rather late in the day — even then some were shot by the Japs and when they did start picking them up undoubtedly they intended that all British ranks should go down with the ship — it was only when some started getting clear that they attempted to pick up those still afloat.

If there is anything else I can do for you please let me know,

    Yours sincerely

Like all commanding officers at this time, Penfold was kept busy with writing to the families of all the men who had fallen under his command.

Fleet, Hants — 12 December 1945

Dear Mrs Brooks,

Thank you for your letter of 30 Nov — I am sorry not to have answered it before — but I have been away and also got some more "next of kin addresses" from war office that I had to write to.

I am very sorry indeed to hear of your illness — I have no doubt the strain and anxiety have helped to bring it on.[264]

I feel that the R.A. Prisoners of war fund Artillery House Earl's Court S W 5 should be able to help you in your difficulties — write to the secretary — I will also do so.

Mrs Penfold joins me in wishing you the happiest possible Christmas under the circumstances, and we hope that the New Year will be a more fortunate one for you.

Yours Sincerely

PS Let POW fund know full details of your family — how old would your boys be now?

Ron Brooks: "The most important aspect to me is how my father's death and all the events of that time affected and shortened my mother's life. Compared with many other people's war experiences my brother and I were relatively fortunate. Looking back at my mother's background from provincial Cork, how she married a British soldier and was transported to the relatively exotic locations of Malta and Hong Kong, makes the tragedy more poignant as her life all fell apart and she was left to cope alone with two young boys far from her home and family. She died from TB in 1949.

I think that Geoff was meant to be going to some sort of technical school but I know that my mother was very worried that he was 'mixing with the wrong sort'. I expect that he was a normal teenager who had had more than a usual few months of freedom from control. On a Travel Identity Card I have for Geoff dated July, 1946 his occupation is given as electrician's mate.

It was about this time that my mother found that she had tuberculosis of the throat. She was confined to bed and was not allowed to speak. She had to communicate in writing with us. We had to observe strict hygiene taking care not to use the same cutlery, dishes etc. as she did. I really don't know how she and Geoff managed. There were no hospital places for her and I don't think any treatment other than bedrest. A nurse came in regularly but I can't remember any domestic help. I was sent off to stay with the family of my Father's elder brother in Fetcham, Surrey. My Uncle Fred and Auntie Em had a son of about eighteen who travelled to work in London each day and a daughter Avril about sixteen. They were very kind to me and I was happy enough at my new school. However, I missed my mother very much. I can remember writing secret letters to her from the local post-office.

I don't know when it was that I returned to Dover. My mother was then allowed out of bed and to speak again. She still had a visiting nurse. It must have been a grim time for Geoff and her. He never spoke to me about it afterwards. My mother had decided to return to Ireland in 1946. Her brother Bertie and his wife Vera offered her a flat they had in a large imposing house they rented in Dublin. My Mother had become very friendly with the nurse who visited her in Dover and she accompanied my mother, brother and I to Dublin. My mother paid for her return fare.

Dublin was a different world, a land of plenty in contrast to the bleak austerity of England. I started school again at the High School, Dublin. This was a fee-paying school but I think I had some sort of a scholarship. I, at long last, was given a bicycle to travel there. Through my Uncle Bertie's contacts, Geoff became an apprentice to be a motor mechanic at a garage in nearby Blackrock. I remember when my mother's father came to Dublin to visit her. They wouldn't have seen each other for about sixteen years. She never went back to Cork where her other two brothers lived.

Strangely, I don't remember my mother having any further treatment for her TB. It was a much feared disease in those days and considered very infectious. We still observed strict culinary hygiene. Although the house was large and imposing it only had one bathroom and the arrangement of our flat on the top floor was not ideal. My Aunt was a chiropodist and ran a business from her surgery on the ground floor. Her mother lived with them and kept house. My mother didn't get on well with her. After less than a year, my mother bought an end of terrace house in a poorer but respectable suburb of Dublin.

I think my mother very much valued her independence but her health was failing. Geoff acquired a motor-bike to enable him to get to work. I was still able to cycle into the High School. Lack of money was quite a problem. I think that she had run through whatever family savings

Epilogue

there were. She advertised in the paper and took in lodgers, mainly bed and breakfast for people visiting Dublin on business. In spite of all this I think the short time we lived in Kimmage as a family were happy months for her. Geoff had settled in well to his apprenticeship and a trade that he enjoyed and I was doing well at school. Through school I had made friends with a family who also befriended and helped my mother and who were to be extremely kind to me.

My mother died in her sleep in September 1949. My mother's youngest brother Arthur was her executor. He and his wife Gladys came up from Cork to sort things out. I went to live for a short time with my Aunt Vera and Uncle Bertie so that I could continue day school. Geoff went to live in a hostel for young men whilst he continued his apprenticeship. This was a very rude shock for him and he soon found digs for himself with a family of undertakers in Dun Laoghaire where he was more settled. He finished his apprenticeship and moved on to London to work. I left the High School and went as a boarder to Mountjoy School in Dublin and spent my holidays with my Uncle Arthur and his family in Cork. My Uncle had a seaside cottage near Roches Point at the mouth of Cork Harbour beneath Fort Carlisle where my father had been stationed in 1927 and where he and my mother had met. I began to learn a little of our family history. I won a scholarship to Trinity College, Dublin where I took a degree in engineering, qualifying in 1956. Margaret, who is from Scotland, was also there studying Social Science. We met and the romance blossomed. I took a job with a consulting engineer in London and we were married in October 1957. We have a family of three children and four grandchildren. Geoff married Jean in 1958. He and Jean have no children. Geoff's asthma caught up with him and he died in 1997."

*   *   *

And what of the remaining survivors who helped with this book?

Frank Bennett of the Hong Kong Signals Company, thinking back to the POWs landing in Shanghai after the sinking, recalled: "Of all the survivors who finished up on that quay-side, I never came across my nephew, and have never seen him since." Frank had intended signing on for 21 years' service, but whilst a POW, finished his allotted Colour Service and was transferred — without knowing it — to the reserve. He found himself demobbed at Guildford, issued with a demob suit and a Post Office savings account book worth 410 pounds sterling — his pay accrued during the war years. Learning to become a civvy, Frank joined his two brothers (Maurice had worked nights for four years in the aircraft industry, and George had spent four years in The Pioneers and The Royal Sussex regiment) in their painting business. At this time he discovered that his father had been raised by a maiden aunt called Johnson, and that his real name was Bennett. He changed his surname to the latter by deed poll. "I am still learning to be a civilian", he said, in a letter of May 2004. "I've just about got the hang of it now. Good luck with the book."

Tom 'Taffy' Evans, the despatch rider of the Middlesex regiment, returned to Hong Kong after the war and remarried. He enlisted in Hong Kong's Dock Yard Police as sergeant, later inspector. On the closing of the dockyards, he was transferred to CSOS Police with six others. After marrying again in 1990, he moved to Manila where he still lives at time of writing. He has a son and a daughter. He summed up his experiences very nicely in the last line of a letter dated 30 August 2003: "Anyway, it's all over now. Lucky me."

Wallace Hastings of the Royal Navy did not have an easy time after liberation. Even the surrender ceremony at Hirohata did not go smoothly. As the only two non-Americans in camp, Hastings and Australian Aircraftman William Blackman had had the job of raising the Union Jack:

"I must tell you about the ceremony. On the day, it poured with rain and my flag fouled the lines when half raised, and by tradition this must not be lowered for correction. It took some time to unravel and by the time this was done the Stars and Stripes flew freely and the whole camp was singing the American nation anthem with Bill Blackman and I crying with frustration and the emotion of the moment."

Fortunately, he was luckier with his marriage: "My fiancée Bonny, to whom I had said goodbye in November 1938 was still waiting for me even after seven years apart and we were married in January 1946." On the recommendation of the American CO in Hirohata Camp, he was Mentioned in Dispatches. He stayed in the navy, and in 1948 was stopped while carrying a bottle with his rum issue in it. In those days, this was considered a smuggling offence, and after this run-in with authority Hastings decided to leave the service.

After a few difficult years of self-employment, which he survived "because my dear wife, Bonny has been with me throughout", he worked for local government for twenty years and then bought a newsagents in 1973. This he sold in 1977, buying another in 1979 in a run-down state. Turning the business around finally gave him enough money to retire.

He has one son, in the computer business, who introduced him to the PC ("with his tuition I am beginning to get the better of the beast. My main complaint is that it cannot spell correctly and some of its grammar is appalling") via which we still communicate today.

Alf 'Nobby' Hunt, who was lucky not to have been killed in the fighting of 1941: "I would say that about two hundred of us were on the *Joseph T. Dickman* (APA13) and the rest went to Australia (mostly the stretcher cases and sick people) and some went to Victoria in Canada and got home from Halifax Nova Scotia on the *Ile de France* landing in Southampton on the 4th of November, the day before us. Also there were a few went via India. Don't know how many.

[We left Manila, and via Hawaii, San Francisco, Phoenix, New York Halifax and Southampton, arrived back in the UK in November 1945].

From there, I was sent home on indefinite leave and all my brothers met me at Stratford station. After two months I was taken into a RN hospital at Bristol where I spent four months recuperating and was then discharged from the service as being unfit for military service due to multiple gunshot wounds.

I then spent three months helping out on my sister's farm and there met my future wife who was a land girl in the Women's Land Army. Then I did a refresher electrical course for nine months and joined a large electrical engineering company in Birmingham. There I spent three years working on electrical installations in different parts of the country.

I then joined a medium-sized engineering company, making steel fabrications up to fifty tons in weight, as the works engineer, in charge of maintenance where I stayed until retirement. I then did a three-year night school course learning Japanese.

In 1954, I was made Chairman and Secretary of the Birmingham Association of FEPOW, these offices I still hold. Also, I was Chairman of the Birmingham branch of the Royal Naval Association for a time in the 70s and am now a life member and also represent the Midlands area on the National Federation of FEPOW clubs.

In April [2004], we shall have been married fifty-six years. We have three sons, 54, 46 and 42 and six grandchildren."

Post-war, Alf remembered two Chinese wireless operators named Joe Siong and Charlie Ong who served on HMS *Cicala* with him. "They were both super lads and I had no success when I tried to contact them after the war."

Ross Lynneberg of the Royal New Zealand Naval Reserve, returned to New Zealand on 27 November 1945. "During the early days of our marriage I had no sense of feeling in my feet so when in bed Bernice had to tell me when the hot water bottle was safe to place my feet on it. She also had the worry of shaking me awake, as I would drop into such a deep sleep that my breathing would apparently stop for some time. Along with this problem, there were nightmares revolving around being captured again by the Japanese and the camp life being relived and discussed with other first time POWs — all the time feeling that this time I would not be getting home. These nightmares recurred occasionally for a number of years — then I seemed to grow away from the dreams.

I worked at the Soap Factory till it was later sold and demolished. During that time, with the financial help of my father, I built a shop and set the wife up as a General Draper in the seaside resort where I was building a larger home over the original one, this being necessary as we had a girl and boy.

After the sale of the factory I spent time as an earthmoving contractor, then on my father dying sold the shop and disposed of the earthmoving machinery, purchased a new caravan, having the one built years earlier parked on a leased section on the edge of Lake Taupo, the purpose was to seek out a source of income nearer the lake. First I wasted many months trying unsuccessfully to negotiate the purchase of a pub. Next I purchased a warehouse being built, only to find I was mixed up with smart lawyers and a similar contractor, hence [it took] another four years before recovering our money. During this time, I took a job with a local body while my wife worked at a tourist hotel in the area. The excavation for an underground Power Station was the last station to be built along the Waikato river so I joined the work scheme as a member of the maintenance workshop crew, finally acting as caretaker for the company for several years after the completion of the hydro scheme, then finally full retirement."

Following retirement, Ross made an interesting discovery. During the Second World War he had been underpaid! The New Zealand pay rate for his rank was higher than the Royal Navy's, so there was an agreement that the Royal Navy would pay the base, and that the New Zealand government would top it up. The New Zealand government indeed paid the top up sum to Ross's father during the years, but due to Ross's paysheet never arriving in Hong Kong (he was advanced HK$30 when he arrived, pending the paysheet's arrival, but the Japanese victory came too swiftly), he was never paid his due by the Royal Navy.

Ross put in a claim to the British government in 1998, which was declined. At the beginning of 2004, he was still owed 238 pounds and 10 shillings (in 1945 currency).[265]

James Miller of the Royal Scots, post-war, worked at the Edinburgh Corporation and at Ferranti. He emigrated to Australia in 1956 and worked at the Weapons Research Establishment, spending most of his time in Logistics in Woomera. Miller met his wife-to-be at a party being held for one of his ex-POW friends who just happened to live next door to her parents. They were married two weeks later, and fifty-eight years on [at the time of writing] are still together. Today they have five daughters (Isabella, Patricia, Christine, Janet and Fiona), ten grandchildren and eight great-grandchildren.

Dennis Morley, also of the Royal Scots: "After the war I did several jobs to make up my mind what I wanted to do with my life. I married a wonderful woman and had a daughter. Unfortunately, she died at the young age of thirty years of cancer. I have travelled to Canada six times with my second wife who unfortunately passed away last year. Together we have travelled over most of England. I went to Hong Kong once and I found it very emotional, especially at the War Cemetery. I finally retired about six years ago still going strong at 84 years old." And on my questioning his change of name from Dennis Hickenbottom to Dennis Morley: "The name change worked like this. My full name was Dennis John Morley Hickenbottom. So, it was just a case of knocking off the end bit officially."

William Grant Shepherd of the Royal Navy recalls: "I arrived home [in Scotland] on November 1st 1945 and fairly soon thereafter I realized that life as a POW had left some scars. The full extent of those scars was not realized until I returned to work as a journeyman mechanic in the plant I left as an apprentice in September of 1940. I soon discovered that my nerves were in terrible shape and I struggled against this condition for the rest of my working life. Thankfully the effects of the condition eventually improved, particularly after I emigrated to Canada in March of 1949, settling in Winnipeg, my home ever since. My first job in Winnipeg was as a machinist in the Canadian National Railways repair shops. I worked here from March 1949 until December 31st 1951. On January 1st 1952 I became a Provincial Civil Servant, having been hired as a Factory Inspector with the Manitoba Government, Department of Labour. In June of 1960, I transferred to another branch of the Department of Labour, becoming an apprenticeship supervisor. I held a number of positions in the apprenticeship division before retiring on March 4th 1982 as acting Director of the Division. Considering my fate during the war years, I feel very lucky to be alive today and to have enjoyed almost 22 years of retirement. Many people have contributed to my ability to do so, none more than my wife and two daughters. My wife Margaret especially, had much to contend with during my days of deep depression. I often wonder what the girls thought when they were young, but I'm sure their mother was a great source of strength for them. Margaret is also a native of Forfar, Scotland and she was brave enough to join me in Winnipeg in April of 1950 solely on the promise of marriage. We were married on July 5th 1950 and are grateful we have smoothed the bumps on the road to matrimonial happiness. During my working career, I have also had patient and understanding supervisors.

I don't think I told you anything about our two daughters. Moira is the elder and was born in Winnipeg in 1953. She and her husband have a son and daughter in that order. Their home has been in Regina since 1982, and both children are in their twenties. Linda is the younger daughter and she too was born in Winnipeg, in 1960. She and her husband have one son who just turned eleven years of age, they live and work in Winnipeg. We are proud of them all — but don't tell them that every day. Honestly though, we have much to be thankful for."

William Spooner of the Royal Scots: "This tale is nearly complete, except that I arrived home, eventually married. We had four children — grandchildren 8, so far, and 3 great-grandchildren, and who sit around, looking bored whenever I mention the war, with expressions that say 'here he goes again'. I have never seen Mick [Myles] again, but have been told that he was thrown out of Hong Kong. I don't know if it was true or not, but with him it was credible. Micky, a loveable rogue, a con man, a man with many faces, a face that one could trust, yet a calculating face, like 'what's in it for me?' But he saved my life. I owe him fifty-seven years of married life to a good lady, who was taken from us recently. I owe him four children all of whom have been a great solace, help and comfort to me, although grieving themselves, for the loss of a loving wife, mother and grandmother." Today, Spooner lives in Basildon, Essex.

* * *

Of the others whose writings and memories are referred to:

Arthur Alsey, who had joined the Royal Scots as a bandsman in May 1933, serving overseas in India (Quetta and Lahore) and Hong Kong before the outbreak of the Second World War, changed units after the war. He stayed in the army, joining the Royal Artillery at Woolwich as a musician. He served there for eighteen months until early 1948. After that, the trail goes cold.

Sam Atkins of the Middlesex (from daughter Barbara Tindle): On 4 September 1945 he was flown to Tokyo and put aboard Hospital boat *Marigold*. Transferred to the British on 5 September, he arrived at Auckland, New Zealand, on 3 October 1945. Leaving Auckland on 20 November 1945, he arrived at Sydney on 23 November and sailed for home on 10 December 1945 aboard the *Aquitania*. "His stay in New Zealand was at a recuperation camp, I believe the powers that be thought they could not send freed prisoners of war home, looking the way they did, so they cared for them and got their weight up to a reasonable level before shipping them home. My father was full of praise for the care and attention he received during his stay in New Zealand."

Sam records his weight on 4 October 1945, one month after liberation, as being 52 kilograms. By the end of October, it had increased to 65 kilograms (between 23 May 1943 to 6 December 1944, his weight had ranged from 52 to 63 kilograms, and towards the end of his captivity, September 1945, it went as low as 43 kilograms). "It surely was a close call when he was liberated, I remember him telling me he was lying on his bed when the Americans came into the camp, and they walked past him twice, thinking he was dead! He certainly was lucky to have survived, as so many did not. His illnesses were also written down, dysentery, beri-beri, chronic bronchitis, asthma, as well as accidents whilst working on the docks at Kobe."

He died on 9 January 1992, at the age of seventy-six.

Jim Fallace of the HKRNVR had served in the Royal Marines in the First World War, then spent twelve years in China in the Tientsin Police Force. He moved to Hong Kong in 1939 and joined the HKRNVR. After escaping the *Lisbon Maru* and the Japanese attempts to round up the POWs, he joined the Royal Indian Navy, though did not go to sea again. In 1947, after ten months with the War Crimes Commission in the Far East, he returned to the UK where he was presented with the Royal Human Society Medal for saving the life of Cadet Laloe when the *Lisbon Maru* sank. Post-war he became a pub landlord, but served the Royal Marines again as a steward in the Officers' Mess from 1956 until he retired in 1972 at the age of sixty-nine. Following 'retirement' he worked at the 'Ship' public house in Deal, Kent. He passed away in Deal in 1998.

Geoffrey Hamilton of the HKVDC and Royal Scots, returned to the UK on the *Empress of Australia* together with several old friends including Chris Man and Martin Weedon. One of the first things he did when he arrived was write to a friend, Frau Anneliese Goerdeler in Germany, and like many returning Far Eastern POWs he discovered that the war in Europe had taken its toll too, of friend and foe alike.

Pre-war, Hamilton had stayed with the family of Dr Karl Goerdeler (Lord Mayor of Leipzig and Riechskommisar of price supervision) for four months, and Goerdeler's son Christian stayed with his parents. Christian had been killed on the Eastern Front in 1943, and Dr Karl Goerdeler — as one of the leaders of the July 1944 bomb plot to kill Hitler — was murdered by the Nazis. Frau Goerdeler and their other four children spent the remainder of the war in concentration camps.

Frau Goerdeler replied: "My dear Geoffrey ... After July 20th 1944 Marianne and I were arrested in Leipzig, Nina and my daughter-in-law (wife of Ulrich) here on the farm, Ulrich on an airport of the Lueneburger Heide and Reinhard at the Italian theatre. For months all of us were in jails and afterwards in different concentration camps ... My husband and his youngest brother Fritz of Koenigsberg whom you also know were murdered on February 2nd and March 1st 1945 after a long time of martyrdom. Then we had to seek the two little sons of Ulrich who were displaced by the Gestapo under another name. At last we found them in the Harz Mountains. It is very kind of your parents, dear Geoffrey, that they will take one of the boys to their home. But they are still very little …"

Dan O'Hanlon of the Royal Navy (from Alf Hunt in 2004): "Danny stayed in the navy until he was forty and then he emigrated to South Africa and joined the South African navy. He learned Afrikaans and finished up at the age of sixty-five as a Commander in charge of all their radar. He died two years ago and I still communicate with Pat his widow who lives in Capetown. He had two sons who were both Lieutenant Commanders in the South African navy."

Hargraves Howell of the RASC (from daughter Adrienne): "After the war he was working for a company dealing with timber — if I remember lately and towards the end of his life, he worked for a stock broking company. He was a dedicated member of the Hong Kong Kennel Club and arranged many dog shows and also Secretary of the Hong Kong Society of Prevention to Cruelty to animals, the result of which we had many exotic animals living in our house from time to time! He died of a stroke on 27th August 1966 on the way to Kai Tak airport where he was taking a puppy to be shipped to England. My mother, Carolyn Howell is perhaps better known by her professional name Carol Bateman under which she ran a ballet school in the Helena May for many years. I was born on 2nd October 1952 and adopted by my parents in 1957."

John Inglis of the Royal Artillery worked in the Manchester area as an instrument mechanic after the war. He was married in 1946 and had a son and a daughter. Suffering from respiratory problems, he was advised to get out of the city, and thus in 1954 gained employment at the United Kingdom Atomic Energy Authority at Windscale, Cumbria. In 1961 he was transferred to British Nuclear Fuels Limited. He retired in 1980, aged sixty-three, and died suddenly on 26 June 1986.

William Poulter of the Middlesex Regiment was repatriated to England to be reunited with his wife Dorothy (Doff) and son Robin who had already returned there by sea after two years in Australia, not knowing if he was alive or dead.

When Bill finished his service in the Army, he was employed as a telephone operator by the Post Office. Another son, Christopher, was born in June 1947. Robin eventually joined the Royal Navy and Christopher, the Royal Air Force.

Four months after his sixty-fourth birthday Bill died of a massive heart attack on 31 July 1973. Doff died of cancer on 1 May 1994.

Andrew Salmon of the Royal Artillery returned to Hong Kong, left the Royal Artillery, and started a career with the Hong Kong Prison Service in 1949. There he had an interesting experience. At Stanley jail he immediately recognized a Japanese man, growing vegetables quietly and humbly in the prison farm. It was the 'beast of Shamshuipo'.

"I think actually he had expected to be sentenced to death. Now here was this man who I had seen slap and beat my fellow prisoners, on the other side of the fence. But he was very different, he would have got down on his knees and polished your shoes if you had asked him. He was just the opposite of how I remembered him during the war. We didn't take any liberties with them but that wasn't to say we didn't feel like doing so."

The skipper of the *Lisbon Maru* was also among the group of about forty Japanese war criminals imprisoned in Stanley, but all of the Japanese prisoners were repatriated a few months after Mr Salmon arrived back in Hong Kong.[266]

Martin Weedon of the Middlesex (from his son Mark): "Martin had been at Harrow and Sandhurst (with Tony Hewitt and Chris Man, of the same Regiment) before joining the Middlesex. He and his wife Liz divorced shortly after the war. Both had become rather different people; for example, Liz couldn't tolerate Martin carrying his camp commandant's samurai sword about (clinging to his possessions, as many ex-POWs did), and both had had 1941 wartime affairs. Martin then married Jean Leslie (a friend of Liz's, both being in the Wrens), and Elizabeth re-married in 1949. Her new husband was Tony Hewitt, previously adjutant of the 1st Battalion the Middlesex regiment, who had successfully escaped from Sham Shui Po with two others.[267]

After the war, Martin left the Army, qualified as a barrister, and worked as a Legal Advisor to William Cory (a coal mining concern), then the Rhodesian Selection Trust (also mining, in Lusaka, then Salisbury). Later, he went into education as Clerk to the Governors of the Greycoat Foundation (as a super-bursar to six schools, to one of which — Queen Anne's, Caversham, both his granddaughters went).

With his new wife, he had a son Christopher (now a chartered surveyor in Somerset) and a daughter Susan (now living in Australia) both of whom also had their own children. Jean, at time of writing, is 82 and living in Wincanton. Liz and Tony are also still around, and living in Buderim, Queensland, Australia.

Retiring aged 60, in poor health, Martin Weedon died just two years later. Prison camp had taken a lot out of him (as it did others)."[268]

Reg Westwood of the Royal Engineers (from Alf Hunt): "After liberation we got split up, he came home on I think the *Ile de France* and got in to Southampton just before us. We kept in touch after the war and met at several reunions, firstly at the Royal Albert Hall and then the Festival Hall. He married Joyce in 1951 and they emigrated to Canada in 1957 where he worked as a Dock superintendent. From there, he moved on to North Battleford where he was chief engineer at a large hospital complex. He retired to Westbank, near Kelowna and lived there until last year. My wife and I have been over to see them on several occasions, we helped them move house and lay out their garden on their last move. Like us, they had three sons and Roger their oldest is now a Rear Admiral in charge of shipbuilding for the Canadian navy. After Reg died, Joyce moved to Chilliwack in BC where she now lives. I regularly communicate to her by email."

Alf Taylor of the Hong Kong Signals Company (from friend Marjorie Bray):[269] "Alf was over ten years older than [my husband], so we think he must have been born around the First World War. He married a daughter of Dr. Atienza (I think after the Second World War). They had a daughter, and mother and daughter went to live in England, leaving Alf in Hong Kong, working as a Land Bailiff with the New Territories Administration. Marie Atienza [his wife's adoptive aunt] was fond of Alf and spent a lot of time with him. Marie had a retirement house on Cheung Chau and I think Alf lived there for a while. Later Austin Coates[270] rented it from her in the seventies."

Robert Wright of the Middlesex retired to Yorkshire and wrote his account of his experiences, *I was a Hell Camp Prisoner*, in 1964.

From the USS *Grouper*:

Rob Roy McGregor was awarded the Silver Star "For conspicuous gallantry and intrepidity in action as Commanding Officer of the USS GROUPER during a patrol in enemy Japanese controlled waters from August 22, to October 20, 1942 ... Daringly pressing home attacks on Japanese shipping, Lieutenant Commander McGregor, with great courage and aggressiveness, maneuvered the GROUPER in hostile waters, sinking two enemy merchantmen totalling 12,000 tons, and damaging one ship of 4,000 tons. Despite Japanese counter efforts of depth charges by surface and aircraft, he handled his vessel with such outstanding skill and excellent judgement that he was able to bring her through without damage and his crew home without injury ..."

Leaving *Grouper* in March 1943, he took command of *Seacat* (SS-399) in July 1944, and of Submarine Division 202 as from January 1945. He stayed in the navy post-war, with a number of significant desk and sea jobs, the final one (before retirement to Coronado, California, as a Rear Admiral) being command of Destroyer Squadron 5.

Married in Manila in 1940 to Mary Elizabeth Osborne, they had three children, Rob Roy Jr., Mary Cameron, and Allison Gay.

John Denning Mason served six further war patrols in *Grouper* before becoming Executive Officer and Navigator of USS *Bugara* (SS-331). Staying with submarines post-war, he held numerous positions, including command of the experimental vessel USS *Baya*, and of Submarine Division 81 from 1954–55. After a posting to Gosport, England, he became Chief of Staff and Aide to Commander Submarine Force, Atlantic Fleet in 1964.

Married to Margaret B. Ross of Norwich, Connecticut in March 1941, they had three children: Harrison D. Mason III, Ross M. Mason, and Matthew C. Mason.

Robert Hamilton Close served three further war patrols in *Grouper*. He was awarded the Bronze Star Medal with Combat 'V' for "outstanding heroism in the line of his profession during the Second and Third War Patrols of the USS GROUPER in which two large and one medium-size cargo ships were sunk and two medium-sized cargo vessels were damaged. As Division Officer and Engineer Officer he distinguished himself during each action by his skill and exemplary coolness, and rendered inestimable assistance to his commanding officer ..."

From December 1943 until October 1944, he commanded USS *Pilotfish*. He stayed with submarines until the end of the war, and then after a period with a training unit took command of USS *Collett* (DD-734) in the Korean War (being again decorated for action at Inchon). After Korea, he took postings in the Philippines (at the Pacific Defense College, Baguio) and Thailand.

He married Virginia M. Lent of Bremerton, Washington, and they had three children: Marian Harriet, Stephen Lent, and Daniel Edward Close.

Edward Rowell Holt left *Grouper* in October 1943 and joined USS *Baya*. In February 1945 he was assigned to USS *Sealion* which was awarded a Presidential Unit Citation. Interestingly, in light of the *Lisbon Maru* experience, that citation reads in part, "Daring and skilled in carrying the fight to the enemy, the SEALION also braved the perils of a tropical typhoon to rescue fifty-four British and Australian prisoners of war, survivors of a hostile transport ship torpedoed and sunk while enroute from Singapore to the Japanese Empire."

Married to Mary Herndon Davis, he lost his life, as related above, in USS *Bullhead*.

*   *   *

Many of the *Lisbon Maru*'s survivors returned to Hong Kong. They had not forgotten the kindness of the Chinese fishermen who had rescued so many, and who in doing so probably encouraged the Japanese to pick up the remainder of those who survived. Major General Chris Man started a fund among the survivors for the Chinese people who had saved their lives. In February 1949, the governor of Hong Kong presented Mr Woo Tung-ling and other islanders a motor fishing launch and some funds. Thirteen *Lisbon Maru* survivors were there that day.

Taffy Evans: "After the war, in February 1949, Captain 'Micky' Man MC (later Major-General) organized a fund among the survivors as a token of gratitude. We held a party at Queen's Pier, Hong Kong. Present were, His Excellency the Governor, Micky Man, Hargraves Milne Howell MBE, Geoffrey Hamilton, Frank Kekewick Garton, J. Hill, Andy Salmon, William Taylor, William Johnstone who escaped from the island, Thomas Gorman, myself Tom Evans, James Robson, J. McDougall, A. Woodhead, and J. Campbell."[271]

Many men received recognition for the services they had performed during the war. Three examples will suffice. Howell was made a Member of the British Empire (MBE) for his role in breaking out of the holds. Lieutenant Norman Brownlow of the Royal Scots was also awarded the MBE, for rescuing men trying to clamber ashore at the islands. RPO Bernard Charles Lilley of HMS *Tamar* was awarded the Distinguished Service Medal (DSM): *London Gazette*, 2 July 1946: "For distinguished service during the Defence of Hong Kong and whilst a prisoner of war in enemy hands." The following information was supplied by the recipient's family: "Following the fall of Hong Kong, R.P.O. Lilly [sic] led a party of sailors into the hills and held out for nearly four weeks before being captured. En-route to Japan as a P.O.W. the ship was torpedoed and badly damaged by an American submarine. Whilst working as a P.O.W. in Japan he had to rely on food thrown to him by passers-by."[272]

*   *   *

And what of the families of the other nine of the ten men we watched drift out to sea, never to be seen again, on 2 October 1942?

William Arthur Barlow has defied all attempts to uncover his roots. A group based in Jacksdale, Nottingham, UK, researched their village war memorial and discovered that one of their men, Warrant Officer Class 2 Barlow, had lost his life on the *Lisbon Maru*. They found the newspaper articles quoted in this text, but have not yet been successful in tracing any of his relatives. His details are included in a special Book of Remembrance presented to their village church, St Mary's Westwood, on 19 July 2003.[273]

William James L. Boyes's entire set of medals (1939–45 and Pacific Stars, War Medal) — unnamed as issued, but with a named Condolence Certificate and box of issue, addressed to his wife in Plympton, Devon was put up for sale by Toad Hall Medals, Newton Ferrers, near Plymouth in November 2003 for £145. What happened between his death, and the sale of his medals sixty-one years later, has evaded amateur sleuthing techniques.

Sidney Charles's wife, Alice, and son, David carried on as best they could without him. But then tragedy struck again; David was accidentally killed — then aged thirteen — along with some sixteen other Royal Marine cadets, when a lorry ploughed into their marching column. Alice would never recover from the double blow.

Thomas Hamill was well remembered by his two brothers and seven sisters. His niece, Mary Barker: "I always remembered mum (Janet) and her sisters talking about Uncle Tommy, what a lovely brother he was, and how he died during the war, having been taken a prisoner of war on the *Lisbon Maru*. Sunk by the Americans. The only other bit of folklore I remember was from one of his mates who was from Tayport, and on the *Lisbon Maru* that they were swimming for their lives, and sharks surrounding them. No idea who the other man was, or how he survived and my uncle didn't."

Andrew Flett would never go home to his wife Isabella, and his four children Ian, Joseph, Alec, and Isobel at their home, Glenelg, Queen Street, Lossiemouth. He would never return to his peacetime occupation, fishing as skipper of the *Plough*. Today, although his bones lie on an unmarked seabed thousands of miles away, he has a gravestone in Lossiemouth. "Sacred to the memory of Andrew Flett who was lost off S.S. *Lisbon Maru* while a prisoner of war in the Far East on 2nd October 1942 aged 44 years. Beloved husband of Isabella Murray. Also their son Joseph M. Flett who died 14th October 1939 aged 16 years. And the said Isabella Flett who died 23rd July 1996 aged 98 years."[274]

Ronald Langley-Bates had three children (Douglas, born 1930, Derek, 1932, and Denise, 1933), who with the advent of war were evacuated with his wife to Australia. Kathleen at first believed the war would soon end and they would be reunited. She never recovered from his death and never went back to England. Like many other Hong Kong widows in Australia, she made a new life for herself and her family thousands of miles away from her original home. She died in 1999 at the age of ninety-one, having worked like a slave to send her three children to good schools, and having finally achieved her ambition of owning her own home at the age of seventy-one.

Her son Douglas remembers: "We went from Hong Kong to the Philippines, being billeted with Americans on a sugar plantation at Carmen del Pampanga for a short while. They were very friendly; mother kept in touch for many years. As the Japanese approached, we were sent on to Melbourne, Australia on the *Johan de Witt*.

Our first 'home' was an old guesthouse 'The Fernery' in Frankston. While there, us children went to the local state schools. Mother then joined forces with another evacuee to rent a big house in a prime location on top of Oliver's Hill overlooking the bay.

She was offered it for 2,000 pounds but did not buy it as we would return to HK one day after the war. The land was later subdivided, and the house sold for $AU500,000. The house is still there today.

After receiving the news of father's death, mother decided on a long stay in Australia until after the war. We moved to a guesthouse in St Kilda and she got two jobs, one as a clerk in the Lost Property section of the Railways and one as a waitress. She was well known in the railways as one who did her job efficiently and honestly, and willing to help others. She worked there for thirty or more years and became a surrogate mother to many of the junior staff.

She saved money and sent us three children to private schools. Both boys went to Trinity Grammar School. As she really did not have a great deal of money, she dressed in her best outfit and went to see the headmaster. She told him her story which touched him so much she was given half fees for her two sons.

Then the guesthouse was sold and she needed to find another home. While looking around, she saw some people moving out of a basement flat in St Kilda near the beach. She rushed back to the guesthouse, quickly packed all the belongings, got a taxi to take her to the flat, moved in and squatted there. The agent was furious and sent for the owner.

I was at boarding school but coming home for the weekend. When I arrived, I found I knew the owner as I was taking his daughter out. Mother told him that if he evicted her she would go to the daily papers with the story of a British war widow with three children callously thrown out into the street. He calmed down and said mother could stay.

The flat consisted of a single room, about 20 feet by 24 in a basement. It was divided at one end into two cubicles. One held a table and small tabletop oven/hotplate, the other a bed. The toilet/bathroom were outside down a passage. It was cold and damp but she made it a home.

From there, as things improved, she took the family to a much better flat in Elwood. She was always struggling for money and could not afford carpet so she bought some carpet under felt to keep the place warmer. I can remember bringing a friend home from University, came from well-off family. Very amused by the under felt.

She supported her children to the limit. Attended all our events — sports meetings, concerts, etc. Came to watch me play lacrosse for my University and helped with the afternoon tea. I will never forget how proud she was as she attended the presentation of my Master's Degree.

But one of her major ambitions was the home, and she finally achieved it. A three-bedroom house with a garden she turned into a real English beauty — roses, camellias, a magnolia, and a pond with goldfish. She was passionate about it. She lived there with my brother Derek who never married.

After she retired and grew older, her health deteriorated — she suffered from atrial fibrillation, hiatus hernia, asthma and severe arthritis. The final blow occurred when my brother died before her. She had never considered it and was shattered. She never adjusted, would go into his room and say 'good morning' and 'goodnight' as if he was still there. Put a fresh flower in there every day.

She had an army of friends from all over. At her funeral, as well as family and friends, we saw ex-workmates, her doctor, dentist, podiatrist and many neighbours."

Percy Albert George Robinson's father had spent nearly two years and five months in hospital as a POW in the Great War, finally being repatriated to England on 7 January 1919. No doubt he held out hope for his son for many months. But there was to be no repatriation this time; his mother and father, in Dagenham, Essex, would wait in vain.

When **Frederick Stanford** was in the camp in Hong Kong, his family's Amah would sneak up to the fences and pass food through to him and his best friend James Clark. When the *Lisbon Maru* was torpedoed, they ended up in the water together. All that Jim Clark ever told Stanford's family was that he was with him one minute, and the next he had drifted away, never to be seen again.

Jim himself endured three years in Japanese camps as a prisoner working in the docks. After the war, and liberation, he found that his wife had died. He then searched for his two sons, whom he found in Australia. He returned to England where he met up with Stanford's wife Alice. They eventually married. They were two people who as friends had shared a common loss, both victims of the war, who found solace in each other. If not deep love, they did at least enjoy many years of companionship until Jim died of cancer in 1973 just after retirement as

Chief Commissionaire at the Industrial Design Centre in the Haymarket. Jim was a quiet, tall, strong accented Scot, dour, but with a heart of pure gold. Although he would never talk about his experiences, his nose (broken by rifle butts three times) and his back were heavily scarred. He always smoked the thinnest roll-up cigarettes, a legacy of his time in the camps when such luxuries were scarce and had to be made to last. He would often chastise Stanford's grandchildren (kindly) for using more than two squares of toilet paper, telling them that it should not be wasted.

George Trinder would never even see his third child, Charles. His pregnant wife, Lena Emily, and his two sons, Bernard and George had been evacuated from Hong Kong in July 1940 to Manila, where Charles was born later in the month. Like the other evacuated families, they were then transferred to Australia. Lena died in 1953 when Bernie was twenty and his brothers George, seventeen, and Charles, thirteen. The three boys, as soon as they were old enough, joined the Royal Australian Navy. Bernie trained as an Aircraft Engineer while in the Navy and joined Qantas in January 1958, continuing to work there until his retirement in 1993.

*   *   *

As for the Japanese: The cruel and unpopular Japanese Interpreter **Niimori Genichiro** was tried in Hong Kong in September 1946 before a war crimes tribunal. He was sentenced to fifteen years' imprisonment. Expecting the death sentence, witnesses claim that he danced for joy.

Kyoda Shigeru, Master of the *Lisbon Maru*, was brought before a court in October 1946, and sentenced to seven years (see appendix), but Lieutenant **Wada Hideo** died before he could be brought to trial.

*   *   *

The submarine *Grouper* survived the war too. Her third patrol, the next after that which led to the loss of the *Lisbon Maru*, lasted from 12 November to the last day of 1942. It was a patrol to Brisbane, Australia, but on the way (on 17 December) she sank the Japanese troop ship *Bandoeng Maru*, which was on its way to bring reinforcements to the Japanese positions in the Solomon Islands.

On her following patrol, from 18 January to 21 March 1943, *Grouper* returned to the Solomons. There, her crew rescued an airman who had spent several days stranded on Rengi Island. Patrols five to eight produced no concrete results in terms of sinkings, though several targets were attacked. However, during these four patrols, *Grouper* rescued another airman, this time on New Britain, and also landed a force of fifty men and all their equipment, who were tasked with waging war behind Japanese lines there. After her eighth patrol, *Grouper* returned to the United States for a much needed overhaul. She berthed at San Francisco on 19 October 1943.

Grouper made four more war patrols before the Japanese surrender brought the war to an end. On the ninth war patrol, starting 22 May, *Grouper* made her last kill of the conflict; in a night surface attack on 24 June she sank the *Kumanoyama Maru*. On her last overhaul, after the twelfth patrol, COMSUBPAC modified her SV air-search radar for periscope mounting and operation at shallow submergence, as a prelude to her expected role in the invasion of Japan. Exactly one month after the plutonium bomb was dropped on Nagasaki, on 9 September 1945, *Grouper* sailed from Pearl Harbour to New London together with submarines *Toro* and *Blackfish*. For the next four years she undertook exercises in the seas around New London, Florida, and the Caribbean. But the *Grouper* had been earmarked as something special in the US Navy's submarine portfolio. A year after the end of the Second World War she became the first American submarine to have a Combat Information Centre installed, and, in 1947, she carried out the first egress and ingress of crewmen from a submerged and underway submarine.

On 5 March 1950, *Grouper* returned to the Mare Island Ship Yard for conversion to become the US Navy's first hunter-killer submarine. Her number was therefore changed from SS-214 to SSK-214 on 2 January 1951. Some six months later *Grouper* emerged from Mare Island equipped with the latest electronic warfare equipment (including radar and sonar) and a snorkel. Attached to Submarine Development Group 2, *Grouper* spent the next eight pioneering many of the submarine versus submarine concepts that would define future hunter-killer antisubmarine warfare. She sailed all over the Atlantic Ocean, taking part in US Navy and NATO exercises from Florida to Scotland.

Recognized as an elite boat, *Grouper* was awarded the Battle Efficiency 'E' rating in 1964. In November 1965, she had her final overhaul, and had various items of equipment updated to prolong her life as a floating underwater sound laboratory. She returned to the Caribbean in mid-1966 for intensive research, again making the Atlantic her home and sailing to Narragansett Bay and Bermuda. At the beginning of 1967, she was at New London resuming research into underwater sound propagation. Finally, her sleek shape looking completely different from the *Gato*-class boat that had been launched nearly thirty years earlier, *Grouper* was decommissioned on 2 December 1968 and sold for scrap on 11 August 1970.[275]

But **Groton, Connecticut**, the American city where the *Grouper* was born, survived and thrived, and holds a dirty little secret of its own.

Home to privateers during the American War of Independence, it became a thorn in the side of British forces. In September 1781, guided to the site by Benedict Arnold, some 800 British regular forces and colonial loyalists attacked the 150 volunteers holding Fort Griswold on the heights outside the town.

It was an unusually fierce battle. The defences were strong, and the defenders determined, but the British troops were disciplined and experienced. Knowing he was beaten, the commander of the defenders gave up his sword in surrender. Eyewitnesses claim that he was then killed with it, and that the British attackers then massacred the other survivors. Before this, the eyewitnesses claim, less than ten defenders had been killed. However, when the fighting ceased it was found that eighty of the garrison lay dead and mutilated and more than half of the remainder were severely wounded.[276]

*   *   *

Hong Kong survives, of course, though the majority of the built-up areas are totally unrecognizable to anyone who was here in 1941. But every now and then, on a remote hillside or the corner of a forgotten alley, reminders of the fighting can still be found; a corroded cartridge case here, the marks of shrapnel or bullets on a stone wall there. Stanley and Sai Wan have their war cemeteries; quiet, beautiful places now, though the Stanley cemetery had itself been a battlefield on the last day of the fighting. Tourists pass through today, looking at the headstones and butterflies, pausing sometimes to read an inscription. There is as yet no memorial to the *Lisbon Maru* in Hong Kong,[277] despite the fact that her loss was so devastating to so many of the population.

The *Lisbon Maru* is, for the moment, still lying where she sank in the East China Sea. Tired businessmen, flying from Shanghai's stylish new Pudong Airport to Hong Kong on the regular Hong Kong Dragon Airways

(Dragonair) Airbus service, unknowingly fly right over her. The UK Hydrographics Office (Wrecks Section) lists her as lying at a depth of fifty-two metres, at latitude 29 57'.000 N, longitude 122 56'.000. But according to the islanders she lies further north, in considerably shallower water of twenty-seven metres; not exactly Full Fathom Five, but still in easy diving depth. Being so far outside UK waters[278] the wreck is not protected, though by definition she is a war grave. But these are busy waters; she may not lie undisturbed forever.

While writing this book, I was contacted by some of the inhabitants of the Zhoushan Archipelago. They are more interested in the *Lisbon Maru* than I had ever guessed. They say that the Chinese Navy dived on the ship in the 1950s, and that a father and son followed in the 1990s — with the son losing his life in the process. Now they want to set up a museum or memorial park, and there are persistent rumours that some elements even wish to raise the wreck. An earlier dive raised the helm, they say, and they want to follow this with a film on the subject.

As for those who were on board, well, in 1990 when I started collecting notes for what would eventually become this book there were probably one hundred survivors still around. When I started serious work on it in 2003, I knew of just eight. By March of that year, that group had been whittled down to seven; by July, I knew of only six. Then, to my surprise, over the next eighteen months five more turned up out of the blue.

Two of those five, Signalmen Maynard Skinner and James Dignan, passed through Hong Kong in mid-2005 while this work was being copy-edited. I met them in their hotel. "While I was in the water", said Skinner, "resigning myself to death, some words from The Tempest were running through my mind: 'Full Fathom Five ...' ". I could not have been more astonished. We recited the remainder together.

* * *

One never knows. The Internet is a wonderful thing, and for at least the next few years there is still a chance that I might receive one or two more emails with the goose-pimple-raising sign-off, "and by the way, I was on the *Lisbon Maru.*"

Tony Banham
Hong Kong
2006

Appendix 1

JUDGEMENT: THE TRIAL OF KYODA SHIGERU

On 20 March 1943, having taken note of the reports of the three escapees from the *Lisbon Maru*, the British government finally sent a strongly worded complaint to Tokyo via the Canadian legation in Berne. It asked for details of a court of enquiry "which they assume the Japanese Government will have appointed" to investigate and punish those responsible for "treatment of prisoners-of-war on board LISBON etc. both at time of and before sinking a flagrant violation of customs and usages of war as regards treatment of prisoners and provisions of Geneva Convention". While stating that the British government appreciated that the Geneva Convention was never ratified by the Japanese government, it added: "these heartless violations of all enlightened naval training call peremptorily for condign punishment of persons concerned."

On 16 May, the Japanese finally replied (their delay appears to have resulted from a hasty internal enquiry into the disaster). Again, the communication was made via neutral Berne:

> Japanese Government is led to conclude that British protests aim to falsify and defame, on unfounded information, worthy and just measures taken by competent Japanese officials at the time of the torpedoing of the LISBON MARU.
>
> British allegations such as the sick abandoned and the prisoners fired upon are beyond the imagination of people having common sense, since the persons escorting the prisoners, and the crew did not leave the prisoners until the last moment, and shared their fate. Some of them perished, victims of the disaster, in trying to save some 900 prisoners.

> This fact proves undoubtedly that British allegations are nothing but lies and absurdities.
>
> Please clarify each point in British protests.

This was added to, some two weeks later, by a radio broadcast — pure propaganda — making even stronger claims:

> Tokio reports (Domei, June 3, 2:00 a.m. EST) in English to the Pacific Zone that Takeo Iguchi, Secretary of the Marine Affairs Board, has "made public the heroism of Capt. Shigeru Kyoda, whose ship, the (illegible) Nippon Yusen Kaisha line LISBON MARU was torpedoed and sunk in the eastern China Sea last October while loaded with British war prisoners. The broadcast says Iguchi stated that at the risk of his own life Capt. Kyoda, again and again, swam to the aid of drowning prisoners, pushed floating wreckage into their grasp so that they could be swept ashore safely. Iguchi added that the prisoners themselves [sic] the Captain's heroic action and were unreserved in expressing praise for his gallantry.[279]

British officials recognized this broadcast for what it was, but they took careful note of the captain's name for action at an appropriate time.

But many others in Britain had far more personal interest in such details. At war's end, P.W. Grant, who we last saw asking after the fate of his Royal Engineer son two years earlier, wrote directly to the Prime Minister asking for action to be taken against the *Lisbon Maru's* master. His letter caused a flood of intergovernmental communications:

Letters should be addressed to—	STOREY'S GATE[280]
The Treasury Solicitor,[281]	ST. JAME'S PARK
And the following reference quoted	LONDON, S.W.1.
on the cover and in the letter:	
WCB/XXXIII(a)PHBK	
Telephone No: Whitehall 1124	12th January 1946

Dear Beaumont,

Ref: U.8210/211/73

I must apologise for delay in replying to your letter of 11th December 1945 under above reference enquiring whether the Captain of the "Lisbon Maru" will be treated as a war criminal.

The reply to the above query is in the affirmative. A Charge has been in draft for some weeks but for various reasons has only just now been completed. In it the Captain of the "Lisbon Maru" appears as one of the accused. His name is understood to be Captain Shigeru Tsuno.[282]

The draft is now being engrossed and will be filed with the U.N.W.C.C. in the course of a day or two. If you have not already replied to Mr. Grant's enquiry, you can I think now do so with every confidence.

Yours Sincerely

R.A. Beaumont, Esq.,
Foreign Office,
S.W. 1.

K 746/746/73

FOREIGN OFFICE
S.W.1.

29th January, 1946.

Sir,

I am directed by Mr. Secretary Bevin[283] to acknowledge the receipt of your letter of the 4th October last to the Prime Minister, asking whether the captain of the S.S. Lisbon Maru would be treated as a war criminal.

2. I am to state in reply that it has for some time been the intention of His Majesty's Government to put forward the name of the captain of the Lisbon Maru to the United Nations War Crimes Commission as a war criminal but that the matter has been subjected to some delay as a result of the difficulty which has been experienced in positively identifying this person by name. The delay in answering your letter under reference is attributable to the same difficulty.

The departments of His Majesty's Government concerned believe that sufficient evidence is now to hand to identify the Captain of the Lisbon Maru and to bring a good case against him, and this is consequently being done.

I am,
    Sir,
        Your obedient Servant

P.W. Grant, Esq.,
  Mostyn Hall,
    Penrith,
      Cumberland

Ref   Mostyn Hall [received 27 Feb 46]
K 746/746/73   Penrith
                                     Cumberland

Dear Sir,

Your letter dated January 29th to hand and observe since receiving your letter I have learnt the full facts about my boy.

I enclose a letter from his Company Commander, also one from a fellow prisoner these will give you some details of how they went, he and the others to their death through the fault of those pigs. I would like to add I have had a visit from another boy who was left in Shanghai to die like my boy. He survived, they were given nothing to help in any way as regards medicines etc. Get that pig who was in charge at Shanghai as well as the captain of 'Lisbon Maru'. Kindly return the enclosed letters at you convenience.

                Yours faithfully
                P.W. Grant

U B244/745/73

                FOREIGN OFFICE
                S.W.1.

                5th March, 1946.

Sir,

I am directed by Mr. Secretary Bevin to acknowledge the receipt of your undated letter enclosing two letters on the subject of your son's death in Japanese hands and to assure you that it is the policy of His Majesty's Government to take all possible steps to ensure that justice is meted out to Japanese who have been responsible for committing crimes against British subjects.

2.   The enclosures to your letter are returned herewith as requested.[284]

    I am,

        Sir,

            Your obedient Servant,

P.W. Grant, Esq.,
    Mostyn Hall
        Penrith,
            Cumberland

Appendix 1

Just over seven months after the date of this letter, on 23 October 1946, at ten in the morning in Hong Kong, Jardine Matheson's East Point Godown fell silent. Hong Kong's commander of Land Forces, Lieutenant Colonel R. C. Laming, brought a Military Court to order. With Laming as President, it had been convened to try one Kyoda Shigeru, a "civilian in the service of the Imperial Japanese Army", and one-time Master of the *Lisbon Maru*, on the following charge:

> COMMITTING A WAR CRIME in that he on the High Seas, on the 1st and 2nd October 1942, when Master of the Military Transport S.S. "Lisbon Maru" and as such responsible for the lives and safety of about 1800 British Prisoners of War on board the said transport when it had been torpedoed and was in a sinking condition, in violation of the laws and usages of war, was concerned (a) in the battening down of the P.O.W. aforesaid in the ships holds whereby many died of suffocation and many underwent mental and physical sufferings and many others were trapped and drowned when the ship sank and (b) in his failure to provide for the use of the P.O.W. available boats and life jackets as a result many of them were drowned after the ship had sunk and many more underwent mental and physical sufferings.

The interpreters read out the charge in Japanese as Kyoda listened. Laming asked, "Shigeru Kyoda, are you guilty or not guilty of the charge you have just heard read to you?"

Kyoda: "I plead not guilty."

It was hardly unexpected. Major Peter Vine, Royal Marines,[285] the counsel for the prosecution, then stood and delivered his opening address.

"Mr President and Members. The case before you today is one of unusual importance. The proceedings and the verdict which you reach will be closely studied not only here in Hong Kong but in Singapore and Tokyo. The Admiralty is also deeply concerned since the issues which I will lay before you are concerned with the fundamental responsibility of a Master of a vessel for the lives and safety of all aboard. The responsibility is not essential to the prosecution of this case, but it will affect very considerably the relative guilt of the accused compared with other persons who are not before you ..."

After twenty-five minutes, he called his first witness — Major Y. H. Chan — to present Kyoda's sworn statement of events on board the *Lisbon Maru*. Having established the provenance of the statement, Vine called a number of other witnesses to read the affidavits of a number of those onboard.

Vine then called his first expert witness, Yokota Minoru, captain of the cruiser *Kashima*. Yokota was 43. He had entered the Japanese Naval Academy in 1920, graduated in 1923, and taken his first command in 1938; it is not clear if the court recognized just how experienced he was.

On 6 November 1941, Yokota Minoru had taken command of the new Japanese submarine I-26. Briefed on the Pearl Harbour attack on 15 November, he departed secretly for the Aleutians on 19 November on the boat's First War Patrol. Ordered then to patrol between Hawaii and San Francisco, the submarine received warning on 2 December that hostilities would commence on 8 December (Japanese time). On 6 December they sighted the 2,140-ton Army-chartered steam schooner *Cynthia Olson* carrying military freight from Tacoma, Washington to Honolulu, Hawaii. At dawn I-26 attacked on the surface, shelling the vessel until it finally settled as the first American merchant ship to be lost to a Japanese submarine during the war.

On 31 January 1944 Yokota Minoru took command of the new submarine I-44. After patrolling off Palau and New Ireland, he was lucky to survive an attack by an American aircraft that left the boat leaking and on the surface, unable to dive.

Relieved by Kawaguchi Genbei on 16 September 1944,[286] Yokota became captain of the cruiser *Kashima* after the war, which was then being used to repatriate Japanese troops, and found itself in Hong Kong at the time of the trial.

Vine's aim was simple. He intended showing that the safety of those on board a ship is, under all and every circumstance, ultimately the responsibility of the master of the vessel. In turn, the Defence strategy — as Vine had guessed — was to show that in Japan at time of war, even the master of a vessel was inferior in rank to the senior military person on board, and therefore had to obey his orders.

Knowing that Kyoda's defence was to be based on 'obeying superior orders', Vine had called Yokota as an expert witness to distinguish between the captain's role, and that of the Commanding Officer of troops on board a ship. After a number of confused exchanges, with at least some of the confusion coming from the interpretation, Vine felt he was not getting the clear responses he was after.

Vine: "I want to know who is responsible for the lives and safety of the troops on board?"

Yokota: "The responsibility for navigation is with the captain of the ship. All other responsibility is that of the OC the troops."

Vine: "Sir, I wish to have this witness treated as hostile."

Laming: "On what grounds?"

Vine: "On the grounds of committing perjury. The evidence which he is giving differs from that of his sworn statement."

Laming: "He has made a sworn statement?"

Vine: "He has, sir."

Laming: "I think we should wait a minute and see if we cannot put the question another way."

Finally, Laming's patient questioning resulted in a clear definition of the respective roles.

Laming: "Would you agree when it comes to saving the lives of people on board the captain is not bound to take orders from the OC troops?"

Yokota: "I agree. I think so."

As the whole trial hinged on this single point, a verdict could almost have been arrived at there and then.

The second day of the trial started late, due to a realization that there may have been a recent precedent for this sort of case. As Laming stated to Vine, "Before your first witness is called, the Court has considered that in view of the important legal issues to be decided, it would be of great assistance to the Court if it is possible to get copies of the judgement in the Nuremberg trial which has just been completed. We believe that the Press has a complete transcript of the whole judgement and I shall be grateful if it is possible to get copies of this transcript so that the Court may take advantage of it to guide it."

Vine then called his second expert witness, Pay Lieutenant Commander Imamura Ichiro, in detention himself at Stanley prison on suspicion of war crimes. As a paymaster, he seemed somewhat out of his depth on questions on the law of the sea, but perhaps like Yokota, whose cruiser had been in Hong Kong at the time, he had simply been available.

Like many Japanese naval men, he showed little respect for the army.

Ichiro: "I don't know anything about the details of the regulations providing the relation between the master and the CO, but I think in many cases in the Pacific War army officers behaved so unreasonably that in many cases the majority of the army officers did everything by duress, by force. They acted very unreasonably. When I was a student of the Imperial University, I heard that in 1936 when the army began to be very influential and strong, there was a cry for expansion of armaments and there was a great demand on the military expenditure. When the demand on the military expenditure became so very great the financial department authorities refused to defray the expenditure and then some of the military who formed the nucleus or the mainstay of the army said, 'Japanese people have hundreds of millions of postal savings. If these postal savings deposits were turned over to the use of the army, then military armaments can be accomplished quite easily.' Such is the irrational act of the army. This is an episode. The episode I have just mentioned will show how irrational army personnel can be, so this amply proves that in many cases the behaviour of the military personnel was beyond the realms of common sense."

The Court decided that this outburst was irrelevant, but could get nothing else but 'common sense' answers from the witness.

Next, the first POW witness, Howell, was called, giving the Court a description of conditions on board, and the events surrounding the sinking. Araki Kaname, the Second Officer of the *Lisbon Maru*, followed him, on the fourth day of the trial.

Araki was the witness best qualified, apart from the defendant himself, to describe the actions of the ship's officers in the incident, but first the Court asked him to describe their functions. He replied: "The first mate is in charge of navigation and administration on the deck under the orders of the master of the ship. The second mate is in charge of everything concerning navigation under the orders and instructions of the master of the ship. The third mate is assistant to the first mate. The chief engineer is in charge of the engine room and he is fully responsible for everything concerning the engine room. The first engineer is in charge of administration of the engine room under the orders of the chief engineer. The second and third engineers are in charge of the maintenance of the engines of the ship under the first engineer's orders. The purser is in charge of administration, general affairs and accounting on board the ship under the master's orders. The wireless operator is in charge of sending and receiving and maintaining the wireless equipment on board the ship under the master's orders. The assistant wireless operator is assistant to the chief wireless officer. These are all the duties of the ship's officers."

The questions and answers again focused on the respective authorities of the senior army officer on board, versus the ship's master. What right had the OC troops to issue orders to the crew in an emergency? He had the right to order the master to lower the boats. Even if the OC troops' rank was lower than the master's? Yes, because the master's military rank was only honorary. So, what should the master do if the OC troops gave an order that would endanger those on board? He should endeavour to get the order changed.

A line of questioning about survival equipment and boat drills proved more promising, with Araki readily admitting that all was not well in this department. In normal usage, a life jacket would be issued per person, and they would be required to bring it with them on weekly boat drills. However, it was established that although there were enough life jackets on board for every POW and Japanese soldier, they had never been properly issued.

Araki stated his opinion that the master of the *Lisbon Maru* should have disobeyed the army's order to batten down the hatches of the POWs. He pointed out that disobeying such orders was illegal, but would have been the right thing to do — especially — Araki's logic ran, as Kyoda intended committing suicide by going down with the ship anyway.

Vines: "In the course of your evidence, by your replies both to the prosecutor and in cross-examination and also in reply to questions by the Court, you have given the impression that you believe there may be a higher duty than merely obeying an official order. I am not now referring specifically to the master of the *Lisbon Maru*, but I would like you to answer this on your professional honour as an officer of the Japanese Mercantile Marine. Do you believe that there are times when for the sake of what a man believes to be right and proper that he should disobey an order and do what he thinks is right even though he risks punishment by doing so?"

Araki: "I think that in case an unreasonable order is given and as a result many people could be endangered, if by disobeying this order many people might be happy or would be saved, I think one should disobey the order even though he should be punished later."

Apart from this point, Araki generally painted his commanding officer in a good light. However, he also reported a lack of any apparent communication between Kyoda and the escorting vessels on the subject of trying to save the POWs. This was damning.

Araki's stand as a witness lasted until the end of the seventh day of the trial. On the eighth, another POW witness, Arthur Evans (one of the three escapees), took the stand. He described, authoritatively, the situation from the view of the naval personnel in Number 1 hold. The next day, he was followed by Inspector Joseph Hill of the Police whose description of events in Number 2 hold added little, except noting that he had seen the last Japanese guard on board jump fully clothed, with his helmet on, into the sea. The ninth day's afternoon started with a new witness, Frank Garton of the HKRNVR. Before joining the Hong Kong government in 1924, Garton had served for six years in the British Merchant Navy, a period that included six months' service in the Great War, during which time he had had his first experience of being torpedoed on a freighter.

"It was the last thought on my mind", he said of this second sinking, "that the ship would be torpedoed. I only knew I was en route to another country to do some hard work for the Japanese."

Garton also mentioned that he had only seen POWs, not Japanese guards, on the bridge when he escaped from the hold.

On the tenth day, the court called Hamilton. He gave a more informed view of the events in the second hold.

The following day began with the calling of the fourteenth witness for the prosecution, Euchi Makita, who had translated the defendant's statement. Having verified the translation, he was followed by the third expert witness, Commander G.D.A. Gregory, DSO and bar, Royal Navy. Gregory had joined the navy at the age of thirteen. Now thirty-six, he was captain of HMS *Constance*. Once four questions about his background and authority as a seaman were over, the fifth, pertinent, question was posed. Gregory was clearly prepared for his task:

Vine: "Will you state to the Court, Sir, what you consider are the responsibilities of a C.O. of any vessel at sea?"

Gregory: "I consider that a C.O. of any ship is entirely responsible for the safety of his ship, the safety of his crew, the safety of all passengers and for everything that happens in that ship."

Vine: "Can you elaborate that point, Sir?"

Gregory: "To elaborate that point: Should a superior officer give an order likely to endanger my ship and company I am quite clear in my mind that that order in no way absolves me from the responsibilities for the safety of the ship and for the safety of the people on board."

Araki Kaname was then recalled. The day ended with Mr Takahashi complaining that documents he had sent to Japan for on 16 October had not yet arrived.

The twelfth day of the case opened with Vine closing the case for the prosecution. At the same time, Takahashi argued for an adjournment while his papers ('Operational Field Service Regulations', the regulations specifically concerning the authority of a master of a transport ship requisitioned by the army) were delivered. The Court adjourned to consider this request.

Laming: "The Court has decided that in view of the gravity of the charges made against the accused and the penalties that might be imposed on the accused should he be found guilty that every latitude and every assistance must be given to the defence in order that they may place their defence in the very best way possible."

The Court adjourned, until such time as Tokyo could produce the necessary documents.

When the documents arrived, the Court reconvened on 8 November. However, due to considerations on the necessary translations of the document, a further adjournment until Wednesday, 13 November, was granted. Finally, on that inauspicious day, the defendant himself was called.

After much description of the voyage and life on board up to the sinking, Vine again focused on the protocol concerning the safety of passengers. Once more, he tried to illustrate that the master would have an obligation to ignore any military orders that interfered with that safety.

Vines: "So if a Lance Corporal of the guard had come up to you and said he wanted you to arrange with your crew to put up a gallows on the stern of your ship and hang the prisoners one by one, you would agree to do it?"

Kyoda: "If the unit commander of such a guard should be on board the ship I do not have to obey his orders. I only have to obey the unit commander's orders. If that Lance Corporal is the commander at that time I must obey his orders."

Vine: "So you would obey the order to erect a gallows in the stern of the ship and have the prisoners hanged one by one if the order was given, would you?"

Kyoda: "First of all I would object from a moral point of view."

Vine: "And should the order be repeated and it were made clear that it would be regarded as an act of disobedience if you did not obey would you do it then?"

Kyoda: "Such an order to me as the building of a gallows, such work can be done by the members of the guard or some other person beside the crew. Therefore I would not obey such an order."

Vine: "So you do admit there are orders and there are circumstances in which those orders should not be obeyed?"

Kyoda: "There are times according to the circumstances when such orders are not obeyed."

The 'Operational Field Service Regulations' (paragraph 10, section 3, part 1) seemed to confirm this: "The commanding officer of troops in transit on train or transport has no right to interfere with the departure, arrival or movement of train or transport unless otherwise laid down specifically."

Twice during the examination the name of the *Arandora Star*[287] was brought up, presumably to use that example as a precedent, but as the Japanese witnesses were unfamiliar with the example, that line of questioning could not usefully proceed.

On the seventeenth day of the trial, Kyoda stepped down. The following day, 18 November, Niimori was called. As a defence witness, with his testimony directly contradicting statements made by many other witnesses in areas such as the distribution of life belts, he was of little assistance. The third witness for the defence, an expert on military transportations, Major Ando Tadashi, followed him.

Takahashi, the counsel for the defence: "In case a ship is requisitioned [by the army] what becomes of the position of the crew of the ship?"

Ando: "The crew become civilians attached to the army."

Takahashi: "What position does a civilian attached to the army hold?"

Ando: "They do not hold the status of soldiers but they are employed to carry out any order issued to them by the army."

Cross-examination won from Ando an interesting differentiation between orders and 'private orders' (defined as orders outside the area of duty of the superior giving them). Ando conceded that he would not feel duty-bound to obey such 'private orders'.

Later, a surprise witness was called, the third mate of the *Lisbon Maru*, Hiyama Seinoshin, whom the prosecution had not even known was in Hong Kong.

At that time, 'Document No. 2662, Part 15, Data concerning the Lisbon Maru' was introduced. Found by the Americans after the war at the Merchant Marine Control Beaureau in Japan,[288] these pages related to a Japanese enquiry into the truth of British accusations about the *Lisbon Maru*. The contents were: (1) Gist of the British Protest. (2) The situation at the time of the Disaster of the *Lisbon Maru*. (3) Reference Materials. (4) Decisions.

However, this document was disappointing. It contained nothing useful, being based almost entirely on statements by Kyoda and Niimori. While Kyoda's words stayed close to the facts (with the one exception of stating that the POWs abandoned ship on Japanese orders), Niimori had claimed credit for almost all the things the prisoners had done for themselves, from looking after the sick to organizing food. The fact that — despite Niimori's insistence that Japanese passengers and POWs had had equal opportunities to escape — only one of the former had drowned compared to almost 50 percent of the latter, was ignored in the Japanese enquiry. It concluded that there was no basis to the accusations.

On 28 November, after a six-day adjournment for both sides to prepare their concluding remarks, the Court reconvened for its 23rd day of hearings. The defence's closing address was then read, followed by the prosecution's.

At 12.30 Laming announced: "The Court will now be closed to consider their finding. In view of the large amount of evidence and the important legal points raised by the Prosecution and the Defence, the Court will not re-open until 10.30 a.m. tomorrow morning."

That morning, the 24th, and final, day of the proceedings, Jardine Matheson's East Point Godown was unusually full. In front of a crowded court, Laming announced the verdict:

> "Kyoda Shigeru, you have been found guilty by the Court of the offence charged except with the exceptions which the Court referred to in making their finding. I will remind you and your Defending Counsel again that the sentence is subject to confirmation by superior military authority and that should you wish to appeal against either the finding or the sentence that you must give notice of such appeal within two days, and submit that appeal within fourteen days. The Court have considered very carefully all the attendant circumstances of the case which have been brought out in the evidence and all the arguments put forward by the Prosecution and the Defence and the points urged by the Defence Counsel in his speech in mitigation.[289] The sentence of the Court, therefore on you is that you will go to prison for seven years.
>
> The proceedings of this Court are hereby terminated."
>
> FINDING: Guilty except that the court finds that two and not "many" P.O.W. died in the ship's holds from the effects of the conditions in No. 1 hold and their

already weakened state, and not from suffocation; that others and not "many others" were trapped and drowned when the ship sank, and except for the words "and in his failure to provide for the use of the P.O.W. available lifeboats and life jackets, as a result many of them were drowned when the ship sunk and many more underwent mental and physical sufferings."

SENTENCE: 29 Nov, '46. 7 years' imprisonment.

Judgement had been made. But had justice been done? On whose hands did the blood of 828 men (or 1,073 if all the resulting deaths are included) really lie?

The submariners seem to have been absolved of all blame. Although Selwyn-Clarke, BAAG, and others had tried to get word out, there is no evidence that any solid information that the *Lisbon Maru* was carrying Prisoners Of War reached American submarines before the sinking. CQMS William Poulter of the Middlesex seems to have spoken for everyone on board when he said: "I never heard any man complain of the submarine that sank us, in fact they all agreed it was the right thing to do."

Kyoda Shigeru had been found guilty; the prosecution's attempts to show that his behaviour had been contrary to Japanese standards at the time had been accepted. However, this was despite the fact that it had been clearly established in court that in wartime Japan the captain's authority was less than that of the senior military officer on board. The premise of the trial: "Master of the Military Transport S.S. 'Lisbon Maru' and as such responsible for the lives and safety of about 1800 British Prisoners of War on board the said transport when it had been torpedoed and was in a sinking condition, in violation of the laws and usages of war ..." was itself questionable when the Master clearly did not have overall responsibility in the system prevailing.

While the Master's claims of being an advocate of the POWs in front of Wada and the other military officers cannot be substantiated (and nor can his claims to have tried to aid POWs in their efforts to launch a lifeboat), he was at least involved in the attempts to tow the vessel to shallow water. Whether this attempt was primarily aimed at saving the ship and its cargo rather than the POWs, it may possibly have helped some of the latter to survive.

The fact that of the two counts against him ("(a) in the battening down of the P.O.W. aforesaid in the ships holds whereby many died of suffocation and many underwent mental and physical sufferings and many others were trapped and drowned when the ship sank and (b) in his failure to provide for the use of the P.O.W. available boats and life jackets as a result many of them were drowned after the ship had sunk and many more underwent mental and physical sufferings"), the second was rejected entirely and the first was greatly reduced, suggests that the court did not find him responsible for the deaths of hundreds of men. In fact the sentence of just seven years implied that he was not found fully responsible for any deaths.

The true responsibility, of course, lay in those truly: "in violation of the laws and usages of war". While it is often correctly remarked that Japan had chosen not to ratify the Geneva Convention,[290] it is equally often stated that the Japanese should still have moved POWs — according to the Geneva Convention — in marked vessels.

Therefore, in choosing not to mark ships like the *Lisbon Maru* with the Red Cross, in choosing not to notify neutral powers of their sailing times, and in choosing to carry Japanese troops and war material in the same vessels as POWs, the Japanese authorities had chosen to make them targets for friendly fire.

In fact the truth is more complex. While the Japanese treatment of Prisoners of War was in flagrant violation of the Geneva Convention in almost every aspect, in fact the marking of ships according to the Convention appears to have applied solely to hospital ships. Provisions for the transfer of ordinary POWs were limited to a few lines in the agreement, none of which referred explicitly to transfer by sea. The only immediately relevant clause of the convention appears to be Article 9, which states: "No prisoner may, at any time, be sent into a region where he might be exposed to the fire of the combat zone, nor used to give protection from bombardment to certain points or certain regions by his presence".

The ultimate responsibility for the disaster therefore lay both on Lieutenant Wada, the commander of the POW transportation, and on the brutal military regime of wartime Japan that had no interest in the lives of individuals. But the regime was never put on trial, and Wada died before he could be brought to justice.

Appendix 2

THE HISTORY OF THE LIST OF THE MEN ON THE *LISBON MARU*

(From BAAG files)[291] TSE DICKUAN

Chinese-British subject, born 24.1.1900 in Hongkong, clerk, BAAG 15 June 44 – 31 October 45.

(Award Citation) "After the surrender of Hongkong, this man was given employment in the headquarters of the Japanese department for P/Ws and Internees. After some time in the course of his work he gained access to their official records and Nominal Rolls of British and Canadian P/Ws. Realising that these would be of immense value to us, of his own accord he made copies by taking a few sheets at a time to his home and typing them out. This took some months to complete and throughout this period he did this voluntary work at the risk of his life. When completed he got in touch with the BAAG and offered to hand them over the complete lists.

Within a month of this original contact, the lists were in our hands and provided the first really authentic and complete records we had of the P/Ws, and of the fate of many of them.

He remained on at his post in the Jap P/W office, working for us, but eventually, under the strain, his health failed and he was discharged after a period of illness in hospital, but before he left he laid on the necessary contacts with us whereby we were able to obtain constant and up to date information of the Hongkong P/Ws.

This voluntary work demanded great and sustained bravery and was of the utmost value to us and P/W relatives."

Statement 29.9.45

"... On August 10th 1942 I obtained employment as a typist at the "Intelligence Office" attached to the Prisoner of War Section, HQs, Forfar Road. The staff consisted of the undermentioned: (Tokunaga, Tanaka, Hara, Niimori, Hasigawa, Kochi, Watanabe, Akatayama, Matsuda, Inouye + four Chinese: myself, Arthur Lee, Eugene Mak, Tam Chung Man.

The work of the Chinese staff was purely work in connection with Prisoners of War.

From Nov 1942 when I was given a casualty list to type, I surreptitiously took copies of all papers relating to prisoners. These I hid at my home. I thus managed by the end of 1943 to collect a full list of prisoners of war, casualty lists, etc. When a friend of mine, who was previously employed by the [Canadian Pacific Railway] named John McKenzie (Eurasian) left for Macao in March 1944 I instructed him to get in touch with [His Britannic Majesty's] Consul in order to ascertain if he was prepared to receive message from me. John McKenzie later replied that this would be too dangerous. So I had to give up this idea. In May 1944 I sent my eldest sister to Waichow in order to contact the officer i/c BAAG. But unfortunately she died. On July 7 1944 a cousin of mine named Chan Hong Chung took a letter for me to the officer i/c BAAG Waichow. About ten days later I received a reply signed "Bobbin".[292] This instructed me to deliver all records to him, if the circumstances permitted, and also enclosed some money in order to enable my family to proceed to Waichow. It took me fifteen days and nights of incessant toil to put the finishing touches to my reports. After this I had a breakdown in health. The reports were then put into the lining of an old canvas handbag and this was smuggled through the Japanese lines by my cousin who delivered them to "Bobbin" at Waichow, on or about the 17th August 1944. In August 1944 a new internment camp was opened at Matauchung for the detention of one hundred and sixteen third nationals. As I was very ill I consulted my doctor and obtained one month's leave. During this time I planned my escape. On Sept 19th 1944 I returned to work, although I was still ill. At 10.30 a.m. I purposely dropped from a height of 10 ft. and hurt myself. I feigned unconsciousness and I was sent home to get medical attention. I was given an injection of morphine and slept for two days. When I awoke I feigned madness. After one week a doctor took fluid from my spine and not finding any injury to my brain diagnosed my illness as a "nervous breakdown". On a medical certificate being obtained I was further granted a period of leave up to the end of Sept. 1944.

On 2nd October 1944 I tendered my resignation, together with another medical certificate and luckily this was approved. On Nov 4th 1944 I together with my family left for Taipo. I had in my possession MY5,000 and NC20,000,[293] but when I arrived in Taipo all the MY had been spent in bribery. Owing to trouble between the Govt. troops and communists, I was detained at this place for six days. On Nov 9th a young boy arrived with a message telling me to leave at once. Leaving my wife and family I proceeded to Waichow where I arrived on the 12th. My family, who had been robbed of most of my possessions, arrived on the 15th Nov. 1944. At Waichow I contacted Major Cooper and as a result I maintained communications with a Miss Ho and Mr. Eugene Mak, who had helped me in this work, and thus was able to eventually keep up the records of the Prisoners of War and other intelligence. I later learned that Miss Ho Chun Yue was arrested on Jan 18th 1945 and that no news has since been received of her. Her sister, Miss Ho Bik Wan took up the work and managed with Mr. Mak to maintain communications.

Regarding the arrest of prisoners of war and their subsequent execution or imprisonments, I can give the following details.

About the middle of 1942, four Canadians, amongst who was one named Payne,[294] attempted to escape from North Point Camp. They were arrested and subsequently beheaded.

About the same time a number of prisoners attempted, by tunnelling, to escape from Shamshuipo Camp. They were unfortunately caught. They were made to dig their own graves. After which they were bayoneted. One of the men was I think named Stopworth.[295] 2nd Lt. Tanaka was, on account of his work in the two above-mentioned cases, promoted to full Lieut. He was assisted on these cases by Interpreter Niimori.

About July 1943, Private M. Prata, HKVDC, was arrested on a charge of espionage. He was taken to Tanaka's residence No. 161 Argyle Street and there tortured to death by the water torture. This was administered by two Japanese officers of the Gendarmerie, attached to the Kowloon Police Station, Boundary Street. Tanaka, Niimori and Hasegawa were present. This was witnessed by a maid servant (name forgotten) who informed me of this the following morning. The death of Prata was officially ascribed to "Malaria". I am not sure of the location of the deceased's grave [see addendum below.[296]]

Some time in 1943, Col. Newnham, Lt. Ford (Royal Scots)[297] and Flight Lieut. Gray (RAF) and three Chinese chauffeurs were arrested and subsequently executed. The officers were executed on the 1st December 1943. I have no information regarding this case as it was kept very secret. Although I knew of the arrest of S/Lt. Haddock, I do not know the details of this case.

In Sept. 1943 Commander Craven, L/Cdr Young, Major Boxer, Lieut Dixon, Sgt. Routledge and Pte Hardy were arrested on a charge of espionage and operating wireless transmitters. Lieut Tanaka, Capt Yoko Adjt and interpreter Niimori were connected with this case. Colonel Tokunaga in a communication to Tokyo recommended that the above mentioned persons should receive capital punishment.[298]

A report received at HQs during Aug 1944 showed that Pte F.M. Hale of the HKVDC fell from a veranda and was killed, I do not know the circumstances surrounding this man's death.

I do not know anything regarding the death of Lt. Shrigley.[299] All medical supplies received from the Red Cross were kept by Capt Saito. Whilst such things as shoes, toilet articles and foodstuffs were kept by Capt Kato.

I was never allowed to see the courts martial records of any trials held on prisoners of war.

From time to time I typed Major Cecil Boone's[300] pro-Japanese impressions which were later sent to Tokyo.

The limitation of the number of words allowed in prisoner of war correspondence and the remittance of money to Stanley were proposed by Interpreter Niimori.

Regarding the Lisbon Maru tragedy, Niimori and Sgt. Maj Hayashi Sennosuke were in charge of the prisoners. Niimori, whilst in his cups, boasted that they had blocked up all the gangways so the prisoners could not escape. He also stated that he owed his life to a British officer who saved him from drowning. Regarding prisoners of war acting as informers to the Japanese, I do not know of anyone who acted in this capacity in the Argyle St Officers Camp but I do know that there were two in the Shamshuipo Camp but I have forgotten their names.

Addendum 29th September 1945: Re the death of Pt M. Prata, the girl who witnessed the deed and later informed me is named Yuk Chun. This girl was employed, together with another named Ah Din, as a serving maid at the residence of Lt Tanaka, No 161 Argyle Street, Kowloon. Ah Din was later transferred to the Kitchen and her place was taken by one named Poon Kit Chun. The last named girl's father is the branch manager of Messrs. Singer Sewing Machine Co, Yaumati.

Mak, Eugene
Nationality Chinese, born Hongkong, aged 25, Clerk of works for government contactor, sergeant in Field Ambulance. After he was released from POW camp he was a typist and clerk at POW HQ at Argyle St, up to the surrender of Japan. He was constantly in contact with Major Cooper through Dickson (*sic*) Tse from Sept. 44 to August 45.

Appendix 3

STATISTICS

Hold	Unit	Total	Lost	Lived	Sh'hai	Esc.	Died	Home	%Lost
One	Royal Navy	375	160	215	8	2	72	143	42.67
Two	2nd Battalion, the Royal Scots Regiment	373	144	229	7	0	33	196	38.61
	1st Battalion, the Middlesex Regiment	358	152	206	10	0	56	150	42.46
	Royal Engineers	171	74	97	8	0	37	60	43.27
	Royal Corps of Signals	129	50	79	3	0	20	59	38.76
	Royal Army Medical Corps	21	4	17	5	0	1	16	19.05
	Royal Army Dental Corps (RADC)	3	2	1	0	0	0	1	66.67
	Royal Army Service Corps (RASC)	1	0	1	0	0	0	1	0.00
	Hong Kong Police Force	5	2	3	0	0	0	3	40.00
	Civilians	4	2	2	0	1	0	2	50.00
	Hold total	*1065*	*430*	*635*	*33*	*1*	*147*	*488*	*40.38*
Three	Royal Artillery	376	238	138	3	0	23	115	63.30
Totals		1816	828	988	44	3	242	746	45.59

'Lost' and 'Lived' describe the situation as at the end of 2 October 1942. 'Shanghai' lists those left behind when the majority of survivors were transferred to Moji (and these figures include medical personnel detailed to look after the sick). 'Died' refers to those who died after 2 October.

Note: Approximately seventeen men (including Hunt) of the Royal Navy were in fact in Hold 2, as were perhaps twelve men (including Inglis, Giddons and Bowen) from the Royal Artillery. Here, their numbers are included in 1 and 3 holds. The Royal Navy numbers include the Royal Marines, Dockyard Police, Hong Kong Royal Naval Volunteer Reserve, Merchant Navy, and Hong Kong Dockyard Defence Corps.

Notes

1. A second photo was taken fifteen minutes later but is now missing from the War Crime Trials papers at the PRO. Examination of a poor quality copy at Hong Kong University Library shows that it was taken at the same angle, with most of the vessel abaft the funnel now submerged. A few heads can just be made out lining the bows.
2. In 1942, Bennett was known as Lance Corporal Frank 'Johnny' Johnson.
3. Née Redwood.
4. *Not the Slightest Chance: The Defence of Hong Kong, 1941*, Hong Kong University Press, 2003.
5. Sadly, there were other non-British friendly fire disasters on an even bigger scale. Four months earlier, on 22 June, 1,053 Australians being transferred from Rabaul to Hainan Dao had lost their lives when the *Montevideo Maru* was sunk by USS *Sturgeon*. The *Tango Maru*, on 24 February 1944, was sunk by USS *Rasher* with the loss of 3,000 Indonesian labourers. Over 1,000 Indonesians were also lost on the *Koshu Maru* later that year, with a similar number of Allied POWs of various nationalities being lost on the *Rakuyo Maru* in June, the *Hofuku Maru* in September, and the *Arisan Maru* in October 1944. However, the single largest loss of life was on board the *Junyo Maru*, with 5,620 Indonesians losing their lives when she was sunk by the British submarine HMS *Tradewind* on 17 September 1944.
6. There were six such transportations from Hong Kong to Japan in total. All arrived safely except the *Lisbon Maru*.
7. See Appendix 2: The History of the List of the Men on the *Lisbon Maru*.
8. Goat Island, in San Francisco Bay, is now better known as Yerba Buena.
9. Based at Pearl Harbour from 1931–1939, USS *S-28* (the S boats did not have names) then transferred to San Diego, California. On 7 December 1941, the boat, then a unit of SubDiv 41, was being overhauled at the Mare Island Navy Yard. This work was completed by 22 January 1942, and she returned to her San Diego base to resume her pre-war training duties for the

Underwater Sound Training School. The *S-28* (SS-133), under her new skipper Commander J. G. Campbell — who had been on board less than a month in this, his first command — was finally lost in 1944 while conducting torpedo exercises with the Coast Guard cutter *Reliance*. The precise cause of the boat's loss was never determined.

10 Confusion is often caused by the fact that Pearl Harbour was attacked on 7 December, while Hong Kong, Malaysia, and the Philippines were attacked on 8 December. This is simply an artefact of the positioning of the International Date Line just east of New Zealand (i.e. between Hawaii and Southeast Asia). These attacks, therefore, were in fact almost simultaneous.

11 Some women found positions with the Essential Services at the last minute, thus avoiding the evacuation, and regretted at leisure in Stanley Internment Camp. Others, though considering themselves 100 percent British, were declared 'Eurasian' and rejected by Australia.

12 See photo, 'The Brooks family before the war'.

13 The Crown Colony of Hong Kong consisted of part of the Chinese mainland (the built-up area of Kowloon, plus the New Territories to the north), various outlying islands, and Hong Kong Island itself lying immediately south of Kowloon.

14 Despite the 'Redoubt' label, the position was no more than a handful of sparsely occupied pillboxes and shelters linked by concrete tunnels and open-air passages.

15 Hunt had six brothers and one older sister. Five of the brothers were old enough to see service in the Second World War. Two were pilots in the RAF, one flew Supermarine Seafires in the Fleet Air Arm, one more was in the Royal Navy, and the last served in the 8th Army in North Africa and the Italian campaign. Remarkably, all survived hostilities.

16 The skipper, first lieutenant, and engine room P.O. were John Baxter Colls, George Spedding McGill, and Thomas Elliot respectively. All were lost.

17 Alf's adventures did not stop there. On 23 December, a large shell came over from the island and demolished the house next door to where he and two other survivors from the MTB were held. They were covered with plaster and rubble and several of the Japanese were killed. Alf was put on an old wooden door and taken to Argyle Street "to meet up with about thirty lads that had been captured". He had no medication or bandages for his wounds but they healed up well. In Argyle Street an American doctor took a bullet from his arm and one from his leg using a razor blade. After about three weeks the men were transferred to Sham Shui Po camp.

18 *Tern* was a Bird Class River Gunboat built by Yarrow in 1927. *Cicala* was an Aphis Class River Gunboat built by Barclay Curle in 1916.

19 Shepherd was moved to Queen Mary's Hospital on 23 December for surgery to remove a bullet from his upper thigh. While this surgery was not serious, it led to a spinal infection that took longer to recover from.

20 St Albert's was at the site now occupied by 43 Stubbs Road. Morley adds: "I was admitted to St Albert's Hospital after the Mount Nicholson episode [where he had fought with HQ Company 2nd Royal Scots on the west side of Wong Nai Chung Gap] suffering from what was supposed to be malaria. On looking back with a clear mind I am sure it [was what's] now called battle fatigue, as I was on the go from day one."
21 Presumably 'kurosei': 'kill them'.
22 The officer had been brought in from the battlefield by Peter Allain, Royal Rifles of Canada, and a British solider (thanks to Michael Palmer for this detail). Sister Mary Currie is credited with both following the tradition of wrapping the body in a Japanese flag, and ensuring that the Japanese entering the hospital were made aware of this; they thus spared the hospital's occupants. She was awarded the Royal Red Cross medal.
23 Lieutenant Peter Grounds died and was buried in the gardens of the hotel, outside the pantry. His body could not be identified after the war. The original hotel was knocked down in 1982, but the garage is still there and is in use to this day.
24 Hamilton's diaries are held by the Imperial War Museum in London. All quotes in this work are from that document and his published booklet "The Sinking The Of [sic] Lisbon Maru".
25 CQMS Tierney had been badly wounded in a Japanese bombing attack near Wanchai Gap just after the surrender. He died on 27 December at the Hong Kong Hotel on Pedder Street, which was then being used as an emergency hospital. Today the site is occupied by The Landmark.
26 This number includes all units engaged in the defence, including the police, who were sworn in as militia, and nurses (who often found themselves on the frontline and also suffered casualties).
27 The author, Sergeant Tom Marsh, survived the march, despite having been shot through the head. He also survived the war, having been on the next draft to Japan after the *Lisbon Maru*. This quote comes from a full-length manuscript held by his son.
28 Although the term is not widely used today, in 1941 'Victoria' was regarded as the capital of the Colony. In the twenty-first century, the part of town roughly corresponding to that area is known as Central.
29 Carew, in *Hostages to Fortune*, page 116, maintains that Wigzell died of diphtheria onboard the *Lisbon Maru* before the sinking. The internal files of the CWGC even claim he was buried at Argyle Street in September 1942. However, their official records state he was lost when the vessel sank and has no known grave.
30 The Jubilee Block was a large two-storey complex originally built to house officers. While North Point camp was originally a hastily constructed refugee camp finished in 1938, Sham Shui Po had been a purpose-built barracks and offered a much better standard of building.

31 The author, James Bertram, was a newspaper reporter from New Zealand, who had volunteered at the last minute for service with the HKVDC and fought in the defence of Stanley. Bertram was spared the *Lisbon Maru*, but was on a later transportation to Japan. This quote is from his book, *The Shadow of War*.
32 A strip of cloth wound around the lower leg.
33 Ma Tau Chong camp was on the south side of Argyle Street, Kowloon.
34 In fact, the period as militia only lasted three days. After that, at their own request, they officially became ordinary police again. However, those police captured during their period as militia ended up in Sham Shui Po with the regular POWs.
35 As noted, the majority of British wives and children had been ordered to evacuate to the safety of Australia. However, a number had chosen to find 'essential' work in Hong Kong instead and had stayed. Evacuation was not offered to wives and children who were not recognized as 'British'.
36 Nurse Mary Hope Goodban was wife of Private Gerald Archer Goodban, HKVDC, headmaster of the Diocesan Boys School. Son Nicholas had been born in December 1941, shortly after the Japanese invasion, at Queen Mary's Hospital. This quote is from *At the Going Down of the Sun* by Oliver Lindsay. Selwyn-Clarke was Hong Kong's Director of Medical Services.
37 Official letters relating to Brooks of the Royal Artillery, and Atkins of the Middlesex Regiment will be used as examples throughout this book, though hundreds of other families received almost identical communications.
38 British POWs who had been held temporarily in North Point had already been sent to Sham Shui Po. Etiemble notes, for example, arriving at Sham Shui Po camp after it had been cleaned up: "The entire barracks at Sham Shui Po had been completely ransacked. On arrival from North Point we were put into rooms which I suppose could be classed as liveable conditions."
39 A number of men reported seeing these decomposing remains. However, it seems more than likely that they were Indian soldiers of the 5/7th Rajputs whose bodies had been thrown into the sea by the Japanese.
40 Some claim that the impostor was Marine Eric Horsley, who in fact perished on the *Lisbon Maru*.
41 These POWs would move to Sham Shui Po following the departure of the *Lisbon Maru* draft. Interestingly, many of the Canadians had arrived in Hong Kong on board the *Awatea* that had evacuated so many women and children from Hong Kong. The ship, a famous liner in her day, would be sunk by bombing off Algeria in 1942.
42 Captain Botelho, quoted, commanded 6th Company HKVDC. Botelho stayed in Hong Kong POW camps until the end of the war. This quote appears in *Captive Years* by Birch and Cole.
43 A particularly distressing ailment in which pain in the feet is so extreme that those afflicted cannot sleep.

44 Any of several diseases caused by deficiency of one or more vitamins.
45 In 1964, Wright published an excellent book called *I Was a Hell Camp Prisoner*. All quotes from Wright in this book are taken from that work.
46 Jones had commanded A Company, 2nd Battalion Royal Scots at the Shing Mun Redoubt, and had been captured early in the fighting.
47 The 'squeeze' referred to was the infamous Mimi Lau affair; in fact the blocks of these structures were popularly known as 'Mimi Laus' in Hong Kong long after the war. Mimi Lau had had an affair with Wing Commander Steele-Perkins, which resulted in her family's business being given the contract for much war-oriented construction work. They saved money on the project by using rather less than the traditional amount of cement in the mix. Steele-Perkins died in 1945. Post-war, Mimi Lau is said to have had an affair with another VIP: Richard Nixon, later to be President of the United States.
48 A fellow New Zealander, who would be lost on the *Lisbon Maru*.
49 From papers supplied by Atkins' family.
50 An unpleasant condition known as 'Strawberry Balls', or 'Hong Kong Balls' by those afflicted.
51 Post-war an officer and two sergeants were tried as collaborators. All were acquitted.
52 When American bombers started appearing in the skies above Hong Kong, attacking Japanese ships and installations, the boost to morale was tremendous. However, the first raid was not until 25 October 1942, a month after the *Lisbon Maru* was boarded.
53 Argyle Street Camp was, for a short period, a separate camp for officers. It was soon closed, and the officers moved back to join the men in Sham Shui Po though they remained in a separate area of the camp. The author of this poem was Roger Rothwell.
54 Son of William A. Potter and Florence Potter, of Norwich, Norfolk; husband of Olive Mabel Potter, of Broadwater, Worthing, Sussex.
55 This whole sentence beginning 'Conditions' had been heavily crossed out by the censor, but the majority is still just legible in the original.
56 This number includes Allied civilians.
57 Soon after surrender, the POWs were ordered to sign a chit promising that they would not try to escape. Many refused, and suffered privations until their officers informed them that documents signed under duress were meaningless.
58 According to Howell's testimony at the war crimes trial of Kyoda Shigeru, "At a parade at 9 a.m. [18 September] in the morning, 46 officers' names were called out, of whom about 10 are alive at the moment, and we were detailed within 40 minutes to go to Shamshuipo camp."
59 The remaining Royal Naval and Canadian POWs at North Point were brought across the harbour on 26 September to fill the places vacated at Sham Shui Po by this transportation.

60 A term that refers to ranks other than officers.
61 In 1941 Kai Tak was the RAF's main base in Hong Kong, as well as a civilian airport. It remained in service as Hong Kong's International Airport until replaced by Chek Lap Kok in 1998.
62 It has not proven possible to prepare a definitive list of these men, many of whom presumably died of disease soon after. However, BQMS Albert Reakes is known to have been one.
63 In command of all the POW camps in Hong Kong, Colonel Tokunaga Isao faced a war crimes trial post-war. Found guilty, he was sentenced to death. This sentence was later commuted to life imprisonment.
64 All details of the Japanese side of this story — including time lines, Japanese personnel, cargo, conversations on board, and the state of the vessel at various times — are derived from the war crimes transcripts of the trial of the master of the *Lisbon Maru*, Kyoda Shigeru, in Hong Kong in 1946, WO 234/1114.
65 Fallace's statements are taken from PRO CO 980/67. He not only survived the sinking, but (as will be seen) escaped.
66 Some of the sickest of these men would be removed from the ship before she sailed. It appears that 1,816 were still on board when the *Lisbon Maru* departed.
67 Through Danyll Wills, a Japanese-speaking friend, I asked Takao Okamoto, a Japanese scholar in Kobe, why all Japanese ships are called the '*Something Maru*'. He responded: "Thank you very much for an interesting question. But my answer might disappoint your friend and you, because I could not find any linguistically well-grounded interpretation. Anyway, I'll tell you why the names of most Japanese ships end with 'maru'. The first reason is very simple and convincing. It is almost obligatory to name ships with 'maru' according the law. But the regulations usually come after the recognized tradition. 'Maru' was added as a suffix to the names of pets, armour, flutes (musical instrument) and ships since mediaeval period (please don't ask me when the Middle Ages began and ended in Japan — perhaps from the ninth century). All objects except ships are private things in themselves. So it is highly probable that owners of ships (usually those who were in power or with wealth) named their precious ships with 'maru' (remember that Japanese who are really well-off are essentially atheistic). The most difficult moment is the etymology of 'maru'. The weakest point of Japanese linguistics is an etymology. As long as the origin of Japanese language is the point of dispute, linguistically well-founded etymology of Japanese word cannot be."
68 From Mr. T. Uchida, Manager of Class NK Information Service Department of the Mitsui O. S. K. Lines, Japan. Yokohama Dock Co. Ltd. was later merged with Mitsubishi Heavy Industries Ltd.
69 Kyoda, in the war crimes trial, noted that this damage had been sustained at Ruku.

70 It reads: "MALAY EXP. FORCE AKATSUKI 2948 BUTAI HQ, KAGEYAMA TAI (LISBON MARU)
    Comdr. of UJINAK EMBARKATION HQ.
        (Lt. Gen. SAEKI, Fumiro)
    Comdr. of #3 Shipping Group (SENPAKU HEIDAN)
        (Maj. Gen. SAKURADA, Takeshi)
    Comdr. of #3 DEBARKATION UNIT (YORIKU TAI)
        Lt. Gen. ASAO, Takimasa"
    (ATIS, Comdr. 7th Fleet, SoPacArea, Current Translations, Serial 0457, Captured Document, Dated 2 April 1943) US National Archives and Records Administration (NARA).
71 Although the cargo of gold dust appears clearly in the diagram of cargo loads prepared for the war crimes trial, it is not mentioned in the typed cargo manifest found in the same set of documents. Twice during the trial of Kyoda Shigeru it was hinted that there was a mistake in the description of the cargo, but what the mistake was, was never made explicit.
72 The *Chikuzan Maru* was sunk off Vietnam in 1943. Built as the *Hunter* in Leith, Scotland, in 1907 for use in Australia, she was sold in 1938 to A. P. Moller (Maersk) in Shanghai and renamed *Ariadne Moller*. By coincidence, the *Ariadne Moller* had been caught in Hong Kong by the Japanese invasion, and was scuttled there on 12 December 1941, before being raised by the Japanese and renamed.
73 Normally there would have been eleven officers, but an extra second mate was on board as a passenger, and took Ariki's duties while he was sick. Ariki resumed his duties on 30 September.
74 In fact, Nobby's 'death' was reported to his parents. His name appears on the Naval memorial to the missing in Portsmouth, though at time of writing he is still alive and well.
75 Bailey was no stranger to tight spots. During the fighting in Hong Kong he had been commended for taking an ambulance, with Lieutenant R. Whitfield (RNVR), to rescue wounded at Wong Nai Chung Gap.
76 Readers with elementary mathematical skills, plus some knowledge of the *Lisbon Maru*, will note that this grand total of 1,834 men is slightly higher than the oft-quoted figure of 1,816 (see note 215). There are several possible reasons for the difference (imperfect lists, uncertainties over which sick men were removed from the ship before it sailed, and so forth).
77 The dividing line between civilians and combatants was blurred by last-minute recruitment into the HKVDC and HKRNVR.
78 Howell wrote an account of the sinking for possible publication; today it is held by his daughter. All quotes attributed to Howell in this work are from that document. Niimori was not in fact in command, but was the mouthpiece of those who were.
79 Post-war, Weedon wrote an account of his experiences entitled "Guest

of an Emperor". All quotes attributed to Weedon in this work are from that document.

80 As a foretaste of what is to come, Iles, Hughes, Tivey, Hayward, Hatchett, Gale and Iszard would not survive the sinking. Steele would be picked up from the wreck with a broken back, but would die on the way to Shanghai. Meakin too would die before the year was out. Only Bowles the beri beri sufferer, Gorman, and Wright himself, would survive the war. (Wright's book actually refers to 'Typhoon Sale'. However, no one by the name of Sale was on board, and later he refers to a 'Gale'. The British Army's tradition of simple nicknames makes it all but certain this was in fact Gale.)

81 Alsey's diaries are held by the Imperial War Museum in London. All quotes attributed to Alsey in this work are from that document. It was written longhand in a 1966 diary, but presumably this is a transcript of a fading original.

82 Lance Corporal Harold Sharrock of the Royal Scots. He would not survive the sinking.

83 Alsey was suffering from 'happy feet', or dry beri beri. Next day he stated again, 'my feet keep me awake all night.'

84 The Japanese soldiers occupied part of the upper deck, and also the holds towards the stern of the vessel. Howell refers to them being in the 'afterholds', and Fallace (describing the *Lisbon Maru* as having four holds) states they were in hold 'No. 4 abaft the bridge', adding: 'A number of Japanese men were accommodated in the top half of No. 4 hold, the officers in a space allotted them under the bridge.' This is perfectly correct, but perhaps 'number 4' is best viewed as the third hold (i.e. the Japanese were behind the Gunners). The confusion is caused by the fact that the second hold had two hatches. I have maintained the convention that the second hold was that under hatches 2 and 3, and the third hold was that under hatch 4. As illustration, '*Lisbon Maru* cutaway', shows, there were a number of other holds further after.

85 Presumably a battalion of the 228th Regiment on its way to Guadalcanal. There appears to have been no communication between the British POWs and these Japanese troops. As the former included several Japanese speakers, it seems the two groups were completely segregated at all times.

86 Presumably this was Sergeant Thomas Gorman of the Hong Kong police.

87 In the war crimes trial of 1946, Kyoda Shigeru noted that he had seen a senior POW officer, on board the *Lisbon Maru*, negotiating with Lieutenant Wada through the interpreter Niimori. "I do not know the small details but I think one point which was decided was that food articles were to be issued to the POW and that they themselves would cook the food."

88 Interestingly, all these 'entertainers', with the exception of Green, would survive the war.

89 Although Spooner and others spell the name 'Miles', the formal records state 'Myles'.

90 Japanese for toilet.
91 The culprit survived the war, and Middlesex Regiment tradition has it that he never smoked again from that day till he died.
92 Mulligan eventually escaped to Shanghai where he sat out until the end of the war. He passed away in 1999, shortly after getting back in contact with the Chinese sisters who sheltered him during that period.
93 From his autobiography, *Footprints*. Clark was a particularly strong-willed character. His insistence on aiding POWs ended with his imprisonment and torture from which he never fully recovered.
94 The University of Hong Kong Library, Ride Collection. BAAG were not permitted any encoding equipment, thus all message had to be sent in clear. A basic set of some one hundred code words soon evolved (ALFS was Sham Shui Po, Hbs [Hissing bastards] were Japanese, Selwyn-Clarke was SEPTIC, KELLOG was the Hong Kong Bank, etc.). Where code words did not suffice, the first letters of words were to be read, or other languages were used. The original 'encoded' text of this communication read:

RIDE KWEILIN
FIFTYONE DATED 10/9 STOP. ALFS VALUE SIX HUNDRED IN NAVE AD SOLEM ORIENTEM NOCTE TRES OR QUATRE STOP FURTHER CARGO VALUE ONE THOUSAND BEING ARRANGED FOR MONTH END STOP SOURCE ADDRESSEE YOUR CHIT NUMBER SIXTEEN AND SUBJECT MY L/15 STOP
DUGGIE.

(Note that the city of Kweilin is now spelled Guilin. Duggie was Major Douglas Clague who commanded BAAG Advanced Headquarters at Waichow, 1942–43. The addressee of chit 16 was Edmondston who was a banker still at large at that time at the Sun Wah Hotel. Later he was killed by the Japanese. The subject of L/15 was Selwyn-Clarke).

95 The original read: "MACHIN [Military Attaché CHINA] CHUNGKING FOR RIDE QUOTE DOUGGIE SIXTYFOUR DATED 25/9 STOP CONFIRMATION DUGGIE FIFTYONE DATED TENTH STOP REPORT SIX HUNDRED POWS GOING QUOTE FREDDIE ORANGE ROBERT MONKEY ORANGE SUGAR ACK UNQUOTE TWELVE HUNDRED QUOTE MONKEY ORANGE JAMES EYE UNQUOTE ISLAND NEAR QUOTE JAMES ACK PUDDING ACK NUTS UNQUOTE TODAY STOP IF IN DOUBT ABOVE SUBSTANCE CONSULT ANY MAXIE SPARKER STOP UNQUOTE
OLSEN
                                          2/Lieut.,
Kweilin   for C.O., British Army Aid Group
26.ix.42   37/2 Wen Woo Road"

The final reference is advising asking a radioman's assistance if the code was not understood. Agent 64 was Sergeant Lo Hung Sui, ex 4 Coy HKVDC.

96 Some assert that only one book was on board, but Alsey also recalls reading *J'Accuse*.
97 *Thanet* had escaped Hong Kong on 8 December 1941, some twelve hours after the Japanese attack.
98 Royal Naval losses had not been light in the European Theatre either, and had of course included the pride of the fleet, the *Hood*.
99 *Balao*-class boats would be numbered 285–416. Four *Gato*-class boats survive today: USS *Silversides* SS236 (Muskegon, Michigan), USS *Drum* SS228 (Mobile, Alabama), USS *Cobia* SS245 (Manitowoc, Wisconsin), USS *Cod* SS224 (Cleveland, Ohio).
100 CTF-7 was Rear Admiral Robert H English. The Midway Patrol Group was Task Group TG 7.1. All details of the *Grouper* and her patrols come from the log held at NARA, fiche number 357, available as National Archives Microfilm Publication No. M1752.
101 Duke, in a letter to Clay Blair dated 30 March 1972, stated that "I made a short Top Secret patrol of about two weeks at French Frigate Shoal. The object was to intercept and destroy a Japanese submarine. This patrol was terminated by Midway." Although the log of *Grouper's* First War Patrol starts on 4 June at Midway, the "Description of all Aircraft Sighted" starts on 11 May at "100 miles SW of Pearl Harbor", and from 14 May onwards, "Over French Frigate Shoal".
102 He continued: "I wrote to the RCAF and explained what I had done. However, they replied that I was listed as a deserter. Everything must have been forgiven, as after the war I was sent a war bonus check for time served in the RCAF." Gar did indeed become a skilled private pilot post-war.
103 A wise move, as *Utah* — converted from a Battleship laid down in 1909 into a floating target for USN practice — was lost at Pearl Harbour just weeks later. The wreck and sixty of her crew still lie in Hawaiian waters, largely forgotten as the tourists head for the famous *Arizona* memorial.
104 Although Tokara is the accepted transliteration today, 'Takara' is the name actually used in the log.
105 D-V(G) is found in the *Naval Reserve Register* as one of the Classes of Naval Reserve Officers — Volunteer Reserve (General Service). "D-V(G) — Deck officers, commissioned and warrant, including boatswains, gunners, and torpedo men, qualified for general detail afloat or ashore." The term "S&A, Asst. Elec & Eng." defied the translation attempts of the Naval Historical Center, but their best guess was "Supplies & Administration, Assistant Electrical & Engineering".
106 Ensign is the officer rank between Lieutenant Junior Grade (jg) and Chief Warrant Officer.
107 It is clear that the submarine historian Clay Blair felt that English (commanding CTF-7) relieved Duke of command because of some issue with his abilities. However, Duke received a Bronze Star and a Gold Star

for service on his next appointment, as Navigator & Tactical Officer on the battleship *Pennsylvania*. His personal records were destroyed when *Pennsylvania* was torpedoed at Okinawa, and his records covering later periods were destroyed when his house was flooded in a Florida storm of 1956. Duke's children from his wife's first marriage passed away when young. Note 118 contains details of the Mark 14 torpedo.

108 NARA: National Archives microfilm publications. Pamphlet describing; M 1752.
109 To protect a submarine from magnetically triggered ordnance it was normal procedure to reduce the permanent magnetic field of a boat (deperming) by using external coils carrying a powerful electric current.
110 *Litchfield* was the flagship of Submarine Squadron 4, Submarine Force, Pearl Harbour. At the outbreak of Pacific war, *Litchfield's* duties included escorting submarines both into and out of port. She survived the war and was scrapped in 1946.
111 A small island off the south western tip of Japan.
112 Although the *Grouper's* log makes no attempt to identify this vessel, after the war it has usually been recorded as the *Tone Maru*. However, there is some uncertainty about this identification, as will be seen.
113 Known as Backgammon in the UK.
114 Confusingly, the summary of the submarine's log indicates that the *Lisbon Maru* was spotted at 07.04 at 29-57 north, 122-56 east. This does not fit the body of the log, which times the first encounter at 04.00. However, they note seeing a Japanese aircraft at 30-11 north, 123-17 east — which they also claim is the position where the *Lisbon Maru* was torpedoed. If we assume that the first position was that of the first sighting, and the second position is correct, then this fits exactly. Plotting these positions on a map, we see that the latter could have been reached from the former by steaming for about one hour on 010, and two hours on 060 at just under 9 knots (the speed recorded by the *Grouper*, and the final heading reported when the *Lisbon Maru* came in sight again while *Grouper* waited submerged). According to the Japanese report of positions, it seems that at some point after the torpedo hit, the *Lisbon Maru* continued heading north north west until she came under tow.
115 This was a sensible precaution. USS *Tang* (SS-306) was lost to just such a circular. She had launched a night surface attack on 24 October 1944 against a transport that had been stopped in an earlier encounter. The first torpedo was fired, and when it was observed to be running true, the second followed. It curved sharply to the port, broached, porpoised and circled. Emergency speed was ordered and the rudder was thrown hard over. This resulted in the torpedo striking the stern of *Tang,* rather than amidships. The explosion was violent, and crewmembers as far forward as the Control Room suffered broken limbs. The boat went down by the stern with the after three

compartments flooded. Of the nine officers and men on the bridge, three were able to swim through the night until picked up eight hours later. One officer escaped from the flooded conning tower, and was rescued with the others. The submarine came to rest on the bottom at 180 feet, and the men in her moved forward as the after compartments flooded. All secret documents were burned, and the crew assembled to the Forward Torpedo Room to escape. The escape was delayed by a Japanese patrol, which dropped charges, and started an electrical fire in the Forward Battery. Thirteen men escaped from the forward room, and by the time the last made his exit, the heat from the fire was so intense that the paint on the bulkhead was scorching. Of these escapees, only eight reached the surface, and of these only five were able to swim until rescued. Nine survivors in total were picked up by a Japanese destroyer escort.

116 The torpedoes were fired ten second apart so that, if an earlier torpedo hit its target and exploded, the following torpedoes would not be close enough to be exploded by sympathetic detonation.

117 The *Grouper* was indeed to port of the *Lisbon Maru* when the torpedoes were fired.

118 The Mark 14 torpedo dated from 1931. Intended as a replacement for the Mark 10 that was then in use, it was plagued with faults. At the time of Pearl Harbour, the Mark 14 was in short supply, and all those then in service were fitted with the Mark 6 exploder. This was a particularly poor combination. Four main faults were the primary causes of the torpedo's initial problems: two related to the exploder, and two to the depth setting mechanism of the fish. The depth problem was suspected early on, and in June 1942, COMSUBSOWESPAC (Commander Submarines South West Pacific, Rear-Admiral Lockwood) ordered running tests to be conducted at Frenchman's Bay submarine base outside Perth, Western Australia. These proved the suspicions to be correct, with torpedoes on average running eleven feet deeper than set. However, the US Navy's Bureau of Ordinance at Newport Torpedo Station did not immediately admit the problem, eventually conceding that — due to the warheads being heavier than test heads — the Mark 14 ran with a nose-down attitude. However, they then estimated that they ran just four feet deeper than set. Lockwood, in August, ordered submariners to fire ten feet above their usual settings. Compounding this problem was the fact that the torpedo's depth sensor had been designed for a slower (33 knot, Mark 13) torpedo. The pressure gradient over the torpedo's surface at the higher speeds of the Mark 14 gave the wrong feedback. The sensor was later relocated to a neutral position. Even if the torpedo ran at the right depth, the detonator still could not be trusted. The magnetic exploder had been designed in the northern latitudes and did not work as well at or near the equator. The British and Germans had disabled their magnetic exploders much earlier than the US Navy

ordered theirs disabled. The conventional contact exploder, like the depth sensor, had been designed for the slower Mark 13 torpedo. The new 46 knot Mark 14 torpedo had higher inertial impacts that could cause the firing pin to miss the exploder cap. These problems were all fixed by the end of 1943. Until that time, many Japanese vessels had lucky escapes. Interestingly, Kvalheim always believed that one of the first three torpedoes did hit the stern of the *Lisbon Maru*, but failed to explode, and the Master of the vessel confirmed this.

119 Torpex (TORPedo EXplosive) was a mixture rather than a pure chemical compound such as TNT. The components were TNT 41 percent, RDX (Cyclonite, Hexogen) 41 percent and aluminium powder 18 percent. Torpex was valued because of its increased explosive energy, the higher detonation velocity of RDX as compared to TNT, and the prolongation of the pressure wave thanks to the aluminium. Weight for weight, Torpex is at least 50 percent more effective than TNT as an underwater explosive against ships. Torpex is, however, more sensitive than TNT, and RDX is costly and challenging to make safely. The process of converting to Torpex torpedo warheads started with an order for 20 million pounds in early 1942, with the first Torpex loaded warheads following later that year. The 643 pounds of Torpex in a Mk.14 warhead was at least equal to 960 pounds of TNT, giving nearly twice the destructive power of the original warhead. Torpex saw many other uses during the war, being the explosive chosen by Dr Barnes Wallis for his Tall Boy and Grand Slam heavy bombs, and that which killed Joe Kennedy (elder brother of JFK) in 1944 in a specially converted Liberator flying bomb over the UK, while on a vain mission to destroy the giant 150 mm German 'Super-Gun' site at Mimoyecques near Calais.

120 The guns were variously described as being 4 inch and 12-pounder QFs (QF, Quick Firing, simply means that the round comes in a single piece, rather than a separate shell and cordite bag or cartridge).

121 Six feet. The fact that it still passed under the ship clearly demonstrates the untrustworthiness of the Mark 14.

122 The submarine's log consistently refers to this machine as a 'Davai'. Whichever way it is spelled, this aircraft did not exist. The Mitsubishi 108 type 97 is an aircraft that the Allies incorrectly believed to be in the Japanese inventory. It has not proved possible to identify what type of aircraft the *Grouper* actually observed, though one POW witness described it as a biplane.

123 There is no evidence that this torpedo hit the ship. The Japanese gunners claim to have hit it in the water. Improbable though this sounds (and in keeping with other Japanese propaganda claims to have shot down allied aircraft with rice balls and so forth), it is probably true. Many witnesses, including those aboard the *Grouper*, agree that the torpedo exploded. It did not hit the ship, so a sympathetic detonation caused by a close high-explosive shell could well have been responsible. However, the gunners did not impress

everybody. Lieutenant Bucke of the Royal Signals Corp, in a post-war report noted of the incident: "Forward gunners horribly late into action."

124 56 degrees Centigrade.

125 An Escort Destroyer with a displacement of 1,160 tons, length of 85 metres, speed of 23 knots, and two 4.7 inch guns — *Kuri* was launched on 19 March 1920 and commissioned on 30 April 1920. One of the few of her class to survive the war, she was captured in September 1945 and was destroyed by accident in Korea on 8 October 1945.

126 This had been transferred from the *Toyokuni Maru*.

127 Etiemble had a great deal of respect for Dicks. He continues: "My last memories of 'Q' Dicks are just after the war ended, he was running what passed as our cookhouse and trying to salvage food from the 44 gallon drums that the Americans had dropped without parachutes, and had finished up flat as pancakes."

128 By an interesting coincidence, *Toyokuni Maru* was sunk by *Gato*-class submarine USS *Lapon* SS260 (sister ship to USS *Grouper*) on 8 March 1944.

129 Sunk by USS *Plaice*, 30 June 1944.

130 *Grouper* erroneously believed that the ship sank where she was torpedoed (i.e. at 30-11N, 123-17E). However, after towing an estimated fifteen miles west (from 20.30 on the first to 07.30 on the second), the Japanese NYK Line believed she sank at 30-17N, 123-13E. While 30-17N is believable, 123-13E is too far east, and would have meant the men swimming (later in our story) some twenty miles to the islands! Interestingly, the Master's report states that she was torpedoed at 30/17, 123/13, which is far more believable. While only those who have dived on the wreck can confirm this, a resting place in the region of 30-17N, 129-57E (after towing) seems more likely. The Master himself gave the position of the sinking as "5 or 6 miles from Tofuku Mountain at 352 degrees." It appears this means on a bearing of 352 *from* Tofuku Mountain (Dongfu Shan in Chinese).

131 These names, though they came from the *Lisbon Maru's* second mate, are suspect as *Tone Maru* was reported sunk by USS *Grouper* herself on 21 September 1942. *Unkai Maru No. 10* was sunk by USS *Cobia* (SS-245) northwest of Chichijima on 18 July 1944. The fates of the others are uncertain; the Japanese habit of repeating the same name and adding a number makes them hard to trace. All these gunboats, including the *Toyokuni Maru*, were in fact converted freighters. Kyoda Shigeru also gave the names *Fukoku Maru*, *Wampole*, *Ritsushima*, *Tadashi*, and *Rikan Maru*.

132 He continued: "As these naval personnel have a good knowledge of ships and navigation and if they revolted it would be quite serious." During his war crimes trial it became clear that the main Japanese fear was that these men might man the forward gun and use it against the other Japanese vessels in the area.

133 Henderson did not survive.

134 The use of the nickname 'Tommy Atkins' (often shortened to 'Tommy') to represent the British infantryman dates back, according to the Imperial War Museum, to at least 1743.
135 The butcher's knife, according to Carew, came from Private Speight of the Middlesex, a pre-war butcher's assistant from Croydon. Howell, in his war crimes testimony, described "a collection of bread-knives, razors, and pen-knives which had been sent to me."
136 See photo, 'The sinking of the *Lisbon Maru*'.
137 The deck under the Captain's Bridge, which was itself the deck immediately below the Bridge.
138 One of those shot and wounded in the hold at this time, according to Challis, was Bandsman Plummeridge of the Middlesex. Plummeridge survived.
139 The shot Lieutenant was most probably Potter. In the war crimes trial of Kyoda Shigeru, Howell described how he opened the bulkhead door before Potter was shot, and the gunners started to come out immediately. However, Howell also mentions a dead body lying shot on the deck after he had retrieved Potter.
140 Potter's sacrifice was forgotten post-war by the St John's Ambulance in Hong Kong, and his name is not even on their memorial to those members of their organization who lost their lives during the conflict. However, he is named on the Sai Wan memorial to the missing.

In a letter to Colonel Murray Brown of the Volunteers in 1962, Lieutenant Colonel Lindsay Ride, wartime commander of the Combined Field Ambulance wrote: "The situation concerning Potter was this. The Defence Scheme for Hongkong in 1941 included the formation of the Hongkong Field Ambulance on mobilization being ordered. The duties were the collection of all sick and wounded military personnel from both Kowloon and Hongkong and their evacuation to hospital. The HK Field Ambulance was formed from RAMC, RASC, and HKVDC Field Ambulance units, but these could not fill the establishment required and St. John Ambulance was called upon to help. They did so by setting aside a Military Unit which was attached to the HKVDC Field Ambulance for training sometime in 1940 or 1941. Potter was the officer who came with this unit and was responsible for the discipline, pay, etc. of its members. He was never a member of the HKVDC.

On mobilization he reported with his unit to the HKVDC Field Ambulance for duty, and was posted to the HQ of the HK Field Ambulance with me; he remained at these HQ throughout the hostilities, and came with us when the Japanese put us in the POW camp.

I can't understand why the St. John Ambulance do not recognize him, but that really does not concern us. It can be taken as quite definite that he was attached to the HKVDC Field Ambulance for duty on mobilization, that he served with us throughout the hostilities, and I think this attachment

should be recognized as continuing throughout the period of his internment." The University of Hong Kong Library, Ride Collection (with thanks to Ride's daughter, Elizabeth).
141 Whichever account is more accurate (the latter is from Carew), the body of one of the guards was later found and buried by POWs when they were sheltering on a nearby island (probably either Private First Class Teranishi Seijiro, or Private First Class Sugimura Minoru, as Japanese records show the former drowned and the latter missing). Both accounts may, however, be incorrect, as Japanese eye-witnesses giving testimony in the war crimes trial stated that the last guards had jumped into the sea of their own accord.
142 Eaton did not survive.
143 Langley survived the war.
144 Inglis had boarded with beri beri which had become far worse during the voyage.
145 A post-war interview with John Inglis, RA, appears to confirm this: "We released the men in the other holds and killed the Jap sentries." From a newspaper cutting of unknown provenance.
146 In a post-war letter to Ross' mother, Zaz Pitt wrote: "S/Sgt Ross remained with the sick until the last and then would have swum from the ship without a life-jacket carrying haversack full of medical supplies had he not received a direct order to the contrary from an officer ... [Later, in the discouraging circumstances of Kobe prisoner of war camp hospital] your son displayed the very highest qualities of leadership, courage, devotion to duty, patience, and complete disregard for himself. He inspired confidence in other orderlies and patients, of which I was one. He accepted responsibilities far greater than he would have been called upon to bear in normal times, and absolutely refused to give way or admit defeat although a sick man himself, suffering stomach ulcers from which he died (on May 15th 1944)."
147 Kyoda stated: "On the starboard side I saw about ten POWs trying to lower a sampan. I helped them to lower it. I showed them how the sampan should be lowered." At about 9.40 he jumped into the sea himself, and was rescued by a Japanese patrol boat.
148 Weedon, normally an excellent observer, records Panting's death in a POW Camp in Japan on 12 March 1943. In fact this was Corporal Painting.
149 CWGC records confirm that Allison died soon after arrival in Japan, just three weeks after the sinking.
150 Years later, Rix would be best man at Ross Lynneberg and his fiancé Bernice's wedding.
151 It has been hard to identify many men who were shot in the water, but Carew explicitly mentions Lance Corporal Charles Henry Hatfield, Middlesex Regiment, being killed in this manner.
152 John Edward Pearman. This is quoted from a deposition in the war crimes trial documents.

153 This number is arrived at in the following manner: In both number one and number two holds, Pollock and Cuthbertson respectively had returned to check that all living men had left the vessel. That means that no one had been trapped in either of these holds and drowned, and that the only dead were those who had died earlier of disease, been shot trying to break out, or had fallen from the ladders and died. Estimating those numbers as two for hold one (though both were removed before the sinking), and nine for hold two gives a total of eleven. However, whilst the mortality rate on 1/2 October for the men in holds one and two were an average 41 percent, that for hold three was 62 percent. Making the assumption that the difference (21 percent) reflects the men in the third hold who were unable to escape when the ship went down, in real terms this equates to about 70 men. Assuming that hold three, like the similarly populated hold one, had had two deaths up to that point, the sum of those who went down with the ship can be approximated as 0 + 9 + 70 + 2 = 81. If 1,816 POWs were on the vessel when it departed Hong Kong, and two from hold one were already dead, then around 1,733 would have made it alive into the sea.
154 Interestingly though, the western end of Zhejiang Province had, just six months earlier, hosted many of Doolittle's raiders who had crashed or bailed out in that area after their carrier-launched attack on Tokyo.
155 Neither Edwards nor Hemmingfield, RA, survived.
156 Gunner Spiller died in Japan less than a year later.
157 Hare, Whitham and Green all perished. Whitham was the acting Branch Manager of the Sun Life Assurance Company of Canada in Hong Kong, and lived in Shek O. He had been transferred to the Middlesex from the HKVDC.
158 In rough figures, it seems that about 60 percent of the survivors were picked up by the Japanese, while 20 percent were picked up by the fishermen and 20 percent swam to the islands under their own power.
159 Qingbang Dao and Sing Pan Island (or Tsing Pang Island) are the modern and previous transliterations of the same Chinese name.
160 Wright, and others, mentioned an officer — picked up at nearly midnight — who claimed that hundreds of bodies had been swept passed him.
161 Gunner Haywood confirmed: "A total of 53 of us reached the island. I saw an officer whose name was Officer, and who had been in charge of the venereal department at Hong Kong, get smashed up against the rocks and drowned near the island." Haywood's statements are taken from the war crimes depositions.
162 Howell was familiar with Shanghainese as he had been born and brought up in that city. However, he was lucky to be understood as these islands have a dialect of their own.
163 In April 2005 the government of Zhoushan were kind enough to invite me to visit and meet three of the fishermen involved in this rescue. Shen Agui, with his father and uncle, rescued about seven men in two trips. Guo Ade

rescued about ten. The third, Wang Baorong, said very little but I was told he had personally rescued twenty.

164 In his original report, Fallace refers to Laloe as 'Laolo'. Laloe had been wounded in the Hong Kong fighting by an air attack on *Indira*.

165 Although men were too busy surviving to take a great interest in the geography, it appears that the biggest group landed initially on Qingbang Dao, the nearest island due west of the sinking. Fallace's group was most probably on the then uninhabited island of Xifu Shan.

166 Ferris died sixteen days later.

167 This reference, from Wright, appears to be to one of the three escapers, Fallace, Evans, or Johnstone. He calls this man 'Thurso', but no one of that name had been on board the *Lisbon Maru*.

168 Wright refers to a Royal Scot with four broken ribs, but does not name him.

169 Ross had the advantage of being an exceptionally strong swimmer. One of the founding members of the Titahi Bay Surf Life Saving Club, he took part in many exercises pre-war: "Later the club then held their big swim for the life saving cup — everyone starting from the beach, running into the sea, swimming out around a buoy back to the shore and then a sprint up the beach and over the finish line. I recall at the start of this race that Frank, my cousin living next door to us at Ngaio and not a club member, started off when the gun fired alongside me. I don't recall when I next saw Frank but I finished the race collapsing after the effort, and cursing and swearing, to find Ethel my mother wiping my face with a handkerchief. The result was I became the first holder of the club's surf cup and after research of the records — possibly the last."

170 Like many other survivors, Shepherd could not remember the names of the men with whom he had boarded the *Lisbon Maru*, but recalled the name of the first person he saw afterwards.

171 Shen Agui estimated that a hundred men were ferried from Xifu Shan (though some say Miaozihu Dao) to Qingbang Dao in this exercise.

172 Eight hundred forty-three is the figure often quoted for those who lost their lives that day. However, this estimate was based on the number of men missing when the roll was called at Shanghai on 5 October. In fact, some survivors died between the sinking and that date, and others simply had not been located by that time, and were brought to Shanghai later.

173 See note 153 for an explanation of this figure.

174 Hong Kong's harbour was protected by floating booms. These appear clearly in Pathe newsreel footage taken from the air shortly before the war.

175 The rank of Warrant Officer III, Platoon Sergeant Major, was a short-lived experiment. Trinder was appointed to this position in October 1938.

176 *Hayashio* was a *Kagero* class destroyer. She is not mentioned elsewhere.

177 National Archives and Records Administration (NARA).

178 Miles survived. McGillivray (listed as McGilvery by Carew) did not.

179 Estimates of numbers of men rescued by the Chinese, and those picked up from the sea by the Japanese, vary. However, the general consensus is that three hundred or more made it to the islands (the islanders themselves say 384), and five hundred or more were picked up at sea by the Japanese.
180 In 1996, Fallace received a letter from May-Yung Wang Sun, who remembered her family looking after the three men when she was a girl of fourteen. She now lives in the USA.
181 Fisherman Wang Baorong stated that the three men were initially in his house, but were then moved to a seldom-visited cave.
182 Wright actually refers to an 'Able Seaman Letts'. However, no one of that name was on board, so this was presumably Alexander Looe, Engine Room Artificer 3.
183 Quoted from the war crimes trial of Kyoda Shigeru.
184 Post-war documents make it clear that Niimori and Nomura are two names for the same man. Woosong is the previous spelling of Wusong.
185 Presumably this was the Nakazawa who was used by the Japanese as an interpreter in Hong Kong during the occupation, and appeared in the trial of Colonel Tanaka Hisakasu in September 1946.
186 POWs were sent on working parties to extend Kai Tak's (then Hong Kong's airport) runways for Japanese use.
187 Captain Mathers was not on the *Lisbon Maru*. The quote comes from Jean Mather's book, *Twisting the Tail of the Dragon*.
188 The vessel was known as both the *Washington Maru* and the *Shinsei Maru*.
189 From the war crimes trial of Kyoda Shigeru.
190 Lance Corporal Bertram Poulter, also of the Middlesex Regiment.
191 Cuthbertson contracted diphtheria and died in Japan.
192 The others who appear to have been buried at sea are: Frederick Archer, Robert Bromley and George Makel.
193 These men would spend most of the war in a POW camp in Shanghai, reclaiming cordite from old Japanese shells, before being transferred to the Tokyo area late in the war.
194 Uniquely of all those recorded here, Stewart is commemorated on the New Zealand Naval Memorial in Auckland.
195 All POWs queried stated that the so-called 'interviews' were falsified. They have no merit in terms of understanding the loss of the *Lisbon Maru*, but are interesting as examples of wartime propaganda (see photo, '*Lisbon Maru* survivors landing at Moji').
196 In fact, as Horswell well knew, the Japanese attack on Hong Kong had been punctuated by massacres of captured British, Indian, and Canadian prisoners (and Chinese civilians) from beginning to end. Further, it appears that a greater percentage of Allied fatalities were caused by murder post-capture, than in any other battle of the war. See Tony Banham, *Not the Slightest Chance: The Defence of Hong Kong, 1941*, Hong Kong University Press, 2003.

197 9 October to 15 October, 1942.
198 Jack Etiemble confirmed that the same train delivered POWs to both camps: "It was the same train that took POWs to Kobe and Osaka. In Osaka mainly Royal Navy and Royal Artillery plus a few Royal Scots ... Matheson, James Cockburn, Charles Duthie. Middlesex ... William Ure, Tom Rolfe and Eric Leonard. Royal Signals ... Thomas Wright, Montague Truscott, there were some more ..." All Royal Scots officers with the exception of Hamilton were in Kobe. Bombardier John Inglis recalled that this was the first passenger train to use the new undersea tunnel to Shimonoseki; the Kanmon tunnel officially opened for passengers in November 1942.
199 Kokura no longer exists as a separate entity, having been absorbed into the modern city of Kitakyushu. It was lucky to suffer this fate, having been the original target of the second atomic bomb which, due to poor visibility over the primary target, was eventually dropped on Nagasaki. Kokura was a fortified town, with its suburb Moji guarding the straits of Shimonoseki. Today, Moji is also part of Kitakyushu.
200 Men who perished in these hospitals included: Kokura: John Allison, Frederick Ayres, James Badger, John Foster, Edwin Goodwin, Leslie Mullet. Hiroshima: Ronald Bairstow, Thomas Castle, John Duffy, Frederick Goldsmith, James Harrison, Colin Hart, Edward Hewett, Donald Matheson, Thomas Matthews, Melville Morgan, Ernest Neil, Alexander Taylor, William Tibble, Thomas Wall.
201 Frank Walter Gibbs, a wireless operator.
202 The CWGC lists Wilson and Daly as dying 1/2 October. There are many inconsistencies for those who died in the days immediately following the sinking.
203 ALFS was Sham Shui Po camp, POINTERS was North Point. GEORGE was Hong Kong, thus this quote is presumably from the Japanese English-language propaganda newspaper, Hong Kong News. 'Major' Greenwood was probably Commissioned Telegraphist Norman T. J. Greenwood, RN. The identity of Wrenbrook remains a mystery, as no one of that name was onboard.
204 'Sid' (Harry Hale, Royal Scots) had been dropped off at Shanghai as too ill to travel, and would be one of the few from that group to survive the war. Arthur Alsey had been aboard the *Lisbon Maru* but would survive. Joanie was lucky; her husband (in the HKVDC) had not been aboard the vessel. However, one of Joanie's fellow nurses, Sister Constance Godfrey, did not yet know that she had lost her husband, Lieutenant Alfred Godfrey, who had been in the third hold with the Royal Artillery.
205 Others known to have had the opportunity to broadcast were: Guy Castleton HKRNVR, Frank Cotton HKRNVR, and Fred Woodhead HKPF.
206 Presumably Jupp.
207 Jones' father, a CSM with the Middlesex, was listed as missing in 1915 during the First World War.

208 Normally transliterated as 'Ichioka' today.
209 The war crimes transcripts of the Master's trial note that the names Tsuneda and Kyoda were often confused.
210 Extract from *Japan Times Weekly,* 20 October 1942, quoted from Martin Weedon's book, *Guest of an Emperor.*
211 In my correspondence with Shepherd, he noted: "In the course of your research I expect you have heard of Lt. Colonel H. W. M. Stewart of the Middlesex Regiment. He above all officers impressed me by his dedication in doing all he could to resist the cruelty displayed by the Japanese Military. They physically abused him to the point where he could no longer survive. I hope he received full recognition for the bravery shown during these difficult times."
212 In a diary entry for November, Poulter continued: "Captain Man and Lt Graham of my regiment arrived today along with some other officers. I handed over Col Stewart's cap badge to Capt. Man. This may seem like a trivial thing but to the majority of regular soldiers a cap badge is a thing to be prized."
213 He died on 26 November.
214 In 1952, Evans would be murdered by bandits in Saigon. His friend and colleague John Stericker discusses him at some length in the book *Tear for a Dragon.*
215 This was an official press release. On 21 December the Office of HM Military Attaché, British Embassy, in Chunking sent the following memo to London:

Director Military Intelligence
M.I.2. (2)
The War office
London

Owing to the great interest that the local news agencies have shown in these three escapers, I have issued the attached statement through the Press Attaché of the Embassy. I hope by this means to prevent the appearance of wildly garbled and harrowing accounts of their experiences and to safeguard to some extent their Chinese benefactors on the coast of Chekiang.

The press release itself holds nothing unexpected, but mentions that: "According to a report issued by the Japanese in the 'Hongkong News' there were 1816 prisoners of war on board'." This is presumably the original source of this commonly quoted number.

216 Lloyds weekly casualty reports, 18–24 December 1942. By this time, the three escapees were under firm military control. Evans' Movement Order, for example, states bluntly:

You will report at the Airport Chungking at 0830 hours on 26/12/42 and will embark in a C.N.A.C. plane for Calcutta.
On arrival in Calcutta you will report to the Embarkation Commandant and

will request him to give you a passage to New Delhi. You will show him this letter.

On arrival in New Delhi you will report to Major W. R. P. Ridgway G.S.I.(e) General Headquarters.

You are herewith provided with Rs.50/- for expenses on first arrival in Calcutta. You will show the Customs Officials this letter as your authority for bringing this money into India.

Sd/-

Major R.A.

for H.B.M. MILITARY ATTACHE.

217 At Kobe, each work detail had a nickname. Mintagowa was "Iron Ore", Showa Denki was "Graphite", Dai Ichi Shinko was "Rice Ball Rubber", Higashinada was the "Coal Job", Itsumigumi's was "Sweets", etc.
218 This was Private Fred Slann.
219 I am indebted to Carol Taylor-Cockayne of Jacksdale Heritage for these newspaper clippings.
220 This excerpt is illustrative of several hundred pages from the Colonial Office papers relating to those on board. Brotherston had in fact been lost in the sinking.
221 Cheesewright's pillbox (PB 17, which he had commanded during the battle) still exists in Hong Kong today, buried (but for the topmost metre) in the sand at the western corner of Repulse Bay beach. Picnickers often sit on the roof on summer days, unaware that their seat is anything more than a concrete bench.
222 Private Frank James Bindon, Middlesex Regiment.
223 Man, Ewan, and Challis are Captain Christopher Man, Lieutenant Ewan Graham and RSM Robert Challis. Oddly, Weedon and Man — best friends — shared the emperor's and Hitler's birthday respectively.
224 Meat and vegetables.
225 This card was addressed to: "Prisoners of War Post, Services Des Prisoniers de Guerre, 6213420, Pte. S. Atkins 1st Batt. Middlesex Regt. "C Company, Nanking Barracks, Shamshuipo, Hong Kong, British Prisoners of War, C/O Japanese Red Cross, Tokyo".
226 This may possibly have been Phyllis Harrop, a civilian who had escaped from Hong Kong shortly after it fell to the Japanese and wrote the book *Hong Kong Incident*. Frustratingly, the 'Harrop' part of this lady's signature appears on one of the Admiralty documents, but without the initial.
227 As related by David Stanford.
228 The arrival of a Red Cross parcel, even shared between several men, was a major event for POWs whose major concern was lack of food, both in quantity and variety. Ex-POWs speak of British, Canadian, and US parcels, with the Canadian ones generally getting the highest rating. As an example, the content of a typical American parcel was:

American Red Cross
STANDARD PACKAGE NO. 8
for
PRISONER OF WAR
FOOD
CONTENTS

Evaporated Milk, irradiated	1 14 1/2 oz. Can
Lunch Biscuit (hard-tack)	1 8 oz. Package
Cheese	1 8 oz. Package
Instant Cocoa	1 8 oz. Tin
Sardines	1 15 oz. Tin
Oleomargarine (Vitamin A)	1 1 lb. Tin
Corned Beef	1 12 oz. Tin
Sweet Chocolate	2 5 1/2 oz. Bars
Sugar, Granulated	1 2 oz. Package
Powdered orange concentrate	1 7 oz. Package (Vitamin C)
Soup (dehydrated)	1 5 oz. Package
Prunes	1 16 oz. Package
Instant Coffee	1 4 oz. Tin
Cigarettes	2 20's
Smoking Tobacco	1 2 1/4 oz. package

229 Most of Weedon's rabbits died. His diary states later: "Ceased to look after rabbits — I think it best so."
230 South African film star and comedian, 1909–1956.
231 The fall of Saipan marked the end for Japan. It enabled the capture of the neighbouring island of Tinian, from which the atomic bombs would be launched just over a year later.
232 Nottinghamshire.
233 Four American airmen involved in this raid were shot down into the sea and made their way to Macau. From there they were escorted to the Chinese guerrillas by operative Nelson Mar. Mar, still around at time of writing at the age of 92, was the man who introduced me to the Zhoushan government.
234 Later, on a visit to the author in Hong Kong in 2004, Ron recalled his older brother Geoff telling him that their mother had returned to England rather than Ireland because she never really believed her husband was lost, and thought that if he ever came looking for them, he would come to England.
235 Kobe house was finally hit by incendiaries and burnt out on 5 June. The body of CPO Ray, who had died the night before, was lost in the blaze. The POWs were then moved to Maru Yama camp.
236 Poulter and 123 of his comrades had been transferred to Nomachi. Andrews was Private James H. Andrews, Middlesex Regiment.
237 Ron: "My mother always hoped that by some miracle my father would be

found to be alive at the end of the war. These letters and Lt Col Penfold's [in November] must have put an end to that hope ... I can remember when [she] was visited by the lady in uniform who broke the news to her. My mother and the lady then came into the room where my brother and I were and told us."

238 Notagawa is over one hundred miles from Hiroshima, and considerably further from Nagasaki, so this probably was indeed a secondary explosion.

239 Hamilton confirmed: "Then the Japanese Camp Sergeant told us in a drunken moment that as soon as the Americans landed in Japan all prisoners would be killed. Discreet enquiries from other staff led us to believe that this was true, and indeed we found after the war that several other camps had received similar information." While this story has sometimes been disputed, documentary evidence suggests there is no doubt whatsoever that this was the Japanese 'final solution' to the POW problem.

240 Wllshaw was Chairman of Cable & Wireless.

241 Bearing in mind the number of servicemen, POWs, and casualties, the mind boggles at the number of such letters that must have been produced — and all laboriously hand-typed. To illustrate this, the volunteers of the Central Prisoners of War Agency of the Red Cross, for example, sent over 50 million letters and telegrams during the Second World War, and received almost as many back — making very nearly 100 million communications in total.

242 Eitemble recalled: "Before the Americans came down from Yokohama to arrange for our repatriation, a friend of mine, Danny O'Hanlon had made signal contact with some of the fighter planes, luckily one of the pilots understood and signalled back asking what we required. Danny said food and several hours later back came the fighters and dropped kitbags full of bread etc. Later over came some bombers and dropped forty-four gallon drums of food but without parachutes, luckily they didn't kill anybody but the drums were completely flattened, so no grub. Still, they must have learnt their lesson as later they were dropped by parachute."

243 Etiemble added, when asked for his own recollections of this incident: "I don't think I can give you much help about the POWs falling from the B24. On arrival at Atsugi airfield Yokohama, we were loaded onto the planes but I cannot recall names being taken. It was not until we arrived in Manila that I heard of the bombs doors opening, for some unknown reason and 22 ex-POWs falling to their death. I do not think the Americans were very keen for too many people to know about it."

244 The CWGC entry for Gollege states he was lost on 8 September 1945, but his name was on this aircraft's manifest.

245 Hong Kong POW Major A. C. Houghton, RE, who has a grave in Surrey, also died that day. Interestingly, a note in Admiralty files states: "Believed lost in air crash between Japan and Manila."

246 Unfortunately, the *South China Morning Post* refused permission for two

paragraphs from the original article to be reproduced here, unless a fee relating to the number of copies of this book to be published was paid.
247 The actual date was the 10th.
248 Whitehead states: "Joe Hanley [presumably Gunner Thomas James Hanley] went on to tell me a remarkable tale of how the plane taking him home from Japan ran into a typhoon and he had to bale out over the South China Sea. He dog-paddled in the gloom for almost twenty-four hours and then, when he was on the point of giving up, the lookout on an American [sic] warship spotted his tiny head in the vastness of the China Sea and he was rescued" (Whitehead, "Escape to Fight On", p. 192). As Wright's friend Bill Pope does not appear in any casualty list, it must be assumed that he was also one of the lucky few to be picked up. Clearly they never met again, which is not necessarily surprising, as they would have been repatriated via different routes.
249 Built in 1911, *Maunganui* served as a hospital ship in the Second World War. She picked up these survivors in Keelung.
250 The discrepancy in dates is probably not significant, especially as lists of men who were said to be on board do not match. Note also that a second aircraft (B-24M #44-42052, 'Liquidator' — also of the 494th Bomb Group) carrying Australian ex-POWs crashed on the same date, probably in Taiwan. Although the aircraft is recorded as not being found, the following five men from the crash are buried in Sai Wan Military cemetery, Hong Kong:

Cooper, Ronald Simmons   Gunner   VX58497   4 A/Tk Regt. RAA
Gilding, Jack Livingstone   Corporal SX10013   8 Div. Amb. Sub. AASC
James, Albert Arthur   Sergeant NX/60056 2/19 Bn. Aust. Infantry
Noble, Richard Thomas   Sergeant NX35741   2/30 Bn. Aust. Infantry
Rogerson, Harry   W.O.II   VX35009   2/29 Bn. Aust Infantry

Albert Arthur James was the father of the well-known entertainer, Clive James. According to the first volume of James' autobiography ("Unreliable Memoirs") the plane went down in a typhoon in Manila Bay. However, other sources state that it flew into a mountainside in Taiwan. As CWGC graves in Taiwan were re-interred at Sai Wan post-war, the latter seems more likely. See MACR #14972 and #14936.
251 As just three examples of the fates of this fleet of repatriation vessels, *Admiral Hughes* was built late in the Second World War. This troopship (AP-124) survived many years post-war at Suisun Bay, California. *Joseph T. Dickman* went into trans-Atlantic service with the United States Line in 1922 as *Peninsular State*, and was renamed *Pierce* and then *Roosevelt* in mid-1922. She rescued the crew of the British ship *Antigone* in 1926 and was taken over by the US War Department in 1940 as transport *Dickman*. She took part in the D-Day landings at Utah Beach, and was finally scrapped at Oakland, California, in 1948. She was a "535"-class liner (E.F.C.), 535-ft, 13,869 gross

tons, one funnel, two screws, 644 passengers. *Goodhue* (APA-107) was sold as the freighter *Hawaiian Citizen* post-war, and was scrapped in 1982.

252 The other urn was that of Private Alfred Keeler, who had died on 15 August — the day of the Japanese surrender — and whose remains are now in Acton cemetery. Andrews, for unknown reasons, is commemorated on the Sai Wan memorial as having no known grave.

253 Though in fairness it should be noted that the United Kingdom was still under strict rationing and their people could not be as generous as their New World Allies.

254 Of *Lisbon Maru* survivors who died as POWs, Hamilton states: "114 died in Kobe, 55 in Osaka, 21 in Kokura, 24 in Moji, and an estimated 30 in other places, making a total of 244" (versus the 245 recorded in lists prepared for this work). Those who survived in Kokura were lucky. It would have been hit by the second Atomic Bomb, had bad weather not led to Nagasaki being selected in its place.

255 Hilary Llewellyn-Williams is a poet with four published collections. 'My Father Swimming' appears in her book, *Greenland*, published by Seren (2003).

256 It has not been possible to determine the exact number of these men. At least three (one HKRNVR, one Royal Scots Regiment, and one Middlesex Regiment) appear to have moved to New Zealand and made new lives for themselves there. In fairness to their families, their names will not be recorded here. Some men returned home, but later cut off all contact with their families. At least one (see Martin Booth's biography, *Gweilo*, pp. 127–132) committed suicide.

257 Since those four submarines were in the same general area as *Bullhead*, and two further submarines (*Cod* and *Chub*) also passed through those seas at various times, it is difficult to be sure which Japanese anti-submarine attack was the one that sank *Bullhead*. However, most probably it was one that occurred on 6 August 1945 — the very first day of *Bullhead's* patrol on station — when a Japanese army aircraft attacked an Allied submarine with depth charges. It claimed two direct hits, and observed a large quantity of oil and air bubbles at the water's surface. The position stated was close to the coast of the Indonesian island of Bali. The submarine probably lies there to this day.

258 *Grouper* crewman Carl Kjellin's nephew Barney Deibert, for example, reports: "Apparently he never talked to anyone about his time in service. I get the impression that he wanted to forget it all. I even talked to some of the guys that served in the navy at the same time and they told me that he never talked to them about his service time either."

259 Japan Reinforcement Base Depot.

260 Gar says: "I wanted to retire in Hong Kong but my wife insisted moving back to the Great Northwest where our children resided."

261 Blow the ballast tanks to surface, Vent the tanks to dive; hence, Blow and Vent.

262 Rear Admiral.
263 With kind permission of the West Australian Newspaper.
264 On return to England Mrs Brooks had discovered that she had tuberculosis of the throat, and was confined to bed and not allowed to speak.
265 The British government closed all cases regarding personal pay in the Second World War many years ago. However, to the delight (and surprise) of all who know Ross, he was finally paid his due in August 2004!
266 Shortly before he passed away, Salmon was working with a Dr Christine Henderson on an as yet unpublished account of the sinking of the *Lisbon Maru*.
267 Hewitt's wartime experiences are described in his book, *A Bridge with Three Men*. He passed away in Australia in August 2004 as this book was being written up.
268 Martin's son Mark (also a Harrow student, followed by Cambridge and Harvard) was at one time an advisor with McKinsey & Co. to the governor of Hong Kong, Sir Murray McLehose, in the 1970s. Later, he was a top headhunter in London for over a quarter of a century.
269 Daughter of Major Bottomley, HKVDC. Her husband Denis was District Officer of Tai Po.
270 Author of *A Mountain of Light*.
271 These were: Campbell (Police), Evans (Tom himself, ex-Middlesex, and at this time Hong Kong Dockyard Police), Garton (HKRNVR), Gorman (Dockyard Police), Hamilton (Royal Scots), Hill (Police), Howell (RASC), Johnstone (HKRNVR), Man (Middlesex), Robson (Middlesex), McDougall (Royal Scots), Salmon (Royal Artillery), Taylor (Hong Kong Signals Company), and 'A' Woodhead was presumably Fred Woodhead of the Police.
272 Bernard Charles Lilley was born in West Ham, London, on 8 February 1907. He joined the RN as a Boy 2nd Class aboard HMS *Impregnable* on 30 May 1923. He subsequently served aboard *Valiant*, *Clematis*, *Norfolk*, and *Caledon* where, rising through the ranks, he was made an Acting Petty Officer in December 1935. Accepted as an Acting Regulating Petty Officer (RPO) during April 1936, he transferred to *Leander*. Drafted to Hong Kong and *Tamar* (February 1939 to May 1940), he received his L.S. and G.C. award on 3 April 1940, and after a few months aboard *Dauntless*, returned to *Tamar*, only to be taken prisoner of war by the Japanese in December 1941. Whilst a POW on the books of *Drake*, he received advancement to Master at Arms (MAA) on 22 July 1942. He was pensioned on 24 May 1947.
273 The book, *A Village Remembers*, tells the story of Jacksdale, the Memorial and the men who gave their lives. It is available from Jacksdale Garden Centre. MCM, Main Road, Ironville Post Office, Selston Library, and both Selston Post Offices.
274 Thanks to Donald Stewart for the details. He adds: "Andra went with Joe Gault, another Lossie Skipper, out to the Far East to work the Boom Defences.

Joe stopped at Ceylon, Andra went on to Hong Kong. Joe came back to be a successful fisherman. Bella Flett, Andra's sister, married John Gault and became a trawlerman in Aberdeen."

275 Researchers should be aware that the majority of surviving photos of *Grouper* were taken well after the war and thus show very different lines to those she had in 1942.

276 British records do not mention a massacre, nor the manner in which Ledyard died. I am grateful to the Web site of Michael Meals of the Chickamauga and Chattanooga National Military Park for these details.

277 Though a plaque to the RA personnel lost on board is in the Chapel at St Stephen's in Stanley.

278 The ship is not protected under the British legislation regarding treating such wrecks as war graves, as that legislation only applies to British registered ships.

279 Federal Communications Commission report, 3 June 1943.

280 This correspondence can be found in FO371/57578, The National Archives.

281 The Treasury Solicitor's Department provides legal services to central government departments and other publicly funded bodies in England and Wales.

282 See note 209.

283 Foreign Secretary, 1945-51.

284 Thus they are unfortunately not preserved at the PRO.

285 Peter Alan Lee Vine had obtained, in Singapore shortly after the war, his solicitor's Final Qualifying examination. After this fact was reported in Singapore's the *Straits Times*, he was recruited by Colonel Kieran and Brigadier Davis as a prosecuting officer (Deputy Assistant Judge Advocate General) with the temporary rank of Major. After serving on two trials in Singapore, he was posted to Hong Kong for the *Lisbon Maru* case and one other concerning Taiwan. He returned to Hong Kong after the war and had a long and successful career there with Deacons. He lives in Hong Kong to this day.

286 He was lucky again, as on 29 April 1945 a Grumman Avenger torpedo-bomber sunk the I-44 off Okinawa, with the loss of all 134 men on board.

287 In an amazingly close parallel, the *Arandora Star* had sailed from Liverpool on 2 July 1940, carrying 1,673 people, of whom 374 were the British crew and guards, and the remainder German and Italian internees (plus nearly 100 German POWs). Torpedoed off Ireland by *U-47*, the after engine room was flooded at once and the generators were put out of action. Most of the German and Italians on board rushed on deck from the dark holds, but many refused to board the life rafts which the crew and guards led them to. As the ship sank, the Canadian destroyer HMCS *St. Laurent* arrived and started picking up survivors from the boats, and individuals and small groups from the water (mainly by lowering their own personnel over the sides of the destroyer by rope, to physically drag them up, many being soaked in oil and unable to help themselves). Eight hundred

and five of those on board perished, including almost one hundred of the British crew and guards.
288 Although the document is undated, it presumably relates to an enquiry made shortly after the initial British protest. It was recovered from the files of the First Demobilisation Bureau, Tokyo, on 9 September 1946, and placed with the International Prosecution Section for translation on 17 September. The translation was concluded by 8 November.
289 "The Nuremberg trial has made clear that at least an action in consequence of an order should be considered strongly in mitigation of punishment."
290 In this text the third Geneva Convention, of 1929, plus the relevant parts of the second Convention, 1907 (the Hague Convention), are referred to. The fourth Convention, of 1949, strengthened some of these provisions.
291 Now at the University of Hong Kong Library as The Ride Collection.
292 Major Rob Cooper, BAAG.
293 Military Yen and Chinese National Currency respectively.
294 Sergeant John Payne, executed on 26 August 1942, with Private John Adams, Lance Corporal George Berzenski, and Private Percy Ellis. All were Winnipeg Grenadiers.
295 Private James Stopforth (RAOC), executed on 14 September 1942, with Private Paul Connolly (HKDDC), Private Maurice Dunne (RAOC), Private Victor Branson (1st Middlesex), and Lance Corporal William George (1st Middlesex). Three other men were involved in this escape but lived. *Lisbon Maru* survivor Dennis Morley had actually tried to escape with Connolly previously. Dennis wrote: "Thank you very much for the info on Paul Connolly. My mind is now at rest. Did I tell you that we did make an attempt in the early days but were observed by a sentry and had to get back quick? I knew he would try again but would not put me at risk. He was the best friend I have ever had. Thank you once again."
296 Prata was buried in Hong Kong Roman Catholic Cemetery. Date of death was given as 14 Septemer 1943.
297 Actually Captain Douglas Ford. The executions were carried out on 18 December.
298 They were in fact imprisoned and later released.
299 Shrigley was in the HKVDC pay detachment. He was: "Killed in a fall from a second floor window in Yaumatei while under interrogation." The date of death is given as 28 June 1944. Hale was in the Field Company Engineers of the HKVDC. His death is listed as 26 August 1944. The possibility of an error in one or other date leads to speculation that both may have lost their lives in the same incident.
300 Detested by the POWs for his pro-Japanese stance, Boon was tried as a collaborator after the war. He was acquitted.

Bibliography

PUBLISHED

At the Going Down of the Sun. Oliver Lindsay. London: Hamish Hamilton, 1981.
Bagged in World War 2. Royal Marines Historical Society, Special Publication No. 24.
Beneath the Shadow. James Bertram. John Day, 1947.
Captive Years. Alan Birch and Martin Cole. Hong Kong: Heinemann Asia, 1982.
Death on the Hell Ships. Gregory Michno. Pen and Sword, 2001 (originally published by Naval Institute Press).
The First of Foot: The History of the Royal Scots. A. Muir. Edinburgh: William Blackwood and Sons, 1961.
Footprints: The Memoirs of Sir Selwyn Selwyn-Clarke. Selwyn Selwyn-Clarke. Hong Kong: Sino-American, 1975.
Guest of an Emperor. Martin Weedon. London: Arthur Barker, 1948
The Hidden Years. John Luff. Hong Kong: South China Morning Post, 1967.
Hong Kong Eclipse. G. B. Endacott; edited and with additional material by Alan Birch. Hong Kong: Oxford University Press, 1978.
Hostages to Fortune. Tim Carew. London: Hamish Hamilton, 1971.
I Was a Hell Camp Prisoner. Robert J. Wright. London: Brown, Watson Ltd., 1963
The Middlesex Regiment (Duke of Cambridge's Own), 1919–52. P. K. Kemp. Aldershot: Gale and Polden, 1956.
Not the Slightest Chance: The Defence of Hong Kong, 1941. Tony Banham. Hong Kong: Hong Kong University Press, 2003.
The Sinking The Of [sic] Lisbon Maru. G. Hamilton. Hong Kong, Green Pagoda Press, 1966.
Twisting the Tail of the Dragon. Jean Mathers. The Book Guild Ltd., 1994.

UNPUBLISHED

Testimony provided to author – Miles Howell
Testimony provided to author – Alf Hunt
Testimony provided to author – John Inglis
Testimony provided to author – Ross Lynneberg
Testimony provided to author – James McHarg Miller
Testimony provided to author – William Poulter
Testimony provided to author – William Spooner

Correspondence with Frank Bennett
Correspondence with Jack Etiemble
Correspondence with Tom 'Taffy' Evans
Correspondence with Wallace Hastings
Correspondence with Alf 'Nobby' Hunt
Correspondence with Garfield 'Gar' Kvalheim
Correspondence with Ross Lynneberg
Correspondence with Dennis Morley
Correspondence with William Grant Shepherd
Correspondence with William Spooner

Sam Atkins' Papers

Arthur Alsey's Diary, IWM
Geoffrey Hamilton's Diary, IWM
Barbara Redwood's Diary, IWM
Andy Salmon's Diary, IWM

ADM 1/24284: Sinking of *Lisbon Maru*: naval casualties, 1942–1946
ADM 125/149: Lists of Royal and Merchant Navy casualties from Hong Kong, compiled by P.O. Staley
CO 980/67: Protests to Japanese Government on treatment of prisoners of war in torpedoed Japanese transport *Lisbon Maru*, 1942–1944 (Fallace, Evans, Johnstone's reports)
CO 980/102: Shanghai survivors of the *Lisbon Maru*
CO 980/138: Lists of POWs on board Japanese transport *Lisbon Maru*
FO 371/35945: Torpedoing of the *Lisbon Maru*: reports by survivors, 1943
FO 371/57578: Captain Shigeru Tsuno [sic] of *Lisbon Maru* to be arraigned as a war criminal, 1946
FO 916/770: Sinking of the *Lisbon Maru*, 1943
FO 916/1083: Sinking of the *Lisbon Maru*, 1944
TS 26/803: Hong Kong and at sea: Murder of prisoners lost on sinking of *Lisbon Maru*, 1939–1945

WO 32/11677: Survivors in Osaka and Kobe camps
WO 235/1114: War Crimes tribunals, *Lisbon Maru*
WO 392/23: POW Lists

NARA: Log of *Grouper*, National Archives microfilm publications. Pamphlet describing; M 1752.
NARA: Deck Logs of the USS Grouper (SS-214). Record Group 24, stack 470, row 33. Seven logbooks in all.
NARA: Various records relating to *Lisbon Maru*
Naval Historical Center
University of Wyoming: Clay Blair Collection

The Ride Collection, Hong Kong University Library

Index

Aberdeen Industrial School   12, 13
Admiral Graf Spee   45
Alaska   53
Allison, CPO John, RN   41, 89
Alsey, Sergeant Arthur, Royal Scots   43, 49, 70, 77, 114, 124, 125, 136, 215
Altmark   45
Andrews, Private James H., Middlesex   171
Araki Kaname   39, 79
Argyle Street   24, 27, 28, 32, 35
Atkins, Private Samuel Arthur, Middlesex   25, 26, 36, 155, 156, 160, 166, 167, 171, 177, 178, 179, 180, 186, 215
Australia   6, 22, 31, 44, 105, 106, 130, 137, 151, 166, 168, 178, 187, 193, 196, 198, 199, 200, 201, 205, 211, 213, 217, 219, 223, 224, 225, 226

B24   181, 183
B29   170, 171, 172, 175, 181, 193
Badger, Lieutenant James Spencer, RE   137
Baggs, LSBA Ken George, RN   40, 132
Bailey, Bill   198, 199
Bailey, LSBA Reginald Kenneth, RN   41

Bailey, Boom Skipper Stanford, RNR   120
Bamboo Pier   38
Bandoeng Maru   226
Banham, BSM George Thomas, RA   173
Barlow, BSM William Arthur, RA   102, 150, 151, 165, 222
Barron, CSM John, Royal Scots   184
Bataan   6
Bates, Gunner Sydney Francis, RA   182
Bennet's Hill   12, 13
Bennett, Lance Corporal Frank, Royal Signals   7, 21, 40, 42, 46, 74, 82, 85, 89, 100, 101, 114, 115, 117, 209
Benningfield, Private William, Middlesex   98
beri beri   24, 43, 49, 74, 142, 143, 145, 159, 179, 186, 216
Betts, Sergeant Charles, Middlesex   83, 95
Bevis, CERA Herbert Thomas, RN   74
Bignal, Leading Writer Gordon Howard, RN   164
Bindon, Private Frank James, Middlesex   154
Blackman, Aircraftman William, RAAF   210

Booth, Sergeant James Dunbar, Royal Scots   139
Bournemouth   202
Bowen, Bombardier John, RA   41
Bowen Road Military Hospital   9
Bowers, Sea1c Charles E., USN   69
Bowles, Private William, Middlesex   42
Boyce, Lance Bombardier Samuel John, RA   164
Boyes, CERA William James L., RN   103, 222
British Army Aid Group (BAAG)   47, 48, 49, 134
British Broadcasting Company (BBC)   130, 136
Brooks, Master Gunner Charles Frederick, RA   7, 15, 22, 26, 30, 31, 103, 120, 148, 149, 166, 172, 205, 206
Brooks, Emily   7, 103, 120, 166, 206–209
Brooks, Geoffrey   7, 103, 120, 150, 166, 168, 207–209
Brooks, Ronald   7, 16, 103, 120, 149, 166, 168, 207
Brotherston, Sergeant Andrew, HKDDC   151
Brown, Lieutenant Charles Dixon, Royal Signals   130, 134, 137
Brown, Private Donald   146
Brownlow, 2nd Lieutenant Norman, Royal Scots   222
Bucke, Lieutenant Cyril Edward, Royal Signals   74, 101, 126, 137
Burke, Lance Corporal John, Middlesex   182
Butcher, WO Eric, HKRNVR   120
Butler, Leading Seaman Harry, RN   45
Butterfield & Swire   138

Cable & Wireless   178
Calcutta Maru   39, 79
Campbell, Sergeant William, RE   120
Cane, Lance Corporal Ronald, RE   120
Canton   (*see* Guangzhou)
Casey, Stoker Petty Officer Jeremiah, RN   137
Cassin, Able Seaman Francis, RN   129
Cavill, Corporal Dan, Middlesex   83
Central Intelligence Agency (CIA)   196
Challis, RSM Robert H., Middlesex   118, 151, 155, 160
Charleroi, Pennsylvania   56
Charles, Sergeant Sydney, RE   103, 222
Chatham Barracks   14
Cheesewright, Lieutenant Cyril, Middlesex   152
Chekiang (*see* Zhejiang Province)
Chiang Kai Shek   131
Chichijima   58
Chikuzan Maru   39
Chilcroft, Able Seaman Robert Albert, RN   91
Childs, Gunner Thomas Bernard, RA   81, 91
China Station   14, 23
Chungking   38, 48, 144, 145
Churchill, Winston   6, 131, 160
Clapperton, Private James, Royal Scots   182
Clark, WO III James, Royal Scots   157, 225
Clarke, Gunner John, RA   182
Clarkson, Lieutenant William, RE   112
Close, Lieutenant Robert Hamilton, USN   52, 56, 220
Corregedor   6
Croft, Marine Sydney 'Jake', RN   95
Crowley, Captain J. D., USN   54
Cuthbertson, Captain Norman H., Royal Scots   85, 126, 127, 139

D'Allesantro, James A., USN   69
Daishan   94

INDEX 291

Daly, Private Joseph Hunter, Royal Scots 133
Danjo Gunto 58, 59
Dartford 13
Deering, Able Seaman Bill, RN 45
Denton, Bombardier Joseph, RA 45
Dicks, BQMS Stanley, RA 71, 95
Dignan, Lance Corporal James, Royal Signals 229
diphtheria 32, 43, 46, 49, 64, 82, 127, 132, 142, 145
Domei 124, 130
Dongfu Shan 94
Dongji 95, 96
Doxford, Corporal William, HKVDC 182
Duke, Lieutenant Commander Claren E., USN 52, 56, 57
Dundee 12
Dykema, Ensign John R., USN 52, 56
dysentery 24, 26, 28, 43, 70, 71, 75, 120, 126, 132, 139, 142, 145, 179, 186, 201, 215

East China Sea 89, 94, 123, 140, 228
Eaton, Private George, Middlesex 84
Eccleston, Able Seaman Thomas, RN 40, 101
Edwards, Sergeant James Thomas, RA 95
Empress of Australia 216
Empress of Canada 7, 103
Empress of Japan 106
Empress of Scotland 106
Erim, John USN 69
Etiemble, Gunner Jack, RA 5, 6, 15, 19, 24, 26–28, 35v37, 43, 52, 67, 68, 71, 81, 91, 98, 118, 152, 170, 181, 183, 185, 194, 195, 199–202
Evans, Mr Bill 43, 74, 87, 88, 90, 112, 143–145, 156
Evans, Private Tom 'Taffy', Middlesex 15, 66, 68, 71, 97, 183, 210, 221

Fairbairn, 2nd Lieutenant Geoffrey D., Royal Scots 63, 64
Fallace, WO James Wilfred, HKRNVR 38, 43, 44, 73, 74, 86, 90, 97, 110, 112, 113, 143–145, 202, 216
Fergus, Sergeant John, Royal Scots 120
Ferris, Private Stanley Richard, Middlesex 97, 98, 139
Flett, Chief Skipper Andrew, RNR 102, 223
Formosa Straits 55
Fortress HQ 10
Fountain, Sapper Alfred Morris, RE 139
Fukien 143
Fuku Maru #10 72

Gahira Goro 65
Gale, Private John Frederick, Middlesex 42, 75
Garton, Seaman Gunner Frank Kekewik, HKRNVR 221
Geary, Lance Corporal George, Middlesex 98
Gibbs, Mr Frank Walter 132
Giddons, Bombardier Rodney W., RA 41
Gilham, Sergeant Sidney Fred, Middlesex 182
Gin Drinkers Line 8, 10
Glasgow 8, 104, 105
Glenn, F1c Robert W., USN 69
Goat Island 5, 54
Goerdeler, Dr Karl 216
Golden Hill 8
Goodban, Nurse Mary Hope 22
Goodfellow, RSM Isaac, Royal Scots 142
Gorman, Private Thomas, Royal Scots 42
Gorman, Sergeant Thomas, HKPF 44, 221

Graham, Lieutenant Ewan C., Middlesex 101, 154
Grant, Corporal Donald, RE 120, 156
Great Yarmouth 103
Green, Sergeant Ernest Edward 'Dodger', Royal Signals 45, 95
Green Island 11
Greenwood, Commissioned Telegraphist Norman T. J., RN 134, 136
Griffith, Captain Walter T., USN 198
Groton 52, 228
Grounds, Lieutenant Ronald, Middlesex 15
Guadalcanal 38
Guangzhou 11
Guilin 48, 134
Guo Ade 97

Hagger, AB Ken Leslie, RN 132
Hale, Corporal Harry, Royal Scots 124
Halifax, Nova Scotia 184, 185, 211
Halsey, Sir Lionel 11
Hamill, Private Thomas, Royal Scots 104, 223
Hamilton, 2nd Lieutenant Geoffrey C., Royal Scots 16, 21, 24, 32, 100, 118, 127, 133, 136, 138, 154, 157, 160, 170, 176, 194, 216, 217, 221
Hangzhou Bay 89, 94
Hare, Private Charles, Middlesex 95
Harrington, Signalman Desmond, Royal Signals 182
Hastings, LSBA Wallace, RN 13, 14, 40, 49, 65, 75, 86–88, 99, 119, 125, 132, 158, 164, 210
Hatchett, Private Percy John, Middlesex 42, 83, 88
Hawaii 6, 52, 54, 187, 211
Hayashi, Sergeant Major 37
Hayward, Private Walter Alfred, Middlesex 42, 82
Haywood, Gunner George A., RA 91

Heath, WO Charles, RE 120
Heather, Corporal Charles K., Middlesex 66
Hemingway, Ernest 14
Hemmingfield, Gunner Arthur, RA 95
Henderson, CQMS David, Royal Scots 75, 118
Hendy, POSB Norman, RN 41
Hess, MM2c Ralph H., USN 69
Hewitt, Captain Anthony, Middlesex 218, 219
Hickory, North Carolina 56
Higgens, EM1c George W., USN 69
Hiraoka Eikichi 65
Hirohata 164, 210
Hiroshima 132, 134, 172, 173, 195
Hitler, Adolf 115, 216
HMAS *Warramunga* 184
HMS *Bargate* 103
HMS *Cicala* 11, 12, 129, 212
HMS *Ganges* 11
HMS *Implacable* 186
HMS *Indefatigable* 186
HMS *Pembroke* 14
HMS *Prince of Wales* 15, 51
HMS *Repulse* 15, 51
HMS *Royal Oak* 11
HMS *Royal Sovereign* 11
HMS *Seamew* 14
HMS *Taciturn* 194
HMS *Tamar* 14, 40, 74, 103, 129, 137, 187, 222
HMS *Tarantula* 14
HMS *Tern* 12, 74
HMS *Thanet* 51
HMS *Thorough* 194
HMS *Thracian* 129
HMS *Ursa* 183
HMT *Dilwara* 36
Hobson, Sergeant Albert J., Middlesex 98
Hodgson, Sea1c Thomas P., USN 69

Holt, Lieutenant Edward Rowell, USN 52, 56, 61, 64, 65, 72, 193, 196–198, 221
Hong Kong Dockyard Defence Corps (HKDDC) 26, 41
Hong Kong Police Force 21, 44
Hong Kong Royal Naval Volunteer Reserve (HKRNVR) 38, 41, 43, 86, 97, 120, 127, 143, 156, 216
Hong Kong & Singapore Royal Artillery (HKSRA) 41
Hong Kong Volunteer Defence Corps (HKVDC) 9, 10, 14, 19, 21, 23, 48, 124, 182, 216
Hope, Private Arthur, Middlesex 83, 88
Horder, Motor Mechanic Douglas, RN 120
Horswell, Major Sydney James, HKDDC 130, 134, 136
Hosford, Petty Officer Telegraphist Robert, RN 156
Houghton, Captain Alfred C., RE 134
Howell, 2nd Lieutenant Hargraves Milne, RASC 42, 49, 71–73, 78–83, 85, 86, 89, 91, 96–98, 118, 133, 140, 217, 221, 222
Howson, LSBA Ronald, RN 41
Huangpu River 117
Huangxing Dao 94
Hughes, Private William, Royal Scots 42
Hughieson, Telegraphist Jack, RN 132
Hunan 143
Hunt, Telegraphist Alf Dennis 'Nobby', RN 10, 40, 41, 44, 46, 65, 67, 74, 79, 84, 85, 90, 94, 96, 102, 132, 152, 181, 182, 184, 202, 211, 217, 219
Hyakufuku Maru 72
Hymes, Private Johnny, Middlesex 83

IJN *Hayashio* 106
IJN *Kuri* 69, 70, 72

Ikushu Maru 72
Iles, Private Arthur Henry, Middlesex 42
Inglis, Bombardier John, RA 41, 85, 93, 95, 96, 101, 111, 112, 217
Innis, Major Leslie Walrond, RE 98, 139
Ipswich 15, 137
Ile de France 185, 211, 219
Iszard, Lance Corporal George, Middlesex 42
Ito Elzu 66

Jacksdale 102, 103, 150, 165, 222
Jackson, Surgeon Lieutenant Charles Anthony, RNVR 40, 46, 87, 101, 119, 132, 134, 139, 159, 160, 163
James, Sergeant William Richard, RA 182
Jardine's Corner 16
Jardine's Lookout 14
Jennings, Private Francis Arthur, HKDDC 26
Jersey 36, 201
Jintang 94
Johan de Witt 223
Johnson, Frank (*see* Bennett, Frank)
Johnstone, WO William C., HKRNVR 112, 143, 144, 145, 221
Jones, Captain Cyril, Royal Scots 24
Jones, Sapper Norman, RE 45
Jubilee Barracks 12, 21, 29
Jupp, WO John Edmund, HKRNVR 156

Kai Tak 36, 124, 217
Kameoka 164
Kanamoto 152
Kasajima Maru 72
Kelleher, Leading Stoker James, RN 132
Kiangsi 143
Kidder, Jack, USN 198

King, 2nd Lieutenant Ralph M., Middlesex 98
King, Private Thomas Patrick, Middlesex 182
Kipling, Rudyard 164
Kobe 131–134, 138, 139, 147, 158, 160, 161, 164, 169, 176, 200, 216
Kohima, Sergeant 38
Koho Maru #1 72, 79
Kokura 132, 134
Kumanoyama Maru 227
Kvalheim, MM1c Garfield, USN 5, 6, 36, 53–55, 57, 60, 61, 64, 65, 68, 69, 72, 123, 194, 196, 198, 199, 201
Kwangtung 143
Kyoda Shigeru 38, 39, 65–68, 70, 73, 78, 79, 226
Kyoto 176

Laloe, Cadet Mike Francis, HKRNVR 97, 216
Langley, Sergeant Cecil Alec, Royal Signals 85
Langley-Bates, Clerk of Works Ronald, RE 104, 223
Lawler, Eric USN 69
Lees, ERA 3 Alexander, RN 115
Leicester 104
Lewis, LSBA Daniel, RN 41
Lifton, Shipwright First Class Cyril Alfred, RN 74
Lilley, RPO Bernard Charles, RN 222
Lima Maru 38
Link, AS Charles J., USN 69
Little, Signalman John Samuel, RCCS 26
Liuheng 94
Liverpool 11, 165, 168, 172
Llewellyn-Williams, Marine Henry, RN 113, 187
Lloyds 131, 144
London 38, 124, 131, 178–180, 209
Lossiemouth 103, 223

Lynch, Captain Maurice, RAMC 46
Lynneberg, Telegraphist Ross, NZRNVR 9, 10, 23, 24, 43, 67, 70, 74, 75, 84, 86, 89, 99, 101, 115, 175, 176, 186, 212
Lyons Maru 38

Ma Tau Chung 21, 23
Macau 48
Maeda 152
Magazine Gap 16
Malaya 6, 23, 51, 195
Malaysia (*see* Malaya)
Malta 103, 207
Maltby, Major General Christopher 9
Man, Captain Christopher, Middlesex 98, 125, 154, 160, 218, 221
Man, Georgina 'Topsy' 125
Manila 7, 177, 181–184, 186, 187, 206, 210, 211, 220, 226
Mare Island 5, 227
Marigold 215
Mason, Lieutenant John Denning, USN 52, 56, 220
Mathers, Jean 124
Matheson, CSM Donald, Royal Scots 16
Maunganui 183
McCready, LSBA Thomas, RN 40, 132
McDougal, Private J., Royal Scots 221
McFarlane, WO John C., RN 139
McGillivray, Private John, Royal Scots 110
McGregor, Lieutenant Commander Rob Roy, USN 55–57, 59, 61, 63–66, 69, 123, 220
Meakin, Corporal Frank, Middlesex 42
Merchant Marine 41, 138
Miaozihu Dao 94
Middlesex Regiment 6, 9, 10, 12, 14, 15, 19, 24, 25, 27, 35, 40–42, 44, 77, 82, 83, 88, 97, 112, 120, 125, 127,

132, 139, 142, 151, 171, 179, 180, 182, 210, 215, 217–219
Midway   27, 33, 52–55, 57, 58
Miles, Frank   110
Mill Hill Barracks   15
Miller, Private James McHarg, Royal Scots   8, 67, 70, 73, 85, 91, 99, 118, 119, 125, 138, 147, 152, 153, 158, 169, 175, 184, 213
Millican, Petty Officer Joseph, RN   137
Millington, Sergeant Leslie Charles, HKVDC   124
Minatagawa   175
Mitcham   13
Mitsubishi   68, 151, 152
Mizoguchi Miki   65
Moji   48, 127, 129, 131, 132, 134, 140, 141, 145
Morimoto   133
Morioka Maru   38
Morley, Private Dennis, Royal Scots   13, 14, 84, 100, 118, 213
Morrison Hill   14
Mount Parrish   14
Mount Vernon, New York   56
MTB 12   10, 11
Mulcahy, Able Seaman Michael D., RN   129
Mulligan, Gunner James Patrick, RA   47
Murata   138
Mussolini, Benito   115
MV *Awatea*   7, 106
MV *Stirling Castle*   168
Myles, Private Frank 'Mickey', Royal Scots   45, 49, 109, 110, 127, 214, 215

Nagasaki   50, 172, 173, 227
Nakatani   152
Nakazawa   124
Needle Hill   7

Nelson, Private Fred R., Middlesex   98
New Zealand   9, 23, 86, 99, 137, 186, 205, 212, 213, 215
Niimori Genichoro   37, 42, 118, 119, 226
Niioka Gentaru   65
Nippon Yusen Kaisha (NYK) Line   38, 39
Nomura (*see* Niimori Genichoro)
North Point   19, 20, 21, 23, 24, 35, 47, 143
North Saddle Island   59
Norway   53
Notogawa   170, 175–177

O'Brian, 'Obie' USN   69
O'Donnell, Private Fred, Middlesex   96
O'Hanlon, Leading Telegraphist Daniel Joseph, RN   101, 202, 203, 217
Officer, Major John Moore, RAMC   46, 96
Okinawa   181, 183
Osaka   39, 131–134, 136, 138, 139, 142, 147, 152, 156, 158, 160, 164, 169, 170, 175–177, 187, 195, 200, 201
Overy, CSM Richard G., Middlesex   127

Page, Surgeon Lt. Commander John Allison, RN   46
Palmer, Sergeant Reginald, RE   95
Panting, Corporal Hugh Eric, Middlesex   83, 88
Pargeter, Private Ernest Arthur, Middlesex   182
Parkinson, Signalman Robert, RN   91
Peak, The   16
Pearl Harbour   5, 6, 51, 52, 54, 55, 57, 184, 186, 227
Pearman, Marine John Edward, RN   91

Pelham, Lance Corporal Harry J., RE 46, 95, 132, 159
Pellagra 27, 43
Pemberton, SBA Allen, RN 41, 46
Penfold, Lt. Colonel Richard J.L., RA 205
Phipps, Signalman John, Royal Signals 42
Phoenix, Arizona 184
Picton, Corporal Sydney, RE 95
Pitt, Major William N., RA 41
Ploe, MM2c Thomas E., USN 69
Plowman, Staff Sergeant Ernest J., RE 98
Pollock, Lieutenant Joshua Thomas, RN 41, 74, 86, 130, 131, 133, 134
Pope, Private William, Middlesex 182
Portadown 164
Portsmouth 7, 42, 202
Potter, Corps Officer Alan Stanley, St John's Ambulance 29, 30, 70, 78, 80–82
Poulter, Lance Corporal Bertram, Middlesex 126
Poulter, CQMS William, Middlesex 12, 44, 70, 84, 100, 119, 125, 126, 129, 131, 133, 139, 142, 146, 147, 154, 160, 167, 169, 171, 178, 184, 185, 217
Price, Lance Corporal Charles Henry, Royal Signals 182
Punjabis, 2/14th 8
Putuo 94

Qiangtang 94
Qingbang Dao 94, 97, 110, 111
Queen Elizabeth 184
Quinn, Marine John, RN 132

Rajputs 5/7th 8, 10
Rankine, CQMS Duncan, Royal Scots 100
Red Cross 28, 120, 136, 147, 148, 158, 176

Redwood, Nurse Barbara 124, 135
Reeves, Corporal Ronald, Middlesex 120
Remillard, F1c Earl 'Frenchy' D., USN 69
Repulse Bay Hotel 14
Ride, Lt. Colonel Lindsay, HKVDC 48, 134
Rimmer, F2c Wilson 'Pinky' M., USN 69
Rix, Telegraphist John Arthur, NZRNVR 90
RMS *Aquitania* 216
RNH *Gillingham* 14
RNH *Hong Kong* 13, 40
Robins, Sergeant George W., Middlesex 98
Robinson, Sapper Percy Albert George, RE 104, 225
Robson, Private James P., Middlesex 221
Rodgers, Bombardier Joseph, RA 26
Rolfe, Lance Corporal Thomas, Middlesex 95
Rome 123, 124
Roosevelt, Franklin Delano 130, 131
Root, Private Alfred Edward, Middlesex 151
Ross, Staff Sergeant Henry J., RAMC 87, 101, 138
Royal Air Force (RAF) 9, 10, 14, 45
Royal Army Dental Corps (RADC) 41
Royal Army Medical Corps (RAMC) 41, 87, 96
Royal Army Ordnance Corps (RAOC) 41
Royal Army Service Corps (RASC) 41, 42, 217
Royal Artillery (RA) 5, 7, 9, 10, 16, 22, 24, 30, 35, 36, 40–42, 47, 74, 81, 83, 89, 103, 149, 165, 166, 172, 173, 182, 194, 200, 205, 206, 215, 217, 218

Royal Canadian Air Force (RCAF)   5, 53
Royal Corps of Signals (RCS)   7, 40, 41, 42, 45, 74, 88, 126, 130, 137, 182, 209, 219
Royal Engineers (RE)   10, 23, 41, 42, 103, 104, 112, 120, 132, 139, 142, 156, 219
Royal Naval Dockyard Police   41
Royal Navy   9, 10, 14, 15, 19, 40, 41, 45, 86, 119, 132, 133, 139, 156, 210, 213, 217, 218
Royal Marines   132, 144, 187, 203, 216, 222
Royal Rifles of Canada   9, 14, 19
Royal Scots   8, 10, 13, 16, 21, 28, 40–43, 63, 70, 75, 85, 88, 98, 100, 104, 105, 109, 120, 126, 132, 137, 139, 142, 182, 213–216, 222

Sai Ying Poon   21
Saipan   163
Salmon, Sergeant Andy, RA   80, 98, 218, 221
Samura   129
San Diego   5
San Francisco   38, 184, 211, 227
Sasebo, Nagasaki prefecture   39, 58
Seattle   55
Selwyn-Clarke, Dr Selwyn   22, 47
Sham Shui Po   12, 20, 21, 23–25, 27–29, 32, 35, 37, 43, 46–48, 124, 139, 144, 151, 218
Shanghai   33, 44, 47, 50, 59, 72, 93, 96, 107, 110, 114, 115, 117–119, 124–126, 145, 156, 200, 209, 228
Sharrock, Lance Corporal Harold Maynard, Royal Scots   44, 49
Shen Agui   97, 98, 112
Shepherd, ERA William Grant, RN   12, 86, 87, 99, 213
Shih Maru / Fukken Maru   32
Shing Mun Redoubt   8

Shinsei Maru   125, 126, 129
Shore, Lance Corporal Reginald C., Middlesex   182
Shosei Maru   72
Shouson Hill   12
Sing Pan Islands (*see* Qingbang Dao)
Singapore   6, 10, 15, 51, 195
Smith, Lance Corporal Leslie, RE   42
Soden, CSM Edwin J., Middlesex   97, 114, 117, 138, 147
South China Morning Post   103
South China Sea   124, 193
Spiller, Gunner Frederick John, RA   95
Spooner, Private William, Royal Scots   28, 32, 66, 75, 77, 94, 95, 109, 110, 127, 214, 215
St Albert's Convent   13
St John's Ambulance   29, 70
Stanford, CSM Frederick Samuel, Royal Scots   104, 105, 225, 226
Stanley   5, 6, 7, 13, 15, 19, 44, 228
Stanley Camp   21, 22, 41, 43, 124, 125, 167
Star Ferry   11
Steele, Private William Ernest, Middlesex   42, 115
Stevenson, Robert Louis   126
Stevenson, Sergeant James, Royal Scots   137
Stewart, Henry 'Monkey' Moncreif, Middlesex   42, 45, 46, 74, 78–80, 82, 88, 101, 114, 127, 131, 139, 142
Stewart, Telegraphist Murdo, NZRNVR   25, 129
Stone, Sapper Edward, RE   120
Stonecutters Island   38
Stratford-upon-Avon   10
Sugisaki Hirome   65
Sugiyama, Lieutenant   43, 73
Switzerland   154
Symons, Acting Yeoman of Signals Robert, RN   120

Tacoma 53, 196
Taikoo 38
Taiwan 111, 126, 167, 168, 183, 196
Takahasi, Sergeant Major 37
Taohua 94
Taylor, Corporal Guy Ralph, RE 139
Taylor, Lance Corporal William Arthur 'Alf', Royal Signals 82, 88, 90, 97, 98, 111, 112, 115, 219, 221
Tayport 104, 223
Thomas, SBA Gwynfor, RN 41, 120
Tierney, CSM John, Royal Scots 16
Tinian 171
Tivey, Private Richard John, Middlesex 42
Todd, CPO James, RN 120
Tokara Gunto 55
Tokara Jima 55
Tokyo 10, 39, 124, 131, 137, 141, 142, 157, 171, 178, 199, 201, 215
Tone Maru 72
Topcliffe, Signalman Arnold, Royal Signals 98
Toronto 54
Torpedo 6, 57–59, 61, 63–68, 70, 71, 75, 106, 125, 134, 141, 142, 144, 193, 200, 201, 203
Toyokuni Maru 72, 78, 80
Trinder, RQMS George, Royal Scots 105, 226
Tsing Pan (*see* Qingbang Dao)
Tuffs, Able Seaman Edward, RN 95

Ueyama, Sergeant Major 38
Unkai Maru #10 72
US Naval Academy 55, 56
USS *Admiral Hughes* 184
USS *Allen* 54, 55
USS *Arizona* 6, 51, 56
USS *Arkansas* 56
USS *Barbaro* 196
USS *Bashaw* 196
USS *Baya* 220, 221

USS *Blackfish* 227
USS *Breese* 54
USS *Bugara* 220
USS *Bullhead* 193, 194, 197, 198, 221
USS *Cachalot* 52
USS *California* 51
USS *Capitaine* 193
USS *Carp* 196
USS *Childs* 56
USS *Collett* 221
USS *Concord* 56
USS *Cushing* 56
USS *Cuttlefish* 52, 58
USS *Dolphin* 52
USS *Drum* 196
USS *Entemedor* 196
USS *Enterprise* 51
USS *Flying Fish* 52, 58
USS *Fulton* 54, 55, 57, 58
USS *Gato* 52
USS *Goodhue* 184
USS *Gosselin* 184
USS *Grayling* 52
USS *Grenadier* 52
USS *Grouper* 51–57, 59, 60, 63, 64, 67–69, 72, 98, 111, 123, 124, 193, 196–199, 201, 220, 221, 226–228
USS *Gudgeon* 52
USS *Haddock* 58
USS *Joseph T. Dickman* 184, 211
USS *Lexington* 51
USS *Litchfield* 57
USS *Maryland* 51
USS *Monitor* 184
USS *Narwhal* 58
USS *Nautilus* 52
USS *Nevada* 51
USS *New Mexico* 56
USS *Oconto* 184
USS *Oklahoma* 51
USS *Pennsylvania* 51
USS *Pilotfish* 221
USS *Pompano* 58

USS *Portland*   54, 55
USS *Puffer*   193, 194
USS *R-11*   56
USS *Rescue*   184
USS *Russell*   54, 55
USS *S-1*   56
USS *S-28*   5, 54
USS *S-30*   56
USS *S-36*   56
USS *S-44*   56
USS *Saratoga*   51
USS *Seacat*   220
USS *SeaLion*   196, 221
USS *Silversides*   58
USS *Tambor*   52
USS *Tennessee*   51
USS *Tilefish*   196
USS *Toro*   227
USS *Triton*   39
USS *Trout*   52
USS *Utah*   51, 54
USS *West Virginia*   51
USS *Wyoming*   56
USS *Yorktown*   54, 55

Vancouver   184–187
Victoria   20
Victoria Barracks   7
Victoria, British Columbia   184, 211
Vietnam   196, 197
Viner, Private Arthur E., Middlesex   182

Wada, Hideo   37, 72, 73, 81, 118, 140, 226
Wake Island   6, 106
Walkden, Lieutenant Allan Frank, RA   100
Walker, Major Leighton William, Royal Scots   88, 134
Wanchai   13, 42, 197
Wanchai Gap   16
Wanchai Market   14

Washington Maru (*see* Shinsei Maru)
Watts, Signalman Joseph, Royal Signals   120
Weaver, Lieutenant (JG) Albert W., USN   52, 56
Weedon, Captain Martin, Middlesex   35, 42, 101, 126, 138, 139, 142, 143, 148, 151, 154, 160, 161, 163, 167, 171, 218
Wellington   9, 168, 186
Westwood, Corporal Reginald, RE   101, 202, 219
White, Lt. Colonel Simon, Royal Scots   24
Whitehouse, Private Herbert, Middlesex   83, 88
Whitham, Lieutenant James Percival, Middlesex   95
Wigzell, CSM Wallis Frank, Royal Signals   21
Williams, CERA George, RN   120
Wilson, Lance Corporal Charles Edward, Royal Scots   133
Windsor, Ontario   54
Winnipeg Grenadiers   9, 10, 14, 19
Winter, Lieutenant Commander William Jr., USN   52, 56, 61
Wong Nai Chung   6, 10, 13, 19
Woo Tung Ling   112, 221
Wood, Lieutenant Lawrence Arthur, Middlesex   134, 136
Woodhead, Sergeant Fred, HKPF   221
Woolwich   36
Woosung (*see* Wusong)
Wright, Private Robert J., Middlesex   9, 20, 24, 27, 28, 32, 35, 42, 43, 49, 75, 82, 84, 95, 96, 98, 114, 115, 119, 131, 133, 164, 167, 169, 175, 182, 183, 219
Wusong   50, 117, 120, 127, 156

Xifu Shan   94
Yangtze River   59, 80, 89, 94

Yano Mitoshi   72
Yokoate Shima   55
Yokohama   173, 176, 177, 181, 184, 186
Yokohama Dock Company Limited   38
Young, Lieutenant Kenneth Eldred, Middlesex   127

Zhejiang Province   94, 143, 144
Zhongjie Shan   59
Zhoushan Archipelago   79, 94, 113, 143, 229
Zhoushan Island   94
Zhujiajian   94

www.ingramcontent.com/pod-product-compliance
Ingram Content Group UK Ltd.
Pitfield, Milton Keynes, MK11 3LW, UK
UKHW021843140426
5217IPUK00022B/1572